Critical Reaction to *Bubble Schools and the Long Road from Lockdown*

Building on *Lessons from Lockdown*, *Bubble Schools* gives a voice to many of those who have been on the frontline of education and schooling throughout the COVID-19 pandemic - senior leaders, teachers, teaching assistants, support staff, governors, parents, grandparents and the students themselves.

Far more than "another book on education", *Bubble Schools* is a fascinating, thought provoking historical document which should be read by anyone concerned with supporting the "COVID generation" and addressing the inequities in our society – which the pandemic has thrown into sharp relief – in the months and years to come.

Isobel Bryce
Education Consultant and Former Headteacher
Saltash Community School
Cornwall, UK

Even as a sentence drops a third subordinate clause, fine tuning an observation or precisely qualifying one of his bold but convincing assertions, Dr Breslin still manages an enviable directness and clarity. Education professionals will be grateful for his no-nonsense but learned practicality. But not just them. He achieves Orwell's aim: the intelligent working person will understand and enjoy this book, as well as seeing their interests acknowledged and upheld.

Above all, Breslin makes of our common crisis not a sensational drama but a story of many voices which together form a chorus, asking for the best kind of fresh start.

Michael Callanan
Delivery Director
Orwell Youth Prize
Hertfordshire, UK

Further, the stories from parents and students show the true loneliness and isolation that COVID is leaving. A clear need for community that Breslin describes as the job of education is clearly seen through these narratives. He does not simply share stories of the pandemic but offers insights and more importantly, recommendations for each theme highlighted in individual chapters. These recommendations leave the reader with a path forward and hope for the future, a future that is still unknown.

Dr Robyne Elder
Editor
Journal of Educational Leadership in Action
Missouri, USA

I applaud Tony Breslin's new work, *Bubble Schools and the Long Road from Lockdown*, a vivid description of the next stage in the crisis. The book will help educators and beyond to understand the multidimensional repercussions of the pandemic at all levels.

Breslin's second book on the educational impact of the virus again includes the voices of educators and policymakers but this time their perceptions are beyond the initial shock and the social, political, and educational ripples altering the educational experience.

The research is a living documentary and should be read by all those who have a vested interest in education regardless of their role or level. My only hope is that the third book in the trilogy – *Reschooling Society After Lockdown*, focused on life after the pandemic – will be developed sooner rather than later.

Lynda Leavitt
Professor, Educational Leadership
Director, Center for Innovation and Insight
College of Education and Human Services
Lindenwood University
Missouri, USA

Tony Breslin's *Bubble Schools* shines a light on the amazing things our school leaders have done, and continue to do during a tumultuous year in education. He brings first hand insights, analysis and reflection throughout a period of unprecedented change and disruption.

Backed by a series of contributors and extended research, Breslin describes both the small changes to our schooling model and the big ones, and reminds us that the story of the pandemic is not a single narrative of challenge, but a much broader, nuanced picture of achievement, resilience and enduring change across the sector.

Tackling a series of related themes, *Bubble Schools* digests and distils how the sector has continuously adapted to fast changing policy and guidance, and critically he champions a call for a re-set in how we view and measure the role that schools play for our pupils, our parents and our communities.

A compelling narrative and analysis that deserves to be read and actioned.

Michael McGarvey
Managing Director
The Key for School Leaders
Cambridge, UK

Tony Breslin is becoming a prolific author and I am sure that his books will be of great benefit to teachers, parents and the wider community.

Estelle Morris
Baroness Morris of Yardley
Former Secretary of State for Education
UK Parliament

Bubble Schools is no ordinary book about education - it not only captures and preserves the historical impact the pandemic has had on a generation of students, but more importantly gives key insights into how the best creative responses to teaching during the pandemic should and must be leveraged to permanently shift and evolve English education provision in the years ahead.

Cosette Reczek
Parent
London, UK

Tony Breslin has, once again, provided a roadmap to education that will become a must-read for anyone concerned with schooling and education as they have been forever changed by the COVID-19 pandemic.

More than just a collection of data and interviews, Bubble Schools and the Long Road from Lockdown provides an analysis, and an incredibly thoughtful one, of what education means, how the COVID-19 pandemic has impacted that meaning, and the ways in which that meaning could be reformed in meaningful ways in the future.

Breslin's expertise in the field of education is well established, his research is simultaneously nuanced and insightful, and his writing accomplishes the rare feat of being both accessible and informative, making this book, and its innovative recommendations, all the more poignant as we begin to understand what the pandemic years have meant, and could mean, for the future of education.

J. Michael Ryan,
Assistant Professor of Sociology
Nazarbayev University

Bubble Schools and the Long Road from Lockdown

This sequel to Breslin's critically acclaimed *Lessons from Lockdown* explores how school leaders, teachers, parents and pupils have navigated their way through and from lockdown. This is the story of 'doing' schooling against the topsy-turvy backdrop of a pandemic that has caused us all to reflect not just on the purpose and substance of education but also on the world that schools might, in the future, need to prepare children and young people for. Drawing on the voices of more than a hundred pupils, parents and professionals, it captures the range of experiences as teachers and students grappled with new ways of working, policy chaos and the complexity of schooling and teaching in such a landscape.

Bubble Schools is a must-read for all concerned about the shape that our public education systems take as we begin to move forward from a system-shock that has revealed both the strengths and the weaknesses of education policy, system design and long-established classroom practice.

Dr Tony Breslin is an experienced educational leader and a widely published researcher, writer and commentator. A teacher by profession, he is Director at Breslin Public Policy Limited, Chair at Bushey Primary Education Federation and Chair of the Education Committee at Anthem Schools Trust.

Bubble Schools and the Long Road from Lockdown

The Educational Legacy of COVID-19

TONY BRESLIN

Routledge
Taylor & Francis Group

LONDON AND NEW YORK

Designed cover image: © Getty Images

First published 2023
by Routledge
4 Park Square, Milton Park, Abingdon, Oxon OX14 4RN

and by Routledge
605 Third Avenue, New York, NY 10158

Routledge is an imprint of the Taylor & Francis Group, an informa business

British Library Cataloguing-in-Publication Data
A catalogue record for this book is available from the British Library

Library of Congress Cataloging-in-Publication Data
Names: Breslin, Tony, author.
Title: Bubble schools and the long road from lockdown: the educational legacy of
COVID-19 / Tony Breslin. Description: New York, NY: Routledge, 2023. |
Includes bibliographical references and index.
Identifiers: LCCN 2022030573 (print) | LCCN 2022030574 (ebook) |
ISBN 9781032069784 (hardback) | ISBN 9781032069791 (paperback) |
ISBN 9781003204824 (ebook)
Subjects: LCSH: Educational planning–Great Britain. |
COVID-19 (Disease)–Great Britain. |
Social distancing (Public health) and education–Great Britain. |
Educational change–Great Britain.
Classification: LCC LB2806 .B724 2023 (print) |
LCC LB2806 (ebook) | DDC 371.200941–dc23 / eng / 20220713
LC record available at https://lccn.loc.gov/2022030573
LC ebook record available at https://lccn.loc.gov/2022030574

ISBN: 9781032069784 (hbk)
ISBN: 9781032069791 (pbk)
ISBN: 9781003204824 (ebk)

DOI: 10.4324/9781003204824

Typeset in Dante and Avenir
by Newgen Publishing UK

In memory of William Joseph Ryan, my beloved Uncle Bill

11 January 1928 – 4 November 2021

Bill passed away a matter of months before this book entered production.

A native of Kildare in the Republic of Ireland and an inspiration to all who knew him, Bill Ryan had a smile, a handshake and, most importantly, time for anybody and everybody. The world is a better place for the near 94 years that he spent with us. Kind, compassionate and wise, the world would be a better place if we were all a little bit more Bill

A 'COVID-Keep'? Something to do with optimism. We need optimism and that has been taken away because of uncertainty. I would like to be able to see the horizon again – I can't quite see it now. What do we want for our children? I would have thought if we could retain that question it would be of great benefit.

Tony Thorpe. School Governor, Hall Cross Academy, Doncaster, focus group discussion – School Governors and Trustees, 17 April 2021

Contents

Figures

Preface

Bubble Schools and the Long Road From Lockdown is the second in a trilogy of texts that, taken together, seek to capture the educational experiences and opportunities of that period marked out by the scourge of COVID-19, and to assess the legacy that the virus might bequeath to the teachers and learners of the future. The trilogy seeks to do so through the voices of pupils, parents and educational professionals and volunteers, drawing on a growing lockdown literature in the process.

The first text, *Lessons from Lockdown*, had mapped out the challenges of the first schooling lockdown and the shockwaves that it brought to that academic year, a year that concluded on 31 August 2020. There, and here, the main focus is on UK schools but it is hoped that there will be some commonalities that make both texts of interest to a wider international audience.

This book picks up the story on 1 September 2020 and takes us through the academic year that followed and on through the opening term of 2021–22, the overlap being deliberate and aiming to capture the experience of educators, children and young people, and their families, as schools sought to kickstart what, in September 2021, was widely *hoped* to be the start of a post-lockdown era, albeit one reached by a long road from lockdown.

However, as the first draft of this book neared completion early in 2022, and the virus approached its second anniversary, at least on western shores, another iteration of COVID-19, Omicron, threatened that hope. We shall see where it leads, and as readers, you will have *some* idea of this by the time these pages reach you towards the close of 2022. The final text in the trilogy, *Reschooling Society After Lockdown* is due for publication during 2023 or early 2024, but Omicron may have something to say about that.

As with *Lessons from Lockdown*, the starting point for this text is straighforward and threefold: first, that COVID-19 has delivered a shock to our education and training systems, in the UK and beyond, which has the potential to be, and ought to be, long-standing; second, that this shock has ramifications for the pedagogy and purpose of education – the what, the how, and the why of learning; third, that this shock has implications for every kind of educational setting, from preschool to university, from adult and community learning to professional and vocational training, whether the provider is the state, the voluntary sector, or private business.

The extent of this shock should not be underestimated. For educational researchers Sinead Harmey and Gemma Moss:

> COVID-19 has had an unprecedented impact on education in many countries. In Spring 2020, at the height of the first wave of the COVID-19 pandemic, over 1.5 billion young people were impacted by the closure of schools and universities (UNESCO, 2020) [and it was] estimated that 12.8% of enrolled learners worldwide were still out of school due to closures. This estimation does not account for the many nations that have partially reopened schools or moved to online learning; and pupils who are temporarily self-isolating or off sick. This level of disruption to education is unprecedented.
>
> 'Learning disruption or learning loss: using evidence from unplanned closures to inform returning to school after COVID-19'
>
> (Harmey and Moss, 2021)

In her Foreword to the ImpactEd report, 'Pupil learning and wellbeing during the COVID-19 pandemic', published in February 2021, Dame Sue John compares the regular, near-constant change that is part and parcel of the everyday life of education professionals to the system-shock created by the virus:

> Teachers and schools are well used to change. Cohorts of pupils come and go. Governments and policy makers change approach. Over time, the community that a school serves can even shift, subject to demographic and economic forces outside the control of the teaching profession. Most of these changes are subtle and slow-moving. Teachers and schools adapt: often incrementally, often heroically, often with limited resources at their disposal.
>
> This last year has disrupted the pattern. Schools have been faced with rapid change writ large, complete with its own vocabulary

of remote learning; lateral flows and bubbles broken or breached. Teachers and their schools have been at the heart of a national conversation about how the country deals with the most significant crisis in a generation.

(Dame Sue John. Foreword, in ImpactEd, 2021)

As with *Lessons from Lockdown*, while the main focus in this text is on schools, the arguments and evidence set out in the pages that follow are about way more than what happens in our schools, vital though this is. While we concentrate on the statutory years, the perspective taken is one that understands the need for learning to be both lifelong and life-wide, that schools have a pivotal role to play in creating an appetite and capacity for learning, and that they are a part of every individual's learning journey, not a precursor to it. As I argued in the Preface to *Lessons from Lockdown*, too often books and papers that purport to be about education are actually about schooling and, quite specifically, the schooling of children and young people. Again, I want to avoid this ambiguity from the outset: the statutory schooling years are vital in laying the foundations for the fulfilment of potential in adulthood, but education, unlike statutory schooling, has no endpoint and, at any point in time, no boundaries.

And this focus on education being both lifelong and life-wide, and about schooling being about the installation of foundations that will serve individuals and the multiple communities to which they will belong throughout and across their lives is especially vital in light of lockdown. Lockdown, and the enforced non-working, home-working and home-schooling that it has brought for so many of us, has reminded us like never before of the importance of active, learned minds and the ability to both identify, apply and share a range of transferable skills in settings defined by their ambiguities rather than their certainties.

For those of us professionally engaged in the provision of education, lockdown has been inspiring, enabling and humbling in equal measure – *inspiring* because it has called on us to rethink the plethora of tactics and strategies that we have used for so long in our teaching and in the organisation of mass education; *enabling* because it has set free at least some of the creativity that many of us feared had been long brow-beaten out of us by a range of compliance, accountability and assessment processes, and *humbling* because, as professional educators, we have been reminded that many more than us contribute to the process of education; it does, indeed, take a village to educate a child, albeit a village that is variously local, virtual and global. We are at our best when we harness the power and passion of the resultant partnerships, whether they be between teachers and parents, governors and senior leaders, adults and children, or children working in collaboration, whether the challenge be a mathematical equation, an environmental concern or the construction of an imagined landscape in *Minecraft*.

In the penning of the Preface to *Lessons from Lockdown*, I suggested that there would be a strong desire to 'get back to normal', to reinstate life as was (and not just in education) but contended that we should resist this. Following Goffman (1956) and my own earlier work (Breslin, 2001), I argued that:

> Educational institutions – in common with, for instance, hospitals, the military, prisons, the police, care settings, and the bureaucracies of the state and the corporate sector – are relatively total institutions [with] a strong tendency to both reproduce and self-justify their practice across generations. As such, our schools, colleges and universities maximise the feeling of change while minimising its impact, reproducing curricular and other pedagogic practices across generations, rather than responding to emergent need.
>
> (Breslin, 2021)

In this context, I contended that:

> The kind of system-shock delivered by COVID-19 has the potential to fling us from these comfort zones, to make us reassess our practice, to prompt us to ask could and should things be different, and what could 'different' mean? Might 'thinking different' offer us solutions to some of the recurrent challenges at the heart of our education systems, challenges (notably those around inequalities of opportunity and outcome) that, hitherto, have endured in spite of a plethora of educational reforms, especially in the schooling sector?
>
> (Breslin, 2021)

Against this background, the research that underpins this new text mirrors, builds on and returns to that carried out for *Lessons from Lockdown*, although this time I had the benefit of a longer run-in to the writing period, with focus groups and interviews being carried out across a four-month period starting shortly after the 2021 Easter Break.

Again, the research engaged over a hundred participants, including those teaching, or involved in supporting teaching, in the primary and secondary phases, those involved in meeting the needs of children and young people with special educational needs and disabilities, those working in a range of alternative provision settings, school leaders and those involved in school governance, either as governors or trustees, parents, guardians and carers, those teaching in various parts of the independent sector, pupils and students, and a range of policy influencers, policy shapers and policymakers, including those based in teachers' professional associations and in regulatory bodies.

Again, nearly all have been engaged virtually and, again, all have been measured but candid in their responses, and generous and warm in their spirit, whether they have made their contribution through a series of 17 focus-group conversations, or a set of one-to-one discussions, mainly carried out largely during the writing phase, with policy influencers and practice leaders that, again, became a feature of my working day, and often the inspiration for it.

The publication of *Lessons from Lockdown*, in the early weeks of 2021, and the significant media coverage this had brought, helped to bring new participants to the research process, but I also chose to revisit and re-engage many of those who had spoken with us for the earlier book, wondering how their personal and professional lockdowns were panning out.

In addition, international responses to the book had spurred three partnerships that were to bring much to the research process; one was facilitated by Professor Betty Merchant and her colleague, Assistant Professor Juan Nino at the University of Texas at San Antonio, with whom we had held a short series of focus groups involving school leaders and aspiring school leaders in December 2020. Another one was spurred by an invitation from Zoe Camper, Jonathan Tavss and Mitchell Weisburgh, US-based colleagues with a passion for rethinking all manner of traditional practice in the educational sphere and beyond, and co-founders of the Augmented Society Network (ASN). The third partnership was one arising from an invitation to record a podcast with US educators, Professor Lynda Leavitt and Assistant Professor Robyne Elder at Lindenwood University, Missouri, after our shared involvement in the ASN project and the publication of *Lessons from Lockdown*.

As had been the case twelve or so months previous, these conversations were enlightening and wide-ranging, but each concluded with participants invited to transport themselves back to the classrooms they had been familiar with in January 2020, as they faced into another year, one they might have expected to be just like any other, until the juggernaut that is COVID-19 first swung into partial, still-distant view, and then to reflect on three interlinked questions:

1. What, looking back on the classrooms of pre-pandemic schooling, can't you wait to get back to?
2. What, in terms of the schooling that you were involved in offering or experiencing back then, can't you wait to leave behind?
3. What do you envisage we will, or at least *should*, do differently in light of the pandemic?

In the first interview of the *Bubble Schools* research cycle, I got to speak with Tracey Middleton, a school governing clerk who supports multiple school boards in Hertfordshire, England, where I am engaged in the training of school governors. She introduced me to the notion of 'COVID-Keeps'. Although neither of us is sure whether she originated the nicely alliterative phrase, it is a useful badge for those innovative and creative educational practices that might never have emerged had we never had to deal with this awful virus.

And whatever the future of the virus itself, we are certainly not short of other challenges that require our urgent attention, both domestic and international. Thus, against the background of the war in Ukraine, a UK 'cost of living' crisis, a climate emergency and a period of extreme flux in our politics (in the UK, across Europe and in the US), all of which will impact on the form and substance of the education that we offer (and can offer) to children, young people and to learners of all ages, our responsibility to renew our schooling systems remains.

In this context, our ability to hold onto these specific *Lessons from Lockdown*, and these innovations that emerged in our *Bubble Schools*, will determine whether we simply 'get back to normal', or whether our ambitions are greater, and spur us to create the schooling systems and schooling experiences that we – and our children – surely deserve.

Tony Breslin
September 2022

Acknowledgements

I am grateful to the many people who have contributed to the writing of this book.

Special thanks are due to Annamarie Kino and to the Editorial Assistants on the book, Molly Selby and Mouli Sharma, and their colleagues at Routledge, for their encouragement and patience. When I don my school governor or charity trustee hat, or when I train these noble volunteers, I talk about getting the balance between support and challenge right; Annamarie and her team have, again, done so with aplomb, as have their colleagues, Rebecca Willford and Emily Bonden at NewGen Publishing, and Jeanne Brady at Cove Publishing Support Services, who steered the book through the production process.

Particular thanks are also due to the hundred-plus individuals – pupils, parents, teachers, school senior leaders and support staff in primary, secondary and special schools in the state and independent sectors, youth workers, and those working in alternative provision settings, or as school governors and trustees, teacher educators, educational researchers and policy shapers – from the UK and elsewhere who contributed to the many focus groups, one-to-one and small group sessions that have informed and inspired my writing. Three-quarters of these individuals were new to the broader research project and had not contributed to the earlier research for *Lessons from Lockdown*. I am also immensely grateful to those who have invited me to present the findings offered in *Lessons from Lockdown* and in the pages that follow, including groups of teachers, governors and school leaders convened by Governor Services teams in Bury, Leeds and Hull and the West Riding, by Hayes Education, KPMG and Step Teachers, by Claire

Fox and her colleagues at the Academy of Ideas, by Corinne Latham who convenes the excellent HeadSpace conference in Northern Ireland, and by my friends in the Fabian Society Education Policy Group. In addition, I must also thank my many friends in education who have acted as willing sounding boards throughout the process. They have continually informed my thinking and, occasionally, saved me from myself.

The discussions that have been a part of, and emerged from, these sessions have made a vital contribution to my own thinking and to the broader research process. Nick Johnson, Chief Executive at the British Educational Research Association (BERA) and Lizana Oberholzer, Governance Convenor at the British Education Leadership, Management and Administration Society (BELMAS) both provided the opportunity to participate in podcasts and have been sterling supporters of my work throughout. Nick was one of a number of colleagues who read *Lessons from Lockdown* ahead of its publication. I am grateful for the generosity of time and comment that he offered then, as I am to those who have done likewise for *Bubble Schools*. In a similar vein, I am also grateful to the many broadcasters and journalists who have given the book space on page, through speaker, or on screen, and to those who have reviewed either or both texts ahead of, or after, publication.

In addition to these sessions and this support, I have had the privilege – through my role as a governor trainer for Hertfordshire-based HFL Education and, more recently, as a newly appointed National Leader of Governance – of working with over a hundred school or trust governing bodies since the start of lockdown; their insights have informed the analysis and recommendations offered here and served to keep me grounded in the day-to-day challenges that school communities have faced throughout this period.

All of our 'formal' research participants are listed separately in Appendix B. I am thankful not just for the time that every one of these individuals gave us, but the spirit in which they gave this time: openly and open-mindedly, generous with both their time and their ideas, insightful and, in spite of what was often near-exhaustion, essentially optimistically, driven by a belief that in amongst the tragedy of the virus and the reality of lockdown might, as I remarked on the publication of *Lessons from Lockdown*, lie the seeds of innovation and opportunity.

In terms of convening and transcribing the focus groups and interviews, I am especially grateful to Shelley Bray at Tring Typing Services. With Ryan McMahon, the intrepid researcher on *Lessons from Lockdown* who had transcribed the focus group and interview recordings for that book, deep in revision for his final examinations at the University of Cambridge as the research period approached, which ran from April 2021 through to June 2021, I faced the prospect of transcribing my own data, and the endless pressing of 'Play', 'Pause' and 'Rewind' buttons (and the multiple intermittent expletives) that this would involve. Just as I shuddered at the prospect, and with the first planned focus group just days away, David Miller, Head at Pebble Brook School, and a long-standing supporter of my research and writing efforts, suggested I give Shelley a call. Shelley has been fantastic to work with, and as a parent to children at various points in the education system or in the early stages of their careers, she has brought unique and valuable insights to the process. Dave, as always, helped to convene the two meetings of the Special Education and Alternative Provision focus group. And Ryan remains present in these pages; he played the key role in referencing this text and in cataloguing the participants involved.

As with *Lessons from Lockdown*, this book offers primarily a study of the lockdown experiences of educators, pupils and parents in the UK's education systems. However, the narrative presented has been increasingly informed by colleagues from many other settings who came across the earlier text, most notably Professor Betty Merchant and Assistant Professor Juan Nino and their colleagues and the school leaders that they work with at the University of Texas at San Antonio, and with whom I am now working with on a major cross-national study of the educational impact of COVID-19. Amongst many others, I am also indebted to Professor Lynda Leavitt and Associate Professor Robyne Elder at Lindenwood University, who were kind enough to engage me in a podcast focusing on my research, Zoe Camper, Jonathan Tavss and Mitch Weisburgh at the US-based Augmented Society Network who led the production of what I am confident will become an influential set of papers on the future of schooling (Camper, Tavssberger and Weisburgh, 2021), Alex Bell, who hosts the UNESCO World Tour and the network of globally dispersed educators that it brings together, and Assistant Professor Michael Ryan, a sociologist at Nazarbayev University, who is editing an internationally focused series on the pandemic, and its multiple impacts, for Routledge in the United States, including an education collection, *Pandemic Pedagogies* (Ryan, 2022). Each of these individuals and those that joined our international educators' focus group and the three US-UK focus groups organised in partnership with Betty and Juan, have continually reminded me of both the contrasts and the similarities between our different experiences of lockdown. We must continue to share and learn from these, and our proposal that an international network of educational researchers and school and system leaders be formed to facilitate and oversee this process is offered as one means of doing so.

My colleagues on the Governing Board at Bushey Primary Education Federation and, latterly, my new colleagues on the Board of Trustees at Anthem Schools Trust, and the senior staff in each of these organisations, and my many friends across the school and third-sector governance communities, deserve my gratitude and thanks. As I was in the writing of *Lessons from Lockdown*, I am also indebted to those who have worked with me in a plethora of roles across a working lifetime in education, especially my tutors, Barry Dufour and the late Doug Holly at the University of Leicester School of Education and Denis Lawton (who passed away as this text entered production) and Paddy Walsh at the University of London Institute of Education, my many colleagues in the Association for Citizenship Teaching and the Association for the Teaching of the Social Sciences, Sue Armstrong-Brown and the team that she led with such aplomb team at Adoption UK, and the friends I have worked with at Langleybury School in Hertfordshire, The School of St. David and St. Katharine in Haringey, the London Borough of Enfield School Improvement Service, the Citizenship Foundation and Breslin Public Policy Limited. All have played their part in enabling me to understand how our schools work and why education matters. In amongst these, the late Terry Farrell again gets a special mention, a London Head who gave his career to working with young people from often disadvantaged homes, and to moulding young teachers so that we could go on to do likewise.

Throughout the writing period, a range of individuals have been incredibly helpful and have met with me to explore the issues at hand, while others have, simply, kept me going with their insights, their toleration (of my inability to discuss anything else) and their sense of humour. Notable amongst these are Mike Moores, my long-term friend and collaborator at Breslin Public Policy, Mick Callanan, Delivery Director at the Orwell Youth Prize, and another long-term friend, Paddy O'Leary, who was always up for a mid-morning, socially distanced coffee in the garden once the regulations allowed us, Cosette Reczek, who, as she had with *Lessons from Lockdown*, read through the final text, offering forensic, incisive and supportive feedback that I hope I have done justice to, Helen Naughton-Green, who read through all of the interview and focus-group transcripts for *Bubble Schools* before offering the insight that only an international educationalist can, Mary Ann Cooper, inspirational Headteacher at Bushey Primary Education Federation, where, as noted above, I am privileged to be Chair of the Governing Board, and Danny Coyle, the recently appointed Headteacher at Cardinal Wiseman Catholic School in Greenford, to the west of London. In his previous role, as Head at Newman Catholic College in Harlesden, the school which (as Cardinal Hinsley Roman Catholic School) I had attended as a pupil, Danny gave unstinting support to this project, and he continues to do so at Cardinal Wiseman.

In addition, I must thank those who provided pre-publication reviews of a then almost complete text: Isobel Bryce, Michael Callanan, Robyne Elder, Lynda Leavitt, Michael McGarvey, Estelle Morris, Cosette Reczek and Michael Ryan; their insightful comments warmed my spirit as I worked on the final draft and proofed the final copy. I trust that I have done their efforts justice.

Finally, I want to thank my sounding board-in-chief, my wife Ann Bowen-Breslin, another inspirational Headteacher (at Hillingdon Primary School in West London), and a constant source of wise counsel – and much, much more – and our two boys for their unstinting and unconditional support. Their encouragement, patience, tolerance and insight gets me up in the morning and reminds me why this stuff matters. For a second successive year, my study has been their home classroom, and their company my daily fuel.

Needless to say, while the input of those above, and many others, has been invaluable – and for this reason I invoke 'we' rather than 'I' for the greater part of the book – I remain responsible for what is written in these pages, warts and all.

About the author

Dr Tony Breslin is an adviser, writer, media commentator, trainer and public policy analyst specialising in education and participation, and has emerged as an authoritative voice on the impact of lockdown, especially on educational provision.

His work in this field came to the fore with the publication of the prequel to this text, *Lessons from Lockdown: The Educational Legacy of COVID-19*, by Routledge in January 2021, which tracks the experience of teaching, learning and school leadership through the early stages of lockdown in Spring and Summer 2020. He is currently working on the third book in what is set to become a trilogy of lockdown texts, *Reschooling Society After Lockdown*, which is set for publication by Routledge in late 2023 or early 2024, and focuses on how schooling is reinventing itself in the wake of the virus. In addition, during this period he has contributed to a well-received international report, *An Opportunity to Reimagine Learning: Pandemic Catalyst*, edited by colleagues in the Augmented Society Network (Camper, Tavssberger and Weisburgh, 2021) and is working on a comparative project assessing the impact of the pandemic in a range of different national settings under the leadership of Professor Betty Merchant at the University of Texas at San Antonio (UTSA).

His reports, *A Place for Learning: Putting Learning at the Heart of Citizenship, Civic Identity and Community Life* (Breslin, 2016), and *Who Governs Our Schools? Trends, Tensions and Opportunities* (Breslin, 2017), have made important contributions to the debates about the role of adult and community learning and Further and Higher Education in a post-industrial age, and the nature of school governance in an emergent landscape of academies, federations and Multi-Academy Trusts (MATs).

Tony's own experience in governance and as a senior leader in education and the voluntary sector is extensive. A teacher by profession, with experience working in denominational and non-denominational schools and in Further Education, and a curriculum development specialist, he is currently Chair at Bushey Primary Education Federation and a Trustee at Anthem Schools Trust, and was, until recently, a Trustee of Adoption UK. Previously, he has served as Chair of the awarding organisation, Industry Qualifications, the public-speaking social enterprise, Speakers Bank, and the educational charities and membership associations, Human Scale Education and the Association for the Teaching of the Social Sciences.

A former Local Authority School Improvement Adviser, a Chief Examiner at GCSE and a Principal Examiner at A level, he is perhaps best known for his work as CEO at the Citizenship Foundation (2001–10), the influential education and participation charity, now Young Citizens, where he developed the concept of the Citizenship-Rich School, and his work in the governance arena, where his engagement as a Consultant Trainer at HFL Education means that he works with school governors and leaders in primary, secondary and special education on a weekly basis, either in person or virtually. In October 2021, he was appointed as a National Leader of Governance by the Department for Education, one of over sixty experienced governance experts charged with reviewing the quality of governance in maintained schools and MATs in England as part of a national programme administered by the National Governance Association, the membership and support organisation for school governors and trustees in the UK. His recent appointment as a Consultant School Improvement Adviser and Independent Chair of the Post-16 Strategic Review Group in the London Borough of Barking and Dagenham, and his subsequent appointment as Independent Chair of the 'Pathways for All' Strategic Board hosted by Kent County Council, confirmed as this text went to print in autumn 2022, promises to further strengthen the range and reach of his work in schools as school communities navigate, to cite the wording of the title of this text, 'the long road from lockdown'.

Tony is a champion of the social curriculum, professional, technical and vocational education, community engagement and lifelong learning, themes that are common in a wide-ranging publications list featuring over 120 articles, papers and texts, and in the work of the successful social impact consultancy that he leads, Breslin Public Policy Limited.

The optimism of September

1

And the subsequently broken promise of normality

As the dust kicked up by the grading crisis settled and another cohort of young people progressed into Further or Higher Education or into employment or training, most (in spite of the fiasco of the August just past) progressing as they had hoped or at least to a destination of equivalence, and as primary schools continued to go about their work in a way that suggested the system would not fall apart if it was left to fend without the end of phase Standard Attainment Tests that had become a mainstay of UK elementary schooling, it was tempting to think, 'well that was that', and now for some normality.

Certainly, these were this author's thoughts as, late into the night of 31 August 2020, the 'send' button was pressed, and the manuscript for *Lessons from Lockdown: The Educational Impact of COVID-19*, the predecessor text to *Bubble Schools and the Long Road from Lockdown*, was dispatched to AnnaMarie Kino and her team at publishers, Routledge. A job done and a chapter closed. Of course, as the title of this text alludes, it was to prove a somewhat longer road from lockdown than most had anticipated, albeit fired by some kind of summer break and the annual optimism of September – a new school year just begun as John Lennon might have sung, and while trepidation remained in the air, some felt emboldened by the experience of the preceding terms:

DOI: 10.4324/9781003204824-1

> In March it was unexpected, new, 'we haven't been here before', but in September we had been there. I had more confidence. In March, through hard work, we had managed the situation well and I had the confidence I would do it again. In March we didn't have anything to look back on.
>
> (Daniel Coyle, Headteacher, Newman Catholic College, focus group – secondary educators, 13 May 2021)

Cosette Reczek, a parent, colleague and friend who had proofed, and thereby significantly enhanced, *Lessons from Lockdown* in those closing days of August, cast a more wary eye on the journey ahead, in asking:

> But what kind of schools will our children return to, and what kind of schooling?
>
> (Cosette Reczek, parent, in conversation with the author, 29 August 2020)

In England, the government had been keen to help the return to normality on its way. Six months on from the start of that increasingly distant first lockdown in March 2020, the abiding feeling emerging from politicians and newspaper columnists alike was that it was time to 'open up', to get back to work. And so, citizens were urged to 'eat out to help out' (August 2020) and to get back to their city-centre desks, if only to help the micro economies of franchised sandwich bars, coffee shops, eateries and designer outlets that had been spawned at the foot of the towers of glass, steel and neon which now adorn the shiny business districts of almost all UK cities. These creations of the opening decades of the twenty-first century, enabling bankers, lawyers and stockbrokers to pick up a coffee on the way in, a shirt at lunchtime (well, why not?) and a pint after work, while providing the opportunity for some window shopping by their lesser-paid support staff had lost their purpose with the rise of remote working.

Headteacher Mary Ann Cooper remained concerned though:

> It's fine now, the weather's lovely but it's a long term ahead, and staff are still tired and weary, and I worry how things will develop as the nights close in. March was different; there was a sense of novelty, we were blessed with terrific spring sunshine, and the days were opening up. We've got a winter to get through.
>
> (Mary Ann Cooper, Federation Headteacher, Bushey Primary Education Federation, in conversation with the author, 6 September 2020)

And other school leaders shared her trepidation:

> Coming back in the autumn term we thought we were coming back to normality but we (as a staff) always felt that we knew we were heading to another lockdown … (we were) very much anticipating another lockdown.
>
> Steve Mills, Headteacher, White Hill Junior School, Hitchin, and Secretary, Hertfordshire Branch, National Association for Head Teachers, focus group – primary educators, 5 May 2021)

Sure enough, by half-term, a matter of six or so weeks later, the mood was, indeed, changing; 'Eat Out to Help Out', the brainchild of England's then Chancellor of the Exchequer Rishi Sunak, had morphed into 'Drink Up and Get Out'. The local lockdowns that were initially presumed to be the dying embers of a spring and early summer virus, were becoming more numerous and, worryingly, as we shall outline in some detail in these pages, they were afflicting many of the most disadvantaged communities – those whose existence was defined by large, multi-generational families, small cramped homes, and workplaces characterised by employment practices and wage levels that were assumed to be confined to a century past.

The talk was of new variants and 'Circuit-Breakers' – short, sharp, immediate lockdowns designed to stop the virus in its tracks – with active debate focusing on whether schools would or could return after the half-term. This debate crystallised the dilemma for those making decisions. Close schools and the poorest children would (it was assumed) suffer most, not just through so-called 'lost learning' but because many lived in the kind of homes just described. Keep schools open, and the fear was the flames of the virus would be fanned, all this while a vaccine remained some way off, and while the optimism of September seemed some time ago. The half-term break was duly extended in Northern Ireland, Scotland and Wales but not in England. However, on 5 November, a second English lockdown, envisaged as lasting a month and which did not include schools, was announced.

But let us remind ourselves of that September return, and of the bubble schooling, first utilised in the preceding Summer Term, that accompanied it; educationally, there may be all sorts of reasons to dislike the 'bubbling' of the school landscape. Organisationally, however, bubbles were a feat to marvel at, and they deserve exploration accordingly.

Schooling in a bubble

At the heart of any model of mass schooling, is the fluidity and mobility of teaching groups. This is assumed to be most vital in the secondary (or high school) phase, where fans and critics alike have pointed to the 'industrial' organisation of schooling, with its industrial (or 'Fordist' as the management literature might describe it) division of labour and the specialist subject-specific and time-precise teaching (in dedicated rooms, of course) that this facilitates. Geography is in Room 3 in B Block at 2.10 p.m.; French is in Room 17 in Languages Block at 11.15 a.m.; no ambiguity there. As the late Terry Farrell, an experienced and successful London Headteacher, put it to this author many years ago, 'Tony, if you're going to make it as a Head, learn how to timetable first.' Timetables are the internal wiring diagrams of secondary-school life – they both make the machine work and convey multiple messages about status and hierarchy; if the 'Inclusion Unit' (an oxymoron if ever there was one) is a Portakabin at the other end of the school yard and staffed largely by supply teachers, no amount of banners proclaiming the school's commitment to inclusion will arrest the timetabling reality. More subtly, the allocation of newer buildings to particular subjects, or bigger rooms to Heads of Department convey messages, not perhaps about what matters and what does not, but about what matters *most*.

In primary-school settings, where practice is largely based around an 'integrated day' model and a single teacher, the impact of the timetable is less stark, although the mapping of the day and the prioritising of particular subjects such as Mathematics and English still conveys powerful messages about school and societal values, as the National Literacy and National Numeracy Strategies, and the associated Literacy Hours and Numeracy Hours that started just about every English primary school day in the late 1990s, adroitly demonstrated.

The bubbling of the school landscape introduced a whole new layer into the timetabling mix. Thus, when children and young people in England and Wales returned to their classrooms in September 2020, the environment, as Cosette Reczek had predicted, was significantly different. In both the primary and secondary phases, room sizes and the need to retain social distancing often meant that classes had to be smaller, sometimes reduced from thirty to fifteen in size; group work, for years an emblematic marker of progressive practice, gave way to teaching in rows; peripatetic tutors, teaching assistants and those focused on supporting those with Special Educational Needs or Disabilities found themselves unable to sit in the kind of physical proximity to children that the very essence of their relationship-enabled work required, while masks underlined the separation both between teacher and learner and between learners themselves. Reflecting on this, one experienced secondary senior leader observed that:

> The teaching assistants were struggling to be effective in the classroom because they couldn't get close to the pupils they were helping. The teacher area in our classrooms was taped off and physically we had that distance but teaching assistants often sit shoulder-to-shoulder with students and they were feeling they weren't doing a good enough job. I think they felt they were being thrown to the lions by being in the classroom.
>
> (Gemma Absalom, Assistant Headteacher, Parmiters School, Watford, focus group – secondary educators, 13 May 2021)

And in corridors and open spaces inside and out, movement took on a new regimentation, with one-way systems for both children and adults, varied start, finish, break and lunch times, and delineated school yards that ensured children and young people, and associated staff, remained within their 'bubble'. Thus, teachers lost their 'social' (and recuperation) space too, with staff rooms largely off-limits because they invited mixing that breached the overt segregation of the bubbles.

Schools in Scotland start their summer break some weeks earlier than those in England, Northern Ireland and Wales and return to the classroom ahead of their counterparts elsewhere in the UK. Thus, the Scottish restart in August 2020 gave a taste of what was to come. In *Lessons from Lockdown*, Allyson Dobson, the Head at a large Scottish secondary school, provided a vivid description of the 2020 post-lockdown landscape. Given that Scottish schools return for the new academic year three weeks or so earlier than those elsewhere in the UK, she, although not referencing 'bubbles' directly, Dobson signalled what those in schools south of the border and across the Irish Sea could expect in the weeks and term ahead – and how it compared with usual practice:

> Previously, the young people would have come into the dining hall. They would have met their friends. They may have had some breakfast, if they hadn't had breakfast before they left [home]; it was an opportunity to gather and just start [the day] together, we can't do that [now]. And so pupils have to come in and go straight to class. So, at the moment we're actually using, and this is with the agreement of health and safety, all the different fire exits. So, [a pupil] would come straight [in through] the fire exit closest to her Maths class and go straight into class … [a member of the] Senior Leadership Team will be there with

a hand sanitizer, making sure that they're sanitizing hands on entry into the building … [At changeover] the teacher will go round with a spray, spray the desks, the pupils will clean their desk area and their seat … and they'll sit down and they'll begin the learning.
(Allyson Dobson, Headteacher, Dalkeith High School, Dalkeith, research interview, 24 August 2020)

In short, and as we outline in more detail in Chapter 3, 'bubbles', sometimes also referred to as 'pods', acted as sealed social groups. Thus, in the event that a child became infected with the virus, or was identified as being in proximity with somebody with the virus, the bubble would be 'stood down' or 'closed', and the children in it would isolate at home for the recommended period of days, a period that changed across the course of the pandemic. The bubble, therefore, was a closed, self-contained space, and, at least initially, a fairly small closed space. And these were combined with a wider paraphernalia associated with lockdown – bubble-exclusive entrances and exits, the regimentation noted earlier, corridor masks, site-wide social distancing – which, as we have noted, impacted on everything from corridor movement to classroom teaching, the closure of staff rooms (as the adults were also 'bubbled') and the recasting or abolition of a plethora of school events, from assemblies to drama productions, from field trips to sports days, from art exhibitions to parents' evenings.

Against this background, sending home particular groups of children and young people became a feature of schooling not just during the Autumn Term, but across the 2020–21 school year, and into the first term of 2021–22. It is one of the reasons why a key message arising from the research that underpins this book is that no two children, families, classes, or year groups have experienced the same lockdown. The monochrome messaging of the newspaper pages does not do justice to a reality that was far more nuanced and mediated. Some children found themselves in teaching groups, classes, or year groups that were 'stood down' (and sent home) on multiple occasions. Others, sometimes in the same school, got through the year without experiencing anything like this level of disruption, and a minority experienced no disruption at all, other than the disruption of being educated in a sealed unit rather than a much larger and conventionally open school community, and the cancellation of all or most extra-curricular and curriculum enrichment activities.

The pervasive impact of background

This is not to say that being 'stood down', or having one's bubble 'burst' was a 'random' affair. Exposure to health crises is never a random occurrence; for something to be 'random' in the scientific and social scientific sense of the term, every individual in the group concerned must have an equal chance of selection. As the data and demography of the pandemic demonstrates, this is far from the case with COVID-19, as it is with illness in general.

Thus, those who are socio-economically disadvantaged, those in manual employment, those who are unemployed or under-employed (a growing experience for the increasing numbers who find themselves in insecure, unstable and occasional employment, sometimes now described as the 'precariat' rather than the 'proletariat'), those from minority ethnic groups (and notably those from the UK's BAME communities), the elderly and the very young, and those in privately rented or social housing are more likely to have had harsher experiences of the COVID period. They are more likely to have caught the disease, more likely to be hospitalised by it, more likely to end up in intensive care units, and more likely to succumb to the illness.

Thus, while, the virus may show no respect to social standing, it is more likely to strike the poor, unhealthy and otherwise vulnerable both hardest and with the greatest frequency, and this, of course, is the group that is least likely to be *sufficiently* digitally connected to make a success of schooling at home. Moreover, the intersectionalities of these singular indices of disad-vantage magnify the impact of these factors. This young person articulates the impact of such intersectionality cogently:

> Poverty is like a series of doors. One door is being poor, another door is being autistic, another door is being a young carer; another door is living in a bad area … The more doors there are, the more keys are needed to open them and people don't care enough to make the effort to open them all.
>
> (Breslin, Harris and Moores, 2013: 12)

It may, of course, be contended that in the period when COVID was at its most virulent – prior to the development of the vaccine and in the early months of its roll-out in spring 2021 – the greatest impact was on adults, especially older adults and those with pre-existing health conditions, not children, but the point is spurious. Children in disadvantaged settings are the unwitting and blameless victims of the environment they find themselves in. As we shall re-assert several times in these pages: they are less likely to have access to technology and stationery – or a free-from-distraction place to study – in the home, more likely to suffer additional disadvantage as a result of adult family members being hospitalised or having to isolate, and more likely to have lost relatives, neighbours and family friends as a conse-quence of COVID.

Summary

Whatever the optimism of September 2020, it was soon to be dashed. As we shall see, it gave way to a term of disruption-inspired creativity that was to prove different in every setting, and for every school leader, education professional or volunteer, child and family. As a term, it also began to hint at the very different needs that different children and young people would have if and when lockdown does begin to disappear in the rear-view mirror. As this book goes to press a little under two years later, that diversity of need is becoming all the clearer, and it is a theme that is set to infuse these pages. In terms of the pervasive but, as we shall see, often corrosive narratives around 'catch-up' and 'recovery', one size does not fit all. But, then again, in terms of National Curricula, 'Standard' Attainment Tests and assessment models based on a singular form of examination, it never did.

As remarked in *Lessons from Lockdown*, COVID-19 didn't, for the most part, create the inequities that it has exposed. That it is likely to have deepened them is beyond doubt. It may be that this exposure – this post-COVID visibility – that serves to spur politicians and other policy-shapers from denial to decisive action. We shall see.

Recommendations

1.1 If we are to sufficiently personalise learning post-lockdown, research into the educational impact of COVID needs to be focused on capturing the very different and nuanced experiences of different children, families and school communities and, therefore, there should be a focus on in-depth, qualitative research tasked with revealing the intensely personal stories that sit behind lockdown statistics.

1.2 'Catch-up' strategies need to embrace the various curriculum enrichment activities and experiences that children have missed out on during lockdown – activities and experiences that may not feature in the lists of content to be covered in traditional curriculum statements.

1.3 Policymakers and system leaders ought to grasp the new, and undeniable, visibility given by the pandemic to the impact of poverty on educational attainment as an opportunity to reflect on the effectiveness of pre-lockdown policy and practice in 'closing the gap' or 'diminishing the difference' in a post-lockdown world.

1.4 Policymakers and system leaders ought also to grasp the new, and undeniable, visibility given to the impact of other long-standing non-educational factors on educational attainment as a result of the pandemic, as an opportunity to address these socially patterned outcomes.

1.5 Policymakers and system leaders ought to reflect on the 'new vulnerabilities' revealed by COVID and the impact of these on educational outcomes, so that strategies may be developed and piloted to address these new vulnerabilities.

After the grading crisis **2**

What the class of 2020 did next, and what this might mean for Higher Education after lockdown

Lessons from Lockdown was researched and written during Spring and Summer 2020 and offered reflections on an *episode* – a pandemic – that all hoped was coming to a close. As such, it was written as the grading crisis of 2020 unfolded. Two years later, the phrase 'post-pandemic' is disappearing from our language. On 15 June 2021, *The New York Times* used an *Opinion* piece to implore its readers to 'Stop saying post pandemic' and noted that, as the year approached its mid-point, COVID-19 had killed 3.3 million globally, and more in the first five months of 2021 than it had in the whole of 2020. In short, the reality appears to be dawning that COVID may be here to stay and that, as has been the case with many other viruses over the years, we will need to learn to live with it, not least in its so-called 'Long COVID' form.

For the class of 2020, the young people who had been looking forward to progressing into pre-university courses (such as Scottish Highers and A levels elsewhere in the UK), into employment or into Higher Education in the Autumn of that year, it must have seemed this way. Those hoping to secure places at university had lived through the cancellation of written examination papers, the introduction of Centre Assessed Grades, the retrospective imposition of an algorithm to correct alleged 'teacher generosity' (a charge that was – predictably – to be repeated in 2021 and that is challenged in Chapter 6), the subsequent withdrawal of the algorithm

DOI: 10.4324/9781003204824-2

and the reinstatement of the teacher-generated grades (but only after some had already missed out on university places). Those preparing for GCSE examinations had been through a similar experience, not knowing whether they would be able to progress to further studies or training courses as they had planned.

For both, the late cancellation of written papers, announced three months before they had been scheduled to enter the examination hall, was often experienced – in a UK education system that many contend has become overly examination focused – as the denial of a rite of passage. Perhaps for this reason, one of the largest longitudinal studies to date (involving over 60,000 pupils) on the educational impact of COVID-19 on young people in English schools concluded that:

> Throughout 2020, pupils in Year 10 and 11 experienced the greatest challenges with motivation for learning; this did not change when they returned to school after the first lockdown.
>
> (ImpactEd, 2021)

Those seeking access to the workforce had to negotiate an uncertain labour market in which over 6.1 million UK employees remained on the furlough scheme in August 2020 (HMRC, 2020), the government programme that paid up to 80 percent of an individual's wage while they were stood down from employment because of the virus, and in which the number of apprenticeship opportunities had also declined on September 2019 (Camden, 2022). And a significant number of those who progressed to university were about to experience a year they could not have expected.

As this text goes to press in the autumn of 2022, in the aftermath of the annual panic about examination grades and an emergent 'cost of living' crisis that is causing young people and their families to reflect on the possible impact of higher student debt levels, one of the key educational debates is no longer about whether universities will reopen or not (as it had been during the previous academic year), but what will constitute a university education in the years after lockdown.

That, as we discuss throughout these pages, online learning will play some role – and a bigger role – in the delivery of education in every educational phase, including university education, is a certainty, a 'COVID-Keep' for sure, but the balance, or 'blend', between online and offline is unclear. And inevitably, this debate is mixed up with questions about what the value of a university education is, what the interplay between the charges levied for university education and the mode of education delivered should be, and whether broader policy objectives around participation in Higher

Education have a positive or negative impact on the wider schooling system.

As with this wider system, there are several issues at stake here: the effectiveness of different forms of online and offline pedagogy, the role of collaborative, in-the-room learning (especially with expert tutors), the learning that results from the legitimate digressions of seminar discussion (those off-piste, maybe initially off-the-point, forays into related topics or popular culture that no course manual can hope to predict, never mind 'cover', but which enrich both learning and personal development in a multitude of tough-to-quantify ways), the personal development that results from a young person living away from home for the first time (whether in the kitchen or the bedroom, the café, or the bar) and the often lifelong social connections formed during these years, especially vital for those from disadvantaged (or so-called 'non-traditional') cohorts who, without the experience of 'university life' would simply not make these connections. The university years, especially where these are spent away from home in initially unfamiliar settings, are as vital as ever in the development of an individual's social and cultural capital, even if the advantages in terms of economic capital have narrowed as universal education has become the norm, and the number of graduates has increased. Widening participation, that process (and welter of initiatives) whereby tracks into Higher Education for those from disadvantaged and non-traditional backgrounds have been significantly expanded over the past three decades has done much more than produce more graduates. It has widened access for the young people concerned to a whole range of social networks and conduits that were previously, and very literally, the preserve of the middle and upper classes, even if access to elite universities and certain courses remains dominated by those from the independent sector or those from selective or particularly advantaged state schools. As was remarked in *Lessons from Lockdown*, it would appear that those who scan the numbers of graduates emerging from our universities and opine that 'there are too many young people going to university' are talking about *other* people's children. And, for the class who completed A levels in England, Wales, or Northern Ireland, and Highers in Scotland, it was to prove a university experience like no other.

'Going' to university?

Shelley Bray, a PA to the Headteacher of a special school and who has transcribed the multiple focus groups and interviews that inform this text, has viewed lockdown from a number of perspectives, but her primary lens has always been that of a parent. Her rendition of her daughter's experience, both in 'missing out' on the taking of written papers (and with this what has become, as noted, a rite of passage for young people) *and* the sociability that is usually so central to the first year of university life, as one of the class of 2020, is both heartfelt and instructive:

> My daughter was supposed to take her A levels in the Summer last year and had worked so hard for them. She got the grades she needed to get into the university she wanted on the course she wanted but she missed out on that sense of achievement, the 'I did it because I worked hard'. She went to 'uni' but all the lessons were online, no socialising, so she was just sitting in her room on her own. She came home just before the November lockdown and only went back in April this year. Such a disappointing experience after all the hard work, and looking forward to it.
>
> (Shelley Bray, parent, focus group – secondary educators, 13 May 2021)

Given the media reports of student experience that led news bulletins in October and November 2020, Bray's daughter's decision to return home was unsurprising. In the immediate aftermath of 'Freshers' Week' (the annual social jamboree that welcomes new students to the campuses, towns and cities that will be their homes for the next three or more years), *The Guardian* reported that:

> The reopening of universities has so far resulted in reports of coronavirus cases at more than 60 institutions, with entire halls locked down at Manchester Metropolitan and Glasgow universities and thousands of students self-isolating in their rooms.
>
> (Fazackerley, 2020)

Reflecting on the experience, undergraduates were clear that it had not been the one they had expected:

> This first year at uni has been strange – it started off okay in September with nice weather so we could do stuff outside, but then [in] November – we couldn't get out, couldn't go to lectures, everything was online. I had a few tutorials with other people at the beginning but then that stopped happening. It was really hard not meeting other people but I hadn't had a normal uni year before that to compare [it with].
>
> (Louisa, first-year student, focus group – Further and Higher Education students, 3 August 2021)

Lucy, a law student – and a primary Headteacher's daughter – at a university in the North of England, articulated both the experience of students during the Autumn Term of 2020, and the ambivalence that they were met with in local communities. Lucy will have completed her degree by the time this text is published, but one can only assume that the feelings she expresses will have been felt even more acutely by those who were newly arrived as 'freshers':

> The experience of being an undergraduate against the backdrop of the COVID pandemic is complex. On one hand, you are a student, pitied by those around you for being pressurised to meet targets and achieve high (First Class) grades, whilst battling with internet issues and feeling trapped within the bleak walls of your student accommodation.
>
> On the other hand, you are ostracised and painted as an unhygienic 'super spreader', met with disgusted looks, whispers, and backwards steps from older generations, whilst going about your daily business.

And Lucy is critical of the universities in all of this:

> A key aspect that sticks out for me is the attitude of the universities. During my 'normal' (pre-COVID) first year at university, I was constantly reminded that missing a lecture would be 'detrimental to your learning' and that watching video recordings of missed lectures was 'no replacement for in-person learning'. Ironic though it may be, in the climate of COVID, this sentiment was replaced with praise for online learning and the quality of learning available, [perhaps in an attempt to justify] the £9,250 price-tag.
>
> The reality of the online-learning experience was a 'copy and paste' culture, with lecture materials re-uploaded from the years before, rather than new and insightful material. Any gap in learning was excused as an opportunity for independent study. The consensus I have got from those around me, is that university students were forgotten. Unlike other [school] teachers who were expected to attend in-person classes unless they were vulnerable, university lecturers appeared to receive less pressure – why would they want to come in and teach the 'super spreaders of society' anyway?
>
> (Lucy, final year undergraduate (law), written
> submission (by email), 29 November 2021)

And parents who joined the discussion told a similar tale:

My son Oscar went to university in September. There was the fiasco with the grades. He wasn't happy with what he was offered but he still wanted to go to university and get away from home. We suggested a year out to him but then lockdown came. He's taken it in his stride, but it's been difficult to make friends. He's not really met anyone and has missed interaction with people. He can't mix with people on his course.

(Girish Patel, parent, focus group – Further and
Higher Education students, 3 August 2021)

Claudia had worked so, so hard for her A levels – then I think she felt cheated of that sense of achievement because she didn't actually 'take' the exams … She got the grades she needed to get into the uni of her choice on the course of her choice but [after] all those years of dreaming of going to uni, when she got there, it wasn't how it should have been. She actually came home in the end before Christmas because people were dropping like flies with COVID, most of her flatmates had gone home because they were quite local and all lectures were online, so she was just sitting in her room all day on her own.

(Shelley Bray, parent, focus group – Further and
Higher Education students, 3 August 2021)

For those on vocational and professional courses, for whom time on campus would in any case have been limited due to the focus on placement-based learning, the experience was especially isolating, as this young women, preparing for a career in midwifery, explains:

We only actually go to university six weeks of the year – the rest is working in placements. In the first lockdown in March last year everything went online and it was difficult. The things you need to learn need to be done by practising. It's quite an emotional job and you need to care for the women you are treating. Then, when I could go [into] work, it was in a pandemic. We were required to do the set amount of hours even if we had COVID or were isolating – you still had to make those hours up … I spent three weeks isolating but had to work fifty hours a week unpaid to make up the [required placement] time. It was very isolating. We didn't have that class-based chat – discussing your work with each other. That was taken away – you couldn't relieve any stress about the work by chatting to others.

(Daisy, midwifery student, London, focus group – Further and
Higher Education students, 3 August 2021)

The growth of the virus on campuses was attributed by some University Vice-chancellors to the increased numbers at university, the increase as a result of the higher proportion of students achieving the grades set out in offers of places that had been made long before both the pandemic and the grading crisis spawned by the cancellation of written papers. Whether or not this was the case, the outbreaks were perhaps not surprising. Universities in the United States had opened some weeks earlier, during August 2020, with a similar impact, such that, according to the *Guardian* piece cited above, 1,300 US universities and colleges had reported 130,000 cases of coronavirus, an inevitability according to comments attributed to Professor Gavin Yamey, Director at the Centre for Policy Impact in Global Health at Duke University in North Carolina, in the same article:

> Reopening a university is like dumping a cruise ship in the middle of town and letting all the passengers off. It's entirely unsurprising that you're going to get outbreaks.
>
> (Fazackerley, 2020)

In this context, the rapid flight to online teaching and the curtailing of the Autumn Term to enable university students to return home and quarantine in time for a (subsequently significantly curtailed) family Christmas made this a first term like no other.

Towards a more 'open' university sector, or a more delineated one?

Champions of the Open University, an innovation of the English Higher Education system – the brainchild of the social innovator Michael Young and established in 1969 by Harold Wilson's Labour government – that was truly (and almost exactly) fifty years ahead of its time may wonder, when it comes to online learning, what all the fuss is about. In the 1970s, the Open University (or as it is widely known, the OU) pioneered the forerunner to today's online provision with distance learning: mailed-out courses of self-study materials supported by late-night dedicated television programmes on the then-new national TV channel, BBC2, punctuated by periodic weekend residentials. In the UK, the Open University continues to thrive to this day, albeit largely online rather than through the letterbox. Certainly, the OU, immortalised in Willy Russell's classic play and subsequent film, *Educating Rita* (Russell, 1980; Russell, 2003; Russell and Gilbert, 1983), widened participation in that it opened up university education to adults who had grown up in an age when progression to university at the end of formal schooling was reserved for a small minority. The opportunity afforded to adult learners, especially those adults who wanted to study a particular subject to degree level as a means of securing career progression, represented a genuinely new way in which to access Higher Education.

However, Rita was not the typical OU student and the essence of her story is not simply one of gaining a degree or securing career progression, but of the social transformation delivered alongside this process. It isn't just a qualification in English literature, and an 'education' in this narrow sense, that she seeks, as she famously and furiously reminds Frank, her tutor, who appears to bemoan what he sees as the loss of her working-class charm, and the insights that came with this:

> What's up Frank, don't y' like me now that the little girl's grown up … I'm educated, I've got what you have an' y' don't like it … I know what clothes to wear, what wine to buy, what plays to see, what papers and books to read … .
>
> (Russell, 2003)

As is argued throughout this text and in *Lessons from Lockdown*, the social function of the educational institution is as important as its stated educational purpose; indeed, the social transformation is more profoundly *educational* than the formal 'educational' purpose itself. As students, Louisa and Lucy, and as parents, Girish and Shelley, are not bemoaning simply the displacement of the lecture hall by the laptop screen (and some of the students who contributed to the research underpinning this research saw advantages in this mode of delivery, especially the ability to replay and recap on complex issues, or those central to a particular assignment), they are bemoaning the *loss* of the wider package, and the life-experiences, the networks and the cultural capital that this provides access to. It is arguably this, rather than access to a particular career, that is the greatest benefit of a 'university education' to those from so-called 'non-traditional' backgrounds, those sometimes described as the 'widening participation' cohort, those epitomised in Russell's character, Rita, the working-class woman who seeks (and gains) the very education that her tutor, Frank, appears to take for granted.

Again, though, we must not romanticise the pre-lockdown reality; to reiterate, as with other non-educational impacts, lockdown has exposed gaps and inequities that it has not created, although it has often accentuated these. Recent years have seen a significant increase in the numbers accessing a university education, building on a level of participation that was already increasing following then UK Prime Minister Tony Blair, famously calling for a university education for at least 50 per cent of young people.

However, while a plethora of widening participation programmes have increased the numbers accessing Higher Education, the UK's undergraduate population continues to be patterned by phenomena such as social class, gender, ethnicity and disability. And this growth has masked the reality that a 'university education' can mean different things to different learners and that the kind of university education received is, again, patterned by indices of inequality.

In short, pre-lockdown, a student from a disadvantaged background was more likely to attend a Higher Education institution defined as a 'recruiting' university rather than a 'selecting' one, to attend a 'new' university rather than a long-established one, to attend a university with a higher course non-completion (or 'drop-out') rate, and to attend a university with peers who were less likely to have been schooled in the independent sector, such that opportunities for networking and building connections beyond their class of origin was more limited, a reality compounded by the greater likelihood that they would attend a university close to their family home and to live at home during their university years. The risk, of course, is that they graduate *with* the student *debt*, but *without* what many middle-class families would recognise and recall as the student *experience*.

Against this background, one of the ironic levellers of the pandemic period was that many of those (often middle-class) students awarded hard-earned places in elite universities, found themselves denied the learning derived as much from a student life away from home as that imparted in the lecture theatre, as they logged on from the parental home, with their parents only too aware that this was not the student experience that they had expected.

Summary

The young people who survived the UK grading crisis of Summer 2020, as outlined in *Lessons from Lockdown*, cannot have expected an emaciated university education in the year that followed, quarantined in halls of residence or delivered online without the social and developmental benefits associated with on-campus participation in student life. This has thrown up key questions about the nature and purpose of Further and Higher Education in the first half of the twenty-first century, and notably the extent to which it is an online, onsite, or blended experience.

This issue of what a Higher Education amounts to is made more complex where students or their families pay fees to engage in such studies, whether this be in the UK or elsewhere. While it may not necessarily be less expensive for universities to provide online rather than onsite courses (and it will be more expensive to provide both), charging considerable sums for learners who only access the university experience through a screen in a spare room or the corner of a lounge does not feel like value for money. Those universities who only make this kind of offer can expect resistance from the 'consumers' of their 'product' because, in fee-paying settings, that is what the student-academy relationship is transformed into.

Pre-lockdown, disadvantaged students were less likely to gain access to so-called 'elite' universities (and, increasingly, in the UK self-defined as such through the formation of the Russell Group), the universities that offer the greatest opportunity to access a social landscape from which these students have, hitherto, been excluded.

In switching to off-campus learning during lockdown, and with some possibility that this switch may be partially retained post-lockdown, this network access is further restricted, and with it, for *these* students, the potentially transformative social impact of going to university is reduced.

Recommendations

2.1 UK-based students who progressed to Further and Higher Education in September 2020 were drawn largely from the cohort that had experienced the grading crisis of the previous summer; educational researchers should be supported and funded to track the fortunes of this group through to at least their late twenties, as the longer-term impact of their lockdown experiences, at school, college and university, are unlikely to be known until then.

2.2 There may be a case for financially compensating those who have had to pay for Further or Higher Education during the academic years blighted by the pandemic, not because they have not received an education, or the wider university experience, but because they have received something very different to what they had thought they were signing up to – at the very least, national governments and the university and college sectors ought to give urgent attention to this issue and explore the means through which learners might be remunerated if it is found that there is a case for doing so, without threatening the viability or sustainability of the institutions concerned.

2.3 Policymakers, especially those concerned with widening participation, need to consider the risks associated with the emergence of a bipartite university system made up of elite (or 'selecting') universities on the one hand and new (or 'recruiting') universities on the other, each attended by students from different social cohorts.

2.4 System leaders, school leaders and those involved in overseeing university application processes need to promote the value of Higher Education across a border matrix of benefits rather than simply those associated with future employment or earnings.

2.5 Policymakers and system leaders should give serious consideration to the establishment of a national or international Commission on the Future of Further and Higher Education, exploring its purpose, those who engage in it, how participation might be funded and the multiple forms, or optimal form, that it might take.

It all ends in tiers

3

The different experiences of different learners in different settings

The grading crisis of summer 2020, recalled in the preceding chapter and explored in detail in *Lessons from Lockdown*, cast a long shadow over the new academic year. Partly, this shadow was extended through the experiences of the same cohort of young people, now, as just discussed, quarantined in their university halls or working from their bedrooms in the parental home, and partly by the enduring commitment, on the part of Education Secretary Gavin Williamson, to return to 'normal' written examinations in Summer 2021, a commitment, like so many others, inevitably cast aside at the eleventh hour.

Few had expected Williamson to survive the 2020 results season, but the anticipated reshuffle never arrived, and Williamson was to remain in his post for a further academic year. He was finally removed from his position when Prime Minister Boris Johnson 'refreshed' his Cabinet in September 2021, replacing Williamson with Nadhim Zahawi, the minister who had been responsible for the national vaccination programme, widely seen as a rare policy success of the COVID period, and acknowledged as such in a joint report from two prominent Parliamentary Committees; amongst a list of critical conclusions the committees observed that:

DOI: 10.4324/9781003204824-3

> The UK's response, with the notable exception of vaccine develop-
> ment and deployment, has for the most part been too reactive as
> opposed to anticipatory.
>
> (House of Commons, Health and Social Care, and
> Science and Technology Committees, 2021)

We explore the specific experience of the 2021 GCSE and A-level cohorts
in Chapter 7, but it is worth pondering the build-up to these examinations,
during the Autumn Term of 2020 and the Spring Term of 2021, at this stage.
As such, we pick up on a key conundrum that has been outlined in Chapter 1
and which was to help define the academic year as a whole – the juxtapos-
ition of (and inherent contradiction between) *national* examinations and
bubbles, tiers and local lockdowns – and unpick the practical experience of
having to 'open' and 'close' 'bubbles' as the Autumn Term progressed, with
different schools, year groups and classes having very different experiences
of schooling, different levels of course coverage and different levels of
examination preparation.

And the backdrop to these precisely planned and meticulously delivered
processes and this multitude of student and staff experiences was continuing
anxiety, amongst young people and their parents, and periodic illness:

> Our attendance was hit by anxious parents keeping their children
> home, plus kids at home isolating due to track and trace … Teacher
> absence really impacted the school. I had colleagues who were teaching
> eighty-plus kids in the school because of staff isolating, so there were
> a lot of logistics.
>
> (Kathleen McGillycuddy, principal, Broadoak Academy,
> Weston-super-Mare, focus group – secondary educators,
> 13 May 2021)

Later we discuss the impact of managing this turbulence on teachers and
school leaders. Here, the focus is on how this unpredictability was experienced
by children and young people, and their families through what international
educationalist Eliza Green described in one of the interviews that underpins
the analysis offered in these pages 'as the 'hidden home curriculums of lockdown'. Much has been made of the *lost* learning experienced by this cohort
(and rightly so), but too little has been made of what many *did* learn, and
which they might not have learnt, had schools continued to remain open as
normal. Let us turn first, though, to the very different experiences of lockdown across the UK that helped to define the 2020 Autumn Term.

Tiers and bubbles: The multiple experiences of lockdown across the UK

As noted in Chapter 2, a key mantra of this text is that no two children, no two families and no two schools have had the same lockdown. It is more fine-grained than that; in truth, no two year groups or classes and no two staff rooms or subject areas have had the same lockdown. To reiterate, the monolithic experience described by the headline writers and newscasters is a myth and, as such, it is unhelpful to any measured, nuanced understanding of the educational impact of COVID-19. But this is not to say that these experiences, as we have argued in Chapter 1, are not socially patterned by social class, ethnicity, gender, age, disability and residence; as we have shown, they are, and strongly.

In the UK, the first lockdown was superseded by the placing of cities, towns and localities into different 'tiers', to which different post-lockdown arrangements applied. The details of the regulations relating to the different tiers differed in England, Scotland, Wales and Northern Ireland, and were developed by the different national Parliaments and Assemblies, but the principle was universal. The tiering arrangements that were introduced in England on 12 October 2020 are set out in Figure 3.1.

Unsurprisingly, those cities, towns and localities in the North and in the Midlands, those in areas of social disadvantage and/or those with relatively high minority ethnic populations found themselves more likely to be the subject of the local lockdowns that had preceded the tiering framework, as set out in Figure 3.2, and more likely to be amongst the first to be placed in the higher tiers, as set out in Figure 3.3. In due course, local lockdowns were framed as 'Tier 4' areas, with the instruction, albeit with a greater range of professional and occupational exceptions than had applied in the lockdown of Spring 2020, to 'stay at home'.

Further, children and young people at schools in Tier 3 (and later Tier 4) areas experienced the greatest level of disruption to their schooling, either through full school closures or the bursting of bubbles, but even this observation masks an underlying complexity, as this Ofqual analysis of the position (Leahy, Newton and Khan, 2021) in Autumn 2020 confirms:

> Although all schools were expected to remain open irrespective of tier regulations, there were some differences between tiers in terms of the way schools operated ... Government guidance stated that in Tier 1, schools were expected to remain fully open but students in year 7 and above were to wear face coverings in communal areas.

Tier	Descriptor	Practicalities
3	**Very High Alert**	Public houses and other hospitality and leisure facilities are required to close, individuals cannot travel to areas in lower tiers and social mixing beyond the household is not allowed. Some outdoor socialising is allowed in parks and similar places provided that the 'rule of six' and social distancing are adhered to, and schools and shops can remain open.
2	**High Alert**	Those from different households can only mix outside, provided that the 'rule of six' is adhered to and the guidance on social distancing is followed.
1	**Medium Alert**	Any current national restrictions such as those relating to social distancing, the 10 p.m. hospitality curfew and the ban on gatherings of more than six people, indoors and outside, must be adhered to.

Figure 3.1 The 'Tiering' framework in England, introduced in Autumn 2020. Adapted from https://www.bbc.co.uk/newsround/54509311 Retrieved 12th October 2021.

Area	Region (s)	Commencement
Leicester and parts of Leicestershire	East Midlands	29 June 2020
Blackpool with Darwen	North West	25 July 2020
Luton	East of England	25 July 2020
Bradford	North	1 August 2020
Various areas in Greater Manchester, Lancashire and West Yorkshire	North and North West	5 August 2020
Northampton (Glencore Food Processing)	East of England	29 August 2020

Figure 3.2 Areas experiencing a local lockdown (England). Spring 2020–Summer 2021.

In Tier 2, secondary schools were asked to adopt a rota system, and further education (FE) colleges were to limit on-site attendance. This meant that most students experienced a combination of remote and on-site schooling, while vulnerable children and children of critical

Area	Region
Greater Manchester	North West
Lancashire, Blackpool and Blackburn with Darwin	North West
Tees Valley Combined Authority	North East
North East Combined Authority	North East
The Humber	North
West Yorkshire	North
South Yorkshire	North
Leicester and Leicestershire	East Midlands
Derby and Derbyshire	East Midlands
Lincolnshire	East
Nottingham and Nottinghamshire	East Midlands
Birmingham and the Black Country	West Midlands
Staffordshire and Stoke-on-Trent	North Midlands
Warwickshire, Coventry and Solihull	West Midlands
Slough	South East
Kent and Medway	South East
Bristol, South Gloucestershire and North Somerset	South West

Figure 3.3 Initial Tier 3 areas (England): Autumn 2020.

workers were allowed to attend on-site full-time. In Tier 3, secondary schools and FE colleges were required to limit on-site attendance to just children who were vulnerable, those of critical workers, and selected year groups. On 19 December, Tier 4 was introduced in large areas in the south-east of England … In Tier 4, on-site attendance was limited to just vulnerable children and the children of critical workers at all primary and secondary schools. Alternate provision settings and special schools were allowed to remain open to all students (as they also were in Tiers 1 to 3), although that does not necessarily mean they were able to offer a place to all students who would normally be in attendance, as this was likely to have depended on staffing levels, the space available due to social distancing measures, and the unique health risks to individual students.

> Average attendance rates were between 80 to 90% in this phase (Sibieta and Robinson, 2020), but this term is particularly challenging to characterise due to the sporadic impacts of the pandemic on different groups and in different regions … different regions were assigned to Tiers 2 and 3 at different points in time throughout this period, leading to differences in on-site attendance across these regions.
>
> (Leahy, Newton and Khan, 2021)

Against this background, the authors of the report conclude that:

> When schools closed and learning switched to being predominantly remote at the outset of the pandemic, differences between groups of students based on a variety of factors were introduced, and existing disparities deepened. Probably the most prominent of these factors was socio-economic status, with the poorest students' learning time being reduced to a greater extent than the richest. However, even when schools reopened, disparities remained as attendance varied between the most and least deprived areas. There was extensive variation behind the averages reported in the literature about lost time though, at regional, local authority, school and student level. Therefore, it is difficult to generalise across any particular group, as lost time is unique to each individual student.
>
> (Leahy, Newton and Khan, 2021)

Thus, hospitalisation statistics at least for the UK, are mirrored in patterns of school closure and the bursting of 'bubbles'; the poorest children and young people are the most likely to have had their school disrupted between the two national schooling lockdowns (March–May 2020 and January–March 2021), their families are the most likely to have become ill with COVID-19 and to have experienced hospitalisation, and they are the most likely to have lost family and community members to the virus. Drawing on one of a number of case studies, the authors of the ImpactEd longitudinal study cited in the Preface and subsequently observe that:

> … parents of pupils from more economically disadvantaged backgrounds often had irregular work patterns which meant it was harder to establish a routine. Breaks between learning were sometimes

filled with caring responsibilities, including supporting siblings with home learning. In short, there were a range of challenges that went beyond the well-reported need for digital resources. One teacher from BET (Bohunt Education Trust) commented: 'People talk of digital disadvantage but in many cases we are facing furniture disadvantage – there are kids who need a chair, or families who need a bin.'

(ImpactEd, 2021: 16)

Against this background, and to reiterate a point made in *Lessons from Lockdown*, anybody can catch COVID-19 or have their education impacted by it, but some are far more likely to catch the illness than others and some are far more likely to have their schooling disrupted by it. The report from Parliamentarians cited earlier in this chapter is unequivocal about the differential impact of the pandemic, noting in a set of concluding recommendations specifically relating to those from 'at risk communities' that:

The impact of COVID-19 has been uneven across the population, with some sections of society suffering significantly higher illness and deaths than the nation as a whole.

(House of Commons, Health and Social Care, and Science and Technology Committees, 2021: 104)

Perhaps surprisingly, the Members of Parliament make no reference in their recommendations to the educational sphere, but the interplay between disadvantage (in its various forms) and educational access, experience and outcomes is documented across a Sociology of Education literature that spans at least three-quarters of a century. Through the two national schooling lockdowns, COVID-19 impacted on the educational experience of every young person in the UK, but those living in particular settings were far more likely to be additionally impacted by local lockdowns and the bursting of bubbles, and those most likely to feel these impacts negatively were, generally, the least well-placed to mediate them. Why? Because, as we have already noted in the opening chapter, they are likely to live in more cramped accommodation; because they are less likely to have a quiet place or a spare room to study in at home; because their parents are unlikely to be able to work from home, instead earning their (relatively low) income in public-facing, crowded and other high-risk workplace settings, because they are likely to have the worst (or no) internet connectivity, because they are likely to live in device-poor rather than device-rich households. And so on. Again, and focusing on ethnicity in particular, the Parliamentarians on the Health and Social Care and the Science and Technology Committees are clear:

> During the initial phase of the pandemic, Black, Asian and minority ethnic people experienced significantly higher levels of severe illness and death from covid than was typical of the population as a whole. Research conducted so far suggests that the drivers of these elevated levels of impact among Black, Asian and minority ethnic people arise from greater likelihood of jobs that come with higher exposure to covid infection; more challenging social and economic circumstances; more densely occupied housing; and comorbidities from different health conditions. These are classic features of inequality in society and in the economy.
>
> (House of Commons, Health and Social Care, and Science and Technology Committees, 2021: 104–105)

The multiple layering of disadvantage that is generated by the intersections of factors such as social class, employment status, ethnicity, gender, age and disability is all the more powerful in a society where these intersections land on a minority, as they do in many developed, affluent societies, and as they certainly do in both the UK and the US. Where the poor, to recall the analysis offered in *Lessons from Lockdown*, are concentrated with equally disadvantaged peers at the base of a broad triangle, there is, quite literally, solidarity in numbers and a degree of political agency. It is in such societies that the Labour movements of the early and mid-twentieth century emerged, periodically in many of those settings, proceeding to government, or at least to spirited and often effective opposition. To be isolated, in more affluent societies, at the base of a diamond, devoid of the company and the support institutions that might mediate and ultimately address this inequality is not simply to be poor; it is to be powerless.

To say, though, that certain communities and particular social groups are more likely to find themselves in this position and to acknowledge that they have experienced the pandemic very differently is not to suggest that every individual or every household within a particular cohort has had the *same* experience. Rather, the precise mix of impacting intersectional factors is different in every disadvantaged home, as it is in every advantaged home; to make a point that will doubtless be reiterated at various points in this text: nuance is everything in understanding the course and impact of the virus. Moreover, the 'squashing' of the virus in one setting might be a contributor to its emergence elsewhere, perhaps in a group that had seemed hitherto unaffected.

Maybe this offers some kind of explanation as to why what was perceived to be an illness that preyed (and thrived) on the elderly and the vulnerable in Spring and Summer 2020 in settings such as care homes, became a disease prevalent amongst school pupils in the secondary years in Autumn and early Winter 2021. Of course, the similarity might be the institutional environment and the sociability that sits at the core of both settings, albeit much more successfully addressed by the vaccines available to the wider population. In any case, in Summer and Autumn 2020, it was 'bubbles' that middle and senior leaders found themselves organising, and 'bubble schools' that Heads and Principals found themselves leading, and it was bubbles that they most looked forward to waving goodbye to when schools reopened fully in August and September 2021.

So that the definition – and the experience – of such schooling is not lost to history (and so that the odd title of this book might be better understood by those reading it as a history text years from now), it is worth reminding ourselves of what we might mean by a 'bubble' and, therefore, a 'bubble school'.

Bubbles and the organisation of schools

The phenomenon of the 'bubble' first entered the lockdown lexicon as a means of describing the family, social and support groups that individuals could belong to, and those they could admit to their homes and gardens during and in the aftermath of the first schooling lockdown in Spring 2020. From Autumn 2020, the 'bubble' became the de facto mode of school organisation in all educational phases across the UK.

For education professionals, organising and managing bubbles will probably serve as the abiding memory of COVID-19 in UK schools in years to come. Effectively, the use of 'bubble'-based models of organisation enabled the Department for Education to declare schools 'open' in a manner that it considered safe. As both of the Secretaries of State for Education who held responsibility for schooling in England across this period, the Prime Minister, and politicians of every political hue across the UK, had emphasised, and as we note elsewhere in these pages, the priority was to find a way to enable schools to remain 'fully' open because, as the Department for Education put it in one of its regular edicts to school leaders:

> Our priority is for you to deliver face-to-face, high-quality education to all pupils. The evidence is clear that being out of education causes significant harm to educational attainment, life chances, and mental and physical health.
>
> (Department for Education, 2021b)

Fifteen months earlier, accompanying the faltering and patchy school-return that followed the first lockdown in June 2020, described at length in *Lessons from Lockdown*, the UK's Education Departments had advised on the need for bubbles in a series of similar edicts which gave support staff, teachers and school leaders a sense of what was to come; this definition from Northern Ireland's Department of Education was typical:

> Protective bubbles will be used as a key mitigating action where possible. The protective bubble arrangements will be used to segment pupils into a consistent group or groups that arrive together, learn together, play together and eat together, reducing contact throughout the school with other children.
>
> (Department of Education – Northern Ireland, 2021: n.p.)

This outline definition was supported by the following detailed description of how such bubbles would work:

> Protective bubbles will be used to segment pupils into a consistent group or groups as far as is practicable. The purpose of using consistent groups is to limit the number of different interactions in any single day. This will reduce the risk of transmission and improve the ability to focus the tracking and tracing of the virus in circumstances where there is a positive test.
>
> The approach will vary depending on age group. In pre-schools, primary and special schools, it is envisaged that in most cases a relatively straightforward approach can be adopted. A class will act as a single consistent group or bubble, with minimal prolonged interaction with other classes within the school.
>
> At post-primary, the nature of curricular delivery makes it more difficult to implement a single consistent class group or bubble. It should be possible in some schools for Years 8–10, however, others will require limited mixing into different class groups to adhere to legal requirements for practical subjects.
>
> For Years 11–14, it is recognised that a single consistent class group will not be possible, as pupils will be in mixed classes based on their choice of examination courses but schools are encouraged to keep movements and interactions within these year groups to an absolute minimum.
>
> (Department of Education – Northern Ireland, 2021)

In practical terms, and as noted in Chapter 1, these 'bubbles' amounted to sealed groups of pupils, sometimes of typical class size, sometimes smaller (especially in primary schools) and sometimes larger (especially in secondary schools). In primary (or elementary) schools, the number was often effectively defined by the physical size of classrooms, usually built to accommodate thirty or so pupils but now with the requirement that children ought to be socially spaced from each other, often at separate desks or in 'spaced pairs' or staggered rows, able to accommodate about half that number. Thus, the creation of new teaching spaces, as suggested elsewhere in the Northern Ireland guidance, in libraries and school halls was common. As outlined in Chapter 1, groups of children allocated to the same bubble would arrive at and depart from school together, would spend often newly staggered break and lunch times together, and would restrict their movements if not to a certain classroom, then to a certain area of the school.

In secondary schools, the bubbles were often necessarily larger, sometimes based on year groups rather than classes or part-classes, but the intention was similar: to group students into effectively sealed units. Of course, the larger bubbles carried greater risks. Why? Because the impact of a single positive test was the same – to send home the bubble as a whole. Thus, where this might have amounted to half a class in a primary school, it could mean a year group in a secondary. Against this background, *FE News* reported that 623,000 children were absent from school due to the virus on 1 July 2021, with:

- 34,000 pupils with a suspected case of coronavirus, 0.5% of pupils on roll in open schools
- 28,000 pupils with a confirmed case of coronavirus, 0.4% of pupils on roll in open schools
- 471,000 pupils self-isolating due to potential contact with a case of coronavirus from inside the educational setting, 6.3% of pupils on roll in open schools
- 90,000 pupils self-isolating due to potential contact with a case of coronavirus from outside the educational setting, 1.2% of pupils on roll in open schools
- 0.2% of pupils were absent as a result of school closures due to COVID-related reasons.

(FE News, 2021)

Fifteen months earlier, many secondary schools had managed the initial return to school after the first lockdown through a form of blended attendance, with attention focused on those in examination groups and with many students in school on certain days each week, rather than on a conventional full-time basis. In effect, the bursting of bubbles often frustrated attempts to offer a genuinely 'full-time' return from September 2020. And, for some parents this proved almost as disruptive as the home-schooling that many hoped was behind them:

> There were kids testing positive all over the place. My kids, because of contact, were in for a fortnight, then out for a fortnight. It was a shambles ... Back in September we were waiting three days for a test, so your child would cough at school [and] then they would be sent home while you had to wait for [the results from] a test.
>
> (Caroline Graham, parent, focus group – parents and guardians, 10 May 2021)

In any case, and in spite of government calls for it, the focus, when schools returned in September 2020, was less on curriculum catch-up and more on wellbeing. London Head Daniel Coyle explained the rationale for such an approach:

> When we came back in September I changed the timetable completely and had a top-heavy focus on sports, drama, performing arts as we felt the children of this area had missed out on those things. It was all about wellbeing ... We need to keep children in school mentally healthy.
>
> (Daniel Coyle, Headteacher, Newman Catholic College, Brent, focus group – secondary educators, 13 May 2021)

Organisational procedures and curriculum innovations of this type dominated the organisation of schooling across the UK for the second half of the Summer Term in 2020 and across the subsequent academic year; the bubbles were retained, and were arguably somewhat easier to organise, during the periods of restricted school opening that characterised local and national lockdowns, when the children of 'key workers' (howsoever defined) and many of those designated 'vulnerable' continued to attend school. Although there was some variation in the dates and in the tiering frameworks introduced later that Autumn in Scotland, Wales and Northern Ireland, essentially the same model of organisation was employed. Arguably, the impact of 'bubbling' was greatest in secondary schooling where room movement provides what the television presenter Simon Thomas described early in the second lockdown (26 January 2021) to the BBC Radio 5 Live host Nihal Arthanayake as 'the punctuation marks in a child's day' (BBC, 2021), with schools flipping to a model where, other than when specific specialist rooms were needed, the teacher went to the class, rather than the class to the teacher.

Bubbles: The route to calmer schooling?

In the majority of developed education systems, remaining, for the most part, in the same classroom with the same teacher is the daily stock of the child in primary (or elementary) school but secondary (or 'high') schooling cultivates the nomadic spirit in those open to such an idea, and requires this movement from all. Some secondary leaders and practitioners, at least initially, saw some benefits in COVID's quieter corridors, and some found themselves with school sites that better facilitated separation between bubbles:

> We did a great job of converting the school into year group bubbles. We've got a very old site that's evolved over the years so it's [usually] a difficult site to supervise but a great site for bubbles. We can have very distinct entrances.
>
> (Richard Lord, Headteacher, The Deepings School, Peterborough, research interview, 7 October 2021)

And the organisation of large secondary schools into a series of pods, bubbles, or zones that teachers moved to, especially when this was combined with smaller teaching groups and reduced onsite attendance during periods of lockdown or partial closure, combined to produce a new serenity:

> As a consequence of not having 1,000 people crammed in classrooms it was calmer. Children were less agitated. I want to retain some aspects of that calmness. The amount of hours [we put in] to run the school – just moving children around – is exhausting.
>
> (Daniel Coyle, Headteacher, Newman Catholic College, Brent, focus group – secondary educators, 13 May 2021)

Nor was it just school leaders who saw the benefits in this calmness:

> I felt school was calmer. I totally agree there are elements of the problems in corridors that were mitigated by the bubbles. I would like to keep that … .
>
> (Christopher Harris, reading coordinator, Highams Park School, focus group – secondary educators, 13 May 2021)

Daniel Coyle, surveying the bustle of a 'normal' school in October 2021 and looking back on the experience of both bubble schooling and running an urban secondary school with a restricted number of students – the children of key workers and those defined as 'vulnerable' – for much of the foregoing academic year, threw a wry smile at the swiftly lost calmness and conceded:

> Look at this, Tony [the healthy noise and energy of a standard lesson change-over] it's fantastic, but we're not used to it, we're all knackered, we'll get used to it but we're not match-fit yet.
>
> (Daniel Coyle, Headteacher, Newman Catholic College, Brent – in discussion with the author, at the school to be briefed by members of the Student Council, 13 October 2021)

And members of the Student Council at Newman Catholic College, which meets weekly and is drawn from all year groups, concurred with their Headteacher (who was not present) that learning in bubbles had had its advantages:

> Compared with lockdown [the full lockdown of Spring 2020], the bubbles were good, they got us back – we were socialising with friends again.
>
> (Student, Year 8)

> I enjoyed having our own bubble with our own timetable and being together (with friends) most of the time.
>
> (Student, Year 12)

> I liked the bubbles! [During lockdown] we were so scared of going out, socialising, being with friends.
>
> (Student, Year 7)

> I enjoyed the bubbles – everyone had their own building, but we couldn't spend time with our other friends.
>
> (Student, Year 10)

> I liked lockdown's bubbles – you had your own space, and you couldn't be late for lessons, because the teachers came to you.
>
> (Student, Year 10)

All comments drawn from a meeting of the School Council at Newman Catholic College devoted to exploring students' experiences of the lockdown period held on 13 October 2021.

What is notable about these student comments is their focus on what might be described as the 'intimacy' of the bubbles. During the 2020 Summer Term, after the lockdown that had dominated most of the Spring Term, when secondaries had, for the most part, seen only a partial return of students, these young people had enjoyed the stability of their social groups, the sense of ownership that being based in one place had given them, the human-scale size of their pod, and the absence of the near perpetual motion of lesson change-over. One of the (perfectly valid) justifications for moving children from class-to-class in secondary schools is to provide the teacher with an appropriately resourced and themed subject base and an accompanying sense of ownership; perhaps it is not surprising that, on returning to school after the first lockdown, children and young people valued much the same thing.

In this context, it might be reasonable to surmise that 'bubble schooling' so disrupted taken-for-granted normalities, especially the multiple movements of the school day in the secondary phase, that it enabled school leaders, and the school workforce more broadly, to reflect on these normalities, especially in the secondary phase: French and Geography and English and Maths could be taught in the same room and corridor chaos was not an inevitability of school life but, as the year progressed and the novelty wore off, many began to yearn for the corridor-bustle and subject-specific base rooms of old. Daniel Coyle, who had initially enjoyed the calmness that flowed from a reduction in room movement, was among those who now yearned for the sense of identity that they gave to both teachers and their subjects:

> Short term, I want teachers to get [their] classrooms back. I didn't realise how important they were. It's been a real loss to the culture of schools. You could walk into a French classroom eighteen months ago and you knew it was the French room because of the posters, etc.
> (Daniel Coyle, Headteacher, Newman Catholic College, Brent, focus group – secondary educators, 6 July 2021)

And Shelley Bray concurred, but focused on something other than the classroom:

I would like to get the dining room back. The kids used to sit six around a table chattering away, swapping things in their lunchboxes, throwing chips at each other – making friends. Now there are two to-a-table – too far away from each other to have a real conversation – and all facing the front, so just staring at other pupils' backs. It's almost eerie walking through the dining room now. It's too quiet.

(Shelley Bray, transcription lead – Bubble Schools Project,
focus group – secondary educators, 6 July 2021)

Bray brings us back to a recurrent theme of this text: the social function of schooling. In observing the behaviour of the Year 7 students that have joined the school he leads in September 2021, Coyle underlines the importance of such a function, and the consequence of its frustration during the Bubble Schooling era:

A key part of education is socialisation – queuing up, being quiet when you are told to. The Year 7s – it's almost as if they have missed 18 months of socialisation. I have noticed they are a more challenging bunch than normal. One sensible conclusion is the experience they've had has knocked them back. I've certainly noticed that immaturity in Year 7s.

(Daniel Coyle, Headteacher, Newman Catholic College, Brent,
focus group – secondary educators, 6 July 2021)

And this observation was not lost on parents either:

They fell way behind in terms of social interaction because of the loss of that holistic school experience. My son was in this Year 7 group.

(Parent, speaking on condition of anonymity, November 2021)

It was a phenomenon that several secondary educators were to observe during the research detailed here, something put down in part to the absence of the range of transition activities that mark the build-up to the progression to secondary school:

We're not used to having ten to fifteen kids turning up on scooters. We don't get that sort of thing in secondary schools, normally – it was odd … [but] I've got a daughter in Year Six, so I can see it from both angles.

(Richard Lord, Headteacher, The Deepings School,
Peterborough, research interview, 18 October 2021)

This playfulness sat with an apparent contradiction: the contrasting observation that many children at the top end of primary school had developed the kind of independent learning skills that, prior to lockdown, we had often struggled to find in those at a different transition – that is, from school to college or university or workplace.

Of course, these children had developed these independent learning skills because, in a landscape of enforced home learning, they had needed to, even when parents were at home with them, if the expectation was that these parents were 'working from home', as it often was; conversely, they had been less successful in developing the social skills that we have come to expect from children of this age because the atomisation and isolation produced by lockdown and bursting bubbling had frustrated their ability to do so. In England, the resultant anxiety provides one explanation for the continued rise in requests to detail children's needs in EHC (Education Health and Care) plans, particularly amongst those in Year 5 and Year 6, the years that immediately precede transfer to secondary (or 'high') school. Such plans document a child's needs formally as part of a process designed to lock in support for identified children as they progress through their schooling. The growth in EHC plans processed across the pandemic period is illustrated in Figure 3.4.

And there is another take on the apparent social immaturity (or playfulness) of these children on the one hand and their ability to study independently on the other – that, prior to lockdown, we may not have done enough to either develop their capabilities as independent learners in the primary years, or to sustain their exuberance into the secondary phase. This is not to criticise classroom practitioners or school leaders at either level, but to reflect on a system that some might argue is overly driven to quantify and measure progress through school cultures over which 'targets, tests

Year	Total number of EHC plans	New requests for an EHC plan	Number of new EHC plans
2021	473,255	93,302	62,180
2020	430,697	75,951	60,097
2019*	390,109	82,329	53,899

Figure 3.4 The growth in the number of Education and Health Care Plans: 2020–22.

*Pre-pandemic.

Source: Department for Education.

and tables' hold significant sway, and within which certain approaches to learning are predominant.

Emerging from lockdown, our challenge is to develop and apply pedagogies and to build an education system that delivers independent learning skills *and* socialisation, not one as an alternative to the other. Those who thrive, rather than merely survive, in the society of the mid-twenty-first century will need both qualities in equal balance, and, doubtless, in abundance: the ability to learn, unlearn and relearn in an age that will be dominated by portfolio working and multiple careers across the lifespan, *and* the ability to reinvent oneself in multiple settings, at any one point in time and over time.

On course for normality?

Against this background, news that such bubbling, and the associated paraphernalia of distinct entrances, varied starts and ends to the school day, separate lunch and break times, one-way systems and the wearing of face masks was no longer *required* at the outset of the 2021–22 academic year, was widely welcomed by education professionals, even if the Department for Education was clear that the reintroduction of bubbles, in particular, was a possibility, should circumstances change:

> We no longer recommend that it is necessary to keep children in consistent groups ('bubbles'). This means that 'bubbles' will not need to be used in schools. As well as enabling flexibility in curriculum delivery, this means that assemblies can resume and you no longer need to make alternative arrangements to avoid mixing at lunch.
>
> You should make sure your contingency plans (sometimes called outbreak management plans) cover the possibility that it may become necessary to reintroduce 'bubbles' for a temporary period, to reduce mixing between groups.
>
> Any decision to recommend the reintroduction of 'bubbles' would not be taken lightly and would need to take account of the detrimental impact they can have on the delivery of education.
>
> (Department for Education, 2021b)

In August 2020, an earlier attempt to signal the return of pre-lockdown reality – the 'eat out to help out' programme which sought to encourage diners to return to newly reopened restaurants – was followed, later that Autumn, with a second surge in the virus (which we discuss in detail in the next chapter), restrictions on public house opening hours, a second shorter lockdown (during which schools remained open, save for the bursting of bubbles), the quasi-'cancellation' of Christmas and, in the new year, a third substantive lockdown, this time accompanied by the 'closure' of schools.

However, the emergence and successful roll-out of the UK's vaccine programme in the intervening period, brought a greater optimism to the full 'reopening' of 'bubble-free' schools just over a year later in Autumn 2021. We discuss the experiences of young people, and the educational professionals who support their learning and attend to their wellbeing, in returning to 'normal' schooling elsewhere in these pages, but it is worth giving a brief foretaste of that discussion at this stage.

For those at the chalkface, the reversion to long-standing methods for the organisation of schooling had much to promise: the return of a standard school day and traditional pupil-flows around the school site, the casting aside of face masks (or at least their *compulsory* wearing), the reintroduction of assemblies and other large group activities, the re-emergence of curriculum-enrichment activities in the form of school trips and visiting speakers, and the relaunch of extra-curricular programmes, something that Sir Kevan Collins – in his brief period as 'catch-up czar' which we discuss in some detail in Chapter 7 – had seen as so important in enabling young people to rebuild their sociability skills, psychological wellbeing and self-confidence.

The need to work in bubbles, and the placement of areas into particular tiers, had restricted much of this. Thus, while the bubbling of the schooling system had demanded an incredible level of resourcefulness, creativity and resilience on the part of school leaders and the school workforce – efforts that had seen children and young people have their schooling organised like never before – the Bubble School was never set to become a COVID-Keep, and never set to outlive the lockdowns that had spurred its creation; its legacy lies not in that its remnants will be evident in classrooms across the land, and various lands, in decades to come, but in the realisation that schooling can be done differently if there is either the need or the desire to do so.

Summary

As the Autumn Term progressed, the hopes of normality that had been fondly anticipated in September began to peel away. The persistence of local lockdowns and the growth in hospital admissions that accompanied the resurgence in the virus that was evident within weeks of the start of the new academic year, saw bubble-based schooling become the norm for school organisation throughout this period.

While 'bubbles' were challenging to organise and operate, and the use of key communal areas – assembly halls, student common rooms and staff rooms – was often lost, this was a period of incredible innovation in school organisation and a time defined by high levels of 'trial and error' creativity. Bubble-based models were especially complex to organise in secondary schools, where the norm is that the students move to specialist rooms and departmentally located classrooms, but some students, teachers and school leaders initially welcomed the new calmness that this reduction in movement produced; while most secondary practitioners have welcomed the opportunity to return to their specialist bases, and virtually all teachers have welcomed the reopening of staff rooms, there are lessons to be drawn from the sheer diversity of practice during this period.

Children and young people, notably those defined as 'vulnerable', often valued the smaller, more intimate groups that were typical of many 'bubble' settings, and self-reports indicate that these young people made strong progress. The smaller groups and the system-wide focus on vulnerability, howsoever defined, also encouraged teachers to be innovative with pedagogies and enabled them to reach out to those families defined, in ordinary times, as 'hard to reach', innovations and relationships that were to serve all parties well during the second national schooling lockdown that was to follow in the subsequent Spring Term. The dawning of 2021 was to bring no respite from the events of the previous year, but schools, and their leaders, were now equipped with a hastily acquired body of experience and expertise with which to approach it.

Recommendations

3.1 The models of school organisation developed in response to the local lockdowns and bursting bubbles of the Summer and Autumn Terms of 2020, and sustained across the duration of the pandemic, need to be documented and shared system-wide so that the practices undertaken during this period, and the emergent lessons from these, are captured for utilisation in the future.

3.2 At the level of practice, school and curriculum leaders, school improvement advisers and inspectors, and those involved in school governance ought to be encouraged to identify those specific competencies and strategies, developed during the pandemic, that have the potential to become 'COVID-Keeps' as schools emerge from lockdown.

3.3 Retaining elements of the 'calmness' witnessed by many school leaders and young people during lockdown in the post-lockdown landscape ought to be an objective for all schools, as this clearly supports the learning of some children.

3.4 Recapturing the 'trial and error' creativity of Autumn Term 2020 ought to be an objective for all school-based education professionals, but if they are to be successful in this regard, school-based educators will need to feel that they have a licence to innovate from advisers, inspectors and policy leaders.

3.5 As schools emerge from lockdown, and as educational professionals seek to make sense of this period, they need to place a special emphasis on student and parental voice, so that the post-lockdown recasting of schooling is informed by multiple perspectives and a diversity of experiences.

Crisis at Christmas 4

Schools and the second surge

As 2020 drew to a close and the prospect of a lockdown Christmas emerged on the horizon, the ability of both the Prime Minister and the Education Secretary to perform u-turns that a presenter on the popular BBC motoring show, *Top Gear*, might have been proud of again revealed itself.

Throughout November, Boris Johnson had continued to offer the prospect of a family Christmas, albeit curtailed and hemmed in by locally based tiered lockdowns on either side. To some degree, such a festival was held out as a reward for the pain of the foregoing months but, at the last minute, the prize was snatched away, with the Prime Minister announcing on 18 December that, with the surge of the 'Kent' variant of the virus, the Christmas reopening would have to be cancelled, and so, with freezers and fridges already filled, it subsequently was, just two days after his assertion that it would be 'inhumane' to do so – the planned relaxation of tiering regulations for a five-day Christmas was cancelled, and reduced to a single day in most areas, with a new fourth tier introduced in London and various parts of the South East, one that brought with it a 'stay-at-home' order and the closure of non-essential shops.

Throughout this period, the Education Secretary had echoed the Prime Minister's stance on the certainty of Christmas celebrations going ahead, in his own plans with regard to the January reopening of schools. His statement to Parliament on 30 December 2020 is illustrative of both his certainty and his motivation:

> Throughout, we have been adamant that the education of children is an absolute priority, and that keeping schools open is uppermost in

DOI: 10.4324/9781003204824-4

our plans ... Accordingly, we will be opening the majority of primary schools, as planned, on Monday 4th January ... We know how vitally important it is for younger children to be in school for their education, wellbeing and wider development. In a small number of areas, where the infection rates are highest, we will implement our existing contingency framework such that only vulnerable children and children of critical workers will attend face-to-face. We will publish this list of areas today on the gov.uk website. I would like to emphasise that this is being used only as a last resort – this is not all Tier 4 areas – and that the overwhelming majority of primary schools will open as planned on Monday. The areas will also be reviewed regularly so that schools can reopen at the very earliest moment.

(Department for Education, 2021c)

Even after the Prime Minister's 'cancellation' of Christmas, the Education Secretary would not concede that the Spring Term was in jeopardy, continuing to contend that schools would open, as normal, in January; some of them did, but oh so briefly. Williamson had echoed Johnson's words throughout; he was about to echo his u-turn.

To close or not to close? The rise of the 'Kent' variant

During the second half of the Autumn Term, as outlined in the previous chapter, the impact of the so-called 'Kent variant' had been making itself felt in schools with staff absences, the bursting of student bubbles and parental apprehension combining to make the management of schools, especially larger secondary schools, increasingly challenging. And school leaders were not immune from the virus:

I found the last week of that term pretty grim. I got COVID and spent Christmas Day in hospital. The school got hit hard by that variant – lots of pupils and staff off.

(Daniel Coyle, Headteacher, Newman Catholic College, Brent, focus group – secondary educators, 13 May 2021)

In November the new [Kent] strain came in and we ended up closing because the virus ripped through the school. This impacted hugely on us. We reopened at the end of the term but very few pupils came back ... Anxieties among pupils, staff and families shot up ... None of us wanted to close [but] we all had COVID at the same time – me, the Deputy Headteacher and the Assistant Headteacher. In the end we said 'No! We can't carry on.'

> (David Miller, Headteacher, Pebble Brook School, Aylesbury,
> focus group – SEND practitioners and those based in
> alternative education settings, 28 May 2021)

However, with schools as organisations, and individual teachers and teaching assistants, becoming increasingly adept in delivering blended and online learning, there was a new confidence amongst many in the profession that they could at least mitigate the worst impacts of school closures in a way that was unimaginable only a term or so earlier.

Thus, as November blended into December and the virus gathered pace, a number of Local Authorities, Multi-academy Trusts (MATs) and individual schools announced plans to 'close' early for Christmas and to take learning online, enabling children to self-isolate in time for family Christmases that remained in prospect, while continuing to support the children of key workers and those designated 'vulnerable' onsite.

Their rationale, as Greenwich Council Leader Danny Thorpe outlined in an open letter to Headteachers in maintained schools in the borough, was the seemingly exponential growth of the virus; those advocating 'closure' were doing so with a growing digital confidence that meant learning could continue for the four remaining days of term. It is worth reproducing Thorpe's letter in full, as it captures both the substance and the emotion of the moment:

Dear Headteachers

I'm sorry to disturb a weekend, but frankly I know they almost seem a thing of the past given how hard you are working. I've had a number of conversations with heads over the last week and I know how difficult things have been, especially the last week.

It has become clear in the last few days that rates of Covid-19 are rising extremely rapidly, both within Greenwich and across London. The latest data seems to suggest the rate of infection is doubling in the city every 4 days, and last night it was confirmed that Greenwich now has the highest recorded levels of Covid than at any time since the start of the pandemic. Indeed, colleagues from Public Health have advised that Greenwich, with many other boroughs, is now in a period of exponential growth that demands immediate action.

For these reasons, I am asking all schools in Greenwich to close their premises at the end of the day tomorrow with the exception of key workers and vulnerable children, and move to a remote learning offer for the duration of the term.

This is honestly one of the most difficult questions I have wrestled with during all my time as Leader. The DFE are clear this isn't their position and indeed have issued directives to some schools. However, I cannot in all good conscience stand by whilst the numbers are doubling so quickly. If the numbers are indeed doubling every 4 days, they would do so again by this Thursday, exposing more people to risk.

As many of you know, I am a qualified teacher, and as such I know first hand just how important schools are for children, especially the most vulnerable we look after. I know also we are in the middle of the biggest distribution of food and support for families who have had probably the worst year of their lives. I'm determined we will do that in a safe way and the team will be in touch with more details.

It is likely that mass community testing is going to be accelerated in the city in the coming days, and we are already piloting testing within schools to keep people safe. We will be working to ensure we can build and accelerate this to support schools to return safely in January.

I will be sending a letter to you shortly which I would ask you to disseminate via parent mail tonight please, alongside the communications you will need to send.

Finally, can I say again just how much I value and respect the utterly extraordinary work you have done during this year, and I'm sorry that it has come to this at the end of the year. Here's hoping we get reduced rates of infection as quickly as possible.

With best wishes,
Councillor Danny Thorpe
Leader
Royal Borough of Greenwich
13 December 2020

The figures were indeed bleak. Thorpe penned his note to Heads, having been advised by Public Health colleagues that, the previous Friday, 3,670 children and 314 teaching staff in the authority were self-isolating with the illness. But Secretary of State Gavin Williamson and his Schools Minister, Nick Gibb, were unmoved. They saw this as another (and an unwarranted) interruption to children's schooling.

Thus, the week before the Christmas 'holiday' began brought a set of press headlines unimaginable at the onset of the pandemic, in which the

Department for Education threatened to take legal action against Local Authorities, MATs and individual schools and academies to force them to remain open. The response of the Secretary of State was uncharacteristically swift. Concerned with the possibility of a snowballing of such closures nationwide, he argued that:

> It is simply not in children's best interests for schools in Greenwich, Islington or elsewhere to close their doors. I have always been clear that using legal powers is a last resort but continuity of education is a national priority … That's why I won't hesitate to do what is right for young people and have issued a Direction to Greenwich council setting out that they must withdraw the letter issued to headteachers on Sunday (13th December).
>
> (Weale and Quinn, 2020)

The following day, Greenwich relented, the Council's Leader making the following comment in a widely reported press release:

> Yesterday the Council received a Directive from the Government that schools in the borough must remain fully open until the end of term. With COVID-19 cases rising rapidly in the borough, I cannot agree that this is the correct choice for our schools. However, I also cannot justify the use of public funds to fight the decision in the courts. Consequently, I have no choice but to ask our schools to keep their doors open to all students rather than just continuing with online learning.
>
> Response to the Government regarding schools
> Statement from the Leader of the Royal Borough of Greenwich
> Councillor Danny Thorpe
>
> (Thorpe, 2020)

Council leaders in Islington were similarly warned off, and Headteachers in Waltham Forest received a letter from Schools Minister Nick Gibb, emphasizing the need for schools to remain open, drawing an exasperated reaction from that Local Authority's Leader:

> It is disappointing that, during a year when teachers, pupils and parents have made extraordinary efforts to ensure education continues through a once-in-a-lifetime crisis, the minister has chosen to write to our schools threatening them with potential legal action.

Councillor Clare Coghill
Leader
London Borough of Waltham Forest

(Cited in Weale, 2020)

Needless to say, educational professionals on the ground were not impressed with the threatened legal action, with this response from a senior Leader at a special school typifying the mood:

> The staff were really tired and this put added pressure on. The last few weeks before Christmas there was so much pressure on schools – suing those who were going to shut was ridiculous. The impact that had on staff was immense.
>
> (Jane Lovis, Deputy Headteacher, Pebble Brook
> School, Aylesbury, focus group – SEND practitioners
> and those based in alternative education settings,
> 28 May 2021)

The willingness of the Department of Education to go 'head-to-head' with those who had proposed taking learning online in the days before Christmas had not, in the measured terms of Headteachers' Leader Geoff Barton, been helpful:

> It marks a low moment when a government threatens legal action against its own school and college leaders, all of whom have worked tirelessly throughout this crisis to make sense of last-minute and chaotic decisions from Westminster. The government's approach undermines the much-vaunted trust it once said it had for leaders and governors in their communities to make the right decisions on behalf of their pupils, parents and staff.
>
> Geoff Barton, General Secretary, Association for School
> and College Leaders (Cited in Roberts, 2020)

It became all the more galling, given the announcements that the Education Secretary would subsequently make and the new year that followed. A report from a leading think tank – one usually noted for its calm objectivity and political neutrality – summarises, in an uncharacteristically ironic tone, what was to follow: a temporary Department for Education-imposed switch to online learning in secondary schools, initially for the first week after the Christmas break, exactly what the same Department had objected to at the close of the Autumn Term.

Just days later, however, Williamson was to announce that three million pupils in secondary schools would do precisely that – switch to online learning – for the first week of the January term to allow them to set up mass testing for their pupils. That came a mere week before Christmas, with the head teachers and teaching unions branding the testing plan as simply 'inoperable'. Then, on 30 December, five days ahead of the start of the school term, and in apparent response to that reaction, Williamson announced that secondary schools and colleges would remain closed for an additional week, until 18 January, to try to get the testing regime in place. With the virus increasingly out of control he also announced that primary schools in 50 council areas would now not open on 4 January – in other words in a third of the 152 local authorities. That decision, he said, would be reviewed on 18 January.

(Timmins, 2021)

In fact, that review would come somewhat sooner, only days after the Education Secretary's strident Parliamentary address.

And so to the New Year: The term that never was

On Monday, 4 January 2021, primary schools duly opened, as promised – at least in those Local Authority areas where the Department of Education had deemed it safe to do so – while those in secondary schools continued to press ahead with plans to put in place pop-up testing centres for their students.

But the opening was short-lived: for one day only, and in some cases for one of five already scheduled staff professional development days that have been a feature of English schooling since the early 1990s. These five days – 'Baker Days' as older members of the profession still call them – were named after Kenneth Baker, Gavin Williamson's predecessor in the Conservative Governments of the late 1980s and early 1990s. Senior Leaders in secondary settings had spent a significant proportion of their Christmas break establishing the school-based testing arrangements that they had been informed of in the closing weeks of term, an exercise that proved to be a dress rehearsal for a full return of onsite teaching that would not now occur until the middle of March.

At 5p.m. that evening, the Prime Minister led a press conference, broadcast live, in which the inevitable was announced. The government had promised that schools would reopen in January and some had, but the following day they would 'close'; they would, of course, remain open, to the children of key workers and those deemed 'vulnerable'. The Christmas that never was had come to a close and almost a term of online learning lay ahead. However, this term would be very different to the experimental and inevitably faltering efforts of Spring and Summer 2020, as we explore in Chapter 5.

The long shadow of a lost Christmas

Perhaps this wasn't obvious at the time, but for those in education – as for those in any other area of activity – the non-event of a nervously anticipated and subsequently 'cancelled' COVID Christmas would reach far into 2021. Indeed, arguably, its impact was not in January or February, but much later in the year: in June and July as teachers and school leaders reached for the finishing line that is the end of term, and even in September and October, as they held out for the half-term break, never so tired so early in an academic year. Shelley Bray put it this way in an email following one of the focus group discussions that she had transcribed as part of the research for this book; it is worth reproducing in full:

> Tony, you always say in our Zoom meetings that if anybody has anything else to add afterwards to email you their thoughts.
>
> I was thinking about what we'd said about the general [feeling of] fatigue, Covid weariness and low mood that everybody seems to have experienced this year and it struck me that nobody has mentioned that we didn't have Christmas.
>
> If you think about it, even before schools [and] workplaces finish for the Christmas break, the whole of December is pretty much any excuse for a party or get together. There are Christmas Fayres, Christmas lunches, Christmas dinners, works' Christmas parties, meeting up with friends and family for a drink – because it's Christmas – going out for dinner with friends and family – because it's Christmas – carol concerts, Christmas plays … [all this and] the actual Christmas break of spending quality time with loved ones and relaxing – none of it happened.
>
> For me personally, I spent the whole of December at home [isolating] because of having worked closely with Dave [the Head], the SLT [and] teachers who all had Covid – and the school closed for a week because of this. Then, one of my daughters got Covid, then, five days later my son got Covid so I had to start isolating again, then we went into Tier 4 and Christmas was officially cancelled. The rising cases and

deaths were quite frightening – far worse than [in] the first lockdown. So many people I know were in a similar position and December was a pretty miserable and anxious time for everyone, I think.

So, I think, instead of starting January feeling refreshed and ready to go after a nice break with family and friends, everyone was jaded and frightened and wondering how this was ever going to end, and if we'd ever get back to normal.

So, I just wonder whether this lost December fun and [cancelled] Christmas played a part in the weariness this year?

(Shelley Bray, transcription lead, Bubble Schools Project, By email, 4 August 2021)

And, Bray, who surely has a point, omits to add that this cancelled yet exhausting Christmas followed a year that had seen the first schooling lockdown, the delivery of onsite provision during lockdown for particular cohorts of children, the challenge of adapting to delivering learning online for others, the possibility of monitoring visits from the inspectorate (which although 'non-judgemental' and involving a minority of schools were none-theless nervously anticipated by senior leaders), the cancellation of written examinations (and the involvement of secondary educators in a detailed and time-consuming alternative assessment process), the stress of the grading crisis, the emergence and periodic bursting of bubbles, and the conversion of secondary schools (over the Christmas 'break') into testing centres for students who didn't return. Add to this the usual demands of teaching as a profession and school leadership as a role, and the need to deliver all of this in a climate of anxiety amongst pupils, parents and colleagues and a seemingly never-ending stream of sometimes conflicting guidance from the DfE, Local Authorities and MATs, and the measure of the challenge facing educators and school leaders, both at Christmas and across the previous year, becomes clear.

Summary

That, in England, the Department for Education, wedded to delivering the political messaging emerging from both Downing Street and the Education Secretary, ever got to a position where it was threatening legal action against teachers, school leaders and those involved in the governance and local organisation of schooling will remain long in the memory of many in the profession. Every effort ought to be made to ensure that such a situation never arises again. In addition, there needs to be a focus on building system-resilience so that closure decisions are ones that schools can come to autonomously, proportionately, legally and secure in the knowledge that they have the infrastructure to support home – and other offsite – learning and the ability and imagination to recast onsite learning, possibly at the same time, so that education can continue in strained circumstances.

In this context, it is vital that the skills and capacities developed in teachers and learners during this period are captured, shared and enhanced – and institutionalised in curricula and CPD programmes, such that if any such disruption arises again, we have the education systems, governance models, internet connectivity and blended-learning frameworks in place to address the challenges posed, and education professionals ready, confident and sufficiently resilient to meet the challenge.

Recommendations

4.1 Policymakers and system leaders would be wise, as a matter of urgency, to draw up a code of conduct for working with the professionals who deliver educational and other public services on the ground, and this ought to preclude threatening those professionals with legal action in all but the most extreme of circumstances.

4.2 Policymakers and system leaders need to give school leaders and those involved in school governance at a local level far more autonomy on decisions about the opening and closing of school sites in line with local circumstances, while continuing to hold Heads and school-based boards to account for the continuing provision of education for all students.

4.3 There should be a greater focus on the development of study skills in school, college and university curricula, especially in the upper primary, secondary, Further and Higher Education phases.

4.4 Development work undertaken, and skills developed, by teachers during this period so that they are better placed to support home learning, need to be built on with Continuing Professional Development (CPD) programmes that enhance these often new-found capabilities.

4.5 The enhancement in the digital literacy of teachers and learners during this period needs to be utilised as one of the foundation stones for a system that makes optimal use of digital technologies in the post-lockdown era.

Better connected?   **5**

Home-learning second time around

Back in March 2020, as the lockdown juggernaut swung into view, the reaction of colleagues, and of school leaders in particular, was one of bemusement. In *Lessons from Lockdown*, the reaction of Heads and Principals was pretty much unanimous and is worth recalling here:

> Back in the middle of March, in that final week, my overriding feeling was that people were voting with their feet. We lost control of the situation; we are trying to get ahead of situations constantly, because we're leaders. That's what leaders do. We anticipate. We study, we plan … but for the first time, really, and I've been teaching for 32 years now in London, we weren't ahead of the game … Parents were coming to the school door and saying, I'm taking my son away, now; I've just watched the news [and] I'm not happy. Now, when you combine that with the understandable anxieties of staff as well … It became a situation where for the first time as leaders, we really didn't have a clear way forward.
> (Daniel Coyle, Headteacher, Newman Catholic College, Brent, research interview, 17 August 2020 – in Breslin, 2021a: 130)

And for Coyle and his peers, the anxiety continued into the first weeks of lockdown:

> We lived in a vacuum for the best part of ten days, professionally … at home [and] with the family, people in the neighbourhood [were] asking me similar questions: what's going to happen to schools?

DOI: 10.4324/9781003204824-5

Professionally, [Heads were being] bombarded with questions that we simply couldn't answer. And I found that really, really destabilising from a leadership point of view. And … at the same time … you had your own anxieties as well. I look back and I find that was the hardest thing, people voting with their feet, not being able to provide answers for parents, for staff, for yourself, but at the same time having to [wear] that mask of calm authoritative leadership.

(Daniel Coyle, Headteacher, Newman Catholic College, Brent, research interview, 17 August 2020 – in Breslin, 2021a: 130–131)

Ann Bowen-Breslin, who leads a large primary school, also in London, concurred, using almost the same words:

We've all had many stressful periods of headship, but it's the first time where I felt that my skills and knowledge were not enough; I was actually, really, relying on the government and their scientists to tell us the right thing to do.

(Ann Bowen-Breslin, Headteacher, Hillingdon Primary School, research interview, 18 August 2020)

Bowen-Breslin went on to explain the challenge of 'closing' and how school leadership teams adapted to the new landscape that they were required to navigate, often without a route-map:

Given the stress you have about closing a school just for a 'snow day', it was kind of 'this isn't really happening' … in the last week we had parents refusing to send their children into school, which we didn't challenge because we felt that the country was just in such upheaval that we didn't want to add to the stress of parents, and we felt we could understand why they were starting to say, I don't want my child to come in … the government were making their announcements about key workers and vulnerable children … I was really concerned about this … everybody else was being told to stay at home and yet school staff were being told to go to school. And that struck a real nerve … I think the only thing that kept us all calm was the fact that we weren't NHS staff … and we had a vital role as educational professionals … .

(Ann Bowen-Breslin, Headteacher, Hillingdon Primary School, research interview, 18 August 2020)

In short, the strangeness of the situation brought a mix of anxiety and novelty, for leaders, teachers, parents and pupils. While new guidance from the Department for Education and its agencies rapidly became a near-daily occurrence, this did not amount to a coherent 'play book' for the crisis, and the multiple interpretations of each update – from professional associations and other positioned interest groups representing, for instance, parents, governors and teachers' subject communities, from educational influencers and consultant advisers, from Local Authorities and from MATs – often, although well-intentioned, produced more noise than light. As another Headteacher, David Miller, in his reflections on the first lockdown, put it at the time:

> This is all completely new. We're all making it up as we go along but, because of this, we've lost the fear of getting it wrong. That's liberating.
>
> (David Miller, Headteacher, Pebble Brook School, *Lessons from Lockdown* focus group – Special Education and Alternative Provision, 8 July 2020)

Nine months later, at the dawn of 2021, the novelty had disappeared, as, arguably, had a certain amount of *professional* anxiety. As a result, with even less notice than the twenty or so hours given prior to an inspection by Ofsted, the English school inspectorate, schools hit the road running: online lessons, often live-streamed, were up and running within days, something that would have been inconceivable only months before. One school governor, a qualified and experienced teacher who is an established authority in the field of Citizenship Education, reflects on just how differently educational professionals responded to the second national schooling lockdown, enabled by both the experience of the first lockdown and the lessons learned through negotiating more than a term of bursting bubbles and local lockdowns:

> It seemed to me that in January things just seemed to click. I was enormously impressed by the schools I am involved with. There was a real sure-footedness [about] the way things kicked-in in January [when schools were again locked down] and in March [when schools reopened]. The skills that we developed in the first part of the pandemic were refined so the vast majority of lessons moved online. There was a sound number of students in school and levels of involvement from students increased. One of the staff said they felt that they were able to monitor students remotely as well as they were able to do in the classroom.
>
> Tony Thorpe, School Governor, Chair, Curriculum and Performance Committee, Hall Cross Academy, Doncaster, focus group – Governors and Trustees, 17 April 2021)

The trials and tribulations of local lockdowns and 'bubbling' in the preceding term, and the conscious self-up-skilling of the teaching force in terms of digital literacy undertaken by many (but by no means all) schools, had provided the test labs for home-based learning the second time around. Further, the 'trickle-down' of technological equipment – so frustratingly slow during the lockdown of Spring and Summer Terms 2020 – had begun to deliver the device access (if not, necessarily, the connectivity) on which the system still depended, and surely would in the emergent post-lockdown landscape. For this reason, we return to these issues of digital connectivity and device access in Chapters 8 and 9, and, substantively, in the final text in this trilogy, *Reschooling Society After Lockdown*, to be published by Routledge in late 2023 or early 2024.

Parents and schooling: A changing relationship?

During the first lockdown, home-schooling had served as a rude awakening for some parents. Paddy O' Leary, a parent of three school-age children, the site manager at a federation of primary schools, and a retired Metropolitan Police officer, recounts his experience of home-schooling during the first lockdown:

> We did the maths ... I learned how to do fractions again, which is good for me. The maths was easier because it was either right or wrong, you know ... add, takeaway, fractions, multiply. I quite enjoyed it in the end and he enjoyed it ... the English was more difficult for me. It brought back all those horrible comprehension [questions], honestly, you know ... .
>
> (Paddy O' Leary, Site Manager, Bushey Primary Education
> Federation, *Lessons from Lockdown* focus group –
> parents, guardians and carers, 23 July 2020)

O'Leary reminds us that the inclusive intent of most in education is sometimes thwarted by how strange school, and the language of those 'in' education, can seem to those 'outside' the system, especially those who might not have had a great experience of it:

> I left school at 17. And the next time I went back to school was when I [took] this job two years ago. So, a lot of the stuff that teachers [were] sending out, they, because they are in education ... expect that you understand that language. You don't understand it ... because you haven't been back in school for years and years and, and [that's] not

to say that you're not intelligent at all. It's just that you've done something different for so many years, a completely different job … .

(Paddy O' Leary, Site Manager, Bushey Primary Education
Federation, Lessons from Lockdown focus group –
parents, guardians and carers, 23 July 2020)

As is discussed in *Lessons from Lockdown*, some parents had been critical of teachers and schools during the first lockdown and it is undoubtedly the case that the variety of practice left some feeling wholly 'underwhelmed' and others feeling 'bombarded'. This fuelled debates, notably on social media, about the sheer diversity of provision, often between schools serving children from the same communities, and this was a diversity experienced by those in the *Lessons from Lockdown* Parents, Guardians and Carers' Focus Group staged in Summer 2020 and in those groups staged as part of the research process that informs this text.

For those with different children in different year groups, the school run took on a new complexity:

> My youngest was just starting Year 2 so had already had some weeks of being back at school. Year 5 hadn't been in school and had only one hour to see the teacher [online] which was ridiculous. The biggest thing was going back to this environment and not knowing what it was going to be like. They could only go to certain places in the playground and it seemed unfair. The [children] said it was boring because the teachers were trying to recap stuff [that] they had already done. The teachers were trying to get everyone back to speed. There were no Christmas plays. It was all a bit sad really. I had to drop the children at different entrances at different times, so I was splitting myself in two.
>
> (Ruth Dwight, parent, Lessons from Lockdown focus group –
parents, guardians and carers, 23 July 2020)

For those going through the transfer from primary (or elementary) school to secondary (or high) school, many of the rites of passage associated with this progression were lost, and the introduction to the setting that would be their educational home for five, six, or seven years was, sometimes, heavily disrupted:

> My son was missing out on so much going to senior school making new friends. He didn't get to see the end of Year 6. He missed out on that and getting to know new friends in Year 7. Teachers on camera. Freezing classrooms because all the windows were open. As the weeks

went on and it became darker and colder the school was freezing. Not a normal start to Year 7.

(Cosette Reczek, parent, focus group – parents, guardians and carers, 10 May 2021)

And while schools could control activity within their walls, the journey to school was beyond their reach, exposing fault lines that were no respecters of meticulously organised in-school bubbles, and posed a particular challenge to large secondary schools:

We live in Bedfordshire, in a village, but it's a huge catchment area. We have 'vertical' [mixed age] forms but they were scrapped to maintain the bubbles ... The kids weren't allowed to mingle in school but were allowed to mingle on the bus because [they came] from all over ... .

(Caroline Graham, parent, focus group – parents, guardians and carers, 10 May 2021)

And, for those with children at more than one school, there was the issue of consistency:

The remote learning at my daughter's school wasn't anywhere near the quality of the remote learning at my son's school. Her schedule was so curtailed and I didn't understand it. She almost ended up teaching herself. It wasn't acceptable.

(Parent, speaking on condition of confidentiality, focus group – parents, guardians and carers, 10 May 2021)

This diversity of provision and experience, coupled with the broader lockdown fatigue that developed as 2021 progressed, inevitably and understandably produced frustration amongst parents, guardians and carers. It led some teachers and school leaders to question the permanence of the positivity that they had, for the most part, witnessed earlier in the course of the pandemic, with the challenges of in-school examination assessment, which we discuss in detail in Chapter 6, bringing tensions to the fore in the secondary phase:

It's just been a massive drain of energy and the frustrations of staff. I detect bitterness, anger and frustration in the profession. I've had more passive aggression from parents in the last few months than in 30 years in the profession – a general discontent.

(Secondary school Headteacher, speaking on condition of confidentiality, focus group – secondary educators, 6 July 2021)

But Heads understood the varied reactions from different parents and different families:

> We've had demanding parents who have been unreasonable and parents who have been really understanding.
> (Primary school Headteacher, speaking on condition of confidentiality, focus group – primary educators, 14 July 2021)

Nonetheless, the broad conclusion drawn from these discussions and coming through in the focus groups and interviews with parents, school leaders and others, across all phases, was of a greater empathy between home and school, and, for some, there were moments of home-schooling that they would not have wanted to miss:

> We wanted to learn about the Romans, and so we spent a whole week learning all about the Romans and he couldn't get enough of it. So that whole thing about child-led learning really hit home; like, we cannot expect teachers who've got thirty children in a class to be able to do that, but when you're doing it one-to-one at home, if you aren't working, and if you are able to sort of source the things that you need, then it was just absolutely magical … .
> (Fiona Elllis, parent, *Lessons from Lockdown* focus group – parents, guardians and carers, 23 July 2020

Ellis goes on:

> I didn't care what he was learning as long as he was sort of engaging with it. And, you know, and the school [was] very, very good at saying, you know, whatever you're doing is absolutely fine. And that emotional health message kept coming across really loud and clear … .

And the editorial in this weekly federation newsletter, a week into the first lockdown, underlined this message to parents of children in the infant and junior years:

> If we were at school, we would be going into the last week before the Easter holidays. We would be singing Springtime songs, Easter Egg hunting and winding down with the children. Do keep a healthy perspective with learning at home. Children pick up on our fears and anxieties and they hear the news too. They need fun, laughter and normality and they need YOU. YOU with your parent hat on. The teacher

hat definitely suits you, and wonderful things are happening, but you are allowed and should take it off regularly.

(*Bushey Primary Education Federation Newsletter*, Week ending 27 March 2020, author's archives)

During this period in the first lockdown, schools had been criticised for failing to engage with so-called 'vulnerable' students, for whom schools had remained open. Maybe, and as is remarked in *Lessons from Lockdown*, the 'vulnerable' badge did not help, in that to send your child to school during this period, if you were not a designated 'key' worker, was to publicly confess their (and your family's) 'vulnerable' status. In *Lessons from Lockdown*, this Headteacher cited an example:

> One of my mums said that to me, and, uh, she said it in a child protection meeting … Social Services were putting her under pressure about why the children were not [coming] back to school. And she said, 'Well, 'cause everyone is gonna know I'm vulnerable, innit'. And I just, I think I said to her, you're right … I just thought that crystallized [the problem]; it can't be clearer than that.
>
> Headteacher – speaking on condition of anonymity)
> Research Interview
> Summer 2020
> *Lessons from Lockdown: The Educational Legacy of COVID-19*, (Breslin 2021a, p. 149)

In the second substantive lockdown, beginning in January 2021 (after a u-turn that was discussed at length in Chapter 4), schools, again, remained open, but the definitions of both 'key' worker and 'vulnerable' child were softened. This was not done through Department for Education edict or in response to 'guidance' (or the equivalent in Scotland, Wales, or Northern Ireland) but essentially through negotiation between the home and the school.

Thus, many schools did not just admit those officially designated as 'key' workers or 'vulnerable', but were more receptive to appeals from parents, more proactive in 'getting' particular children into school and under more pressure from some parents to accommodate their children. This was especially where families were just *above* the inevitable thresholds that formally govern access to benefits, or entitlement to Pupil Premium support (funding designed to support additional educational interventions targeted at particular 'disadvantaged' groups, care-experienced children and young people and others who have had specific disruptions to their education, and those, where applicable, in receipt of free school meals in English schools), or where there were particular issues at home, issues which the school may well have become aware of during the course of the national and local lockdowns of Spring, Summer and Autumn 2020. Describing the second lockdown, by comparison with the first, Mary Ann Cooper notes:

> We had 40 per cent of our children in school and managing that was key. In the first lockdown I felt we had lost families and pupils I had concerns about, so [we] tried to have those children in. [The term] 'vulnerable' became open to interpretation. We identified children we felt should have been in school … We identified those who needed particular support and had remote meetings with the families to air concerns and how we could support them. After the first lockdown there was more take-up of the offer to have children in.
>
> (Mary Ann Cooper, Federation Headteacher, Bushey Primary Education Federation, focus group – primary educators, 5 May 2021)

It is reasonable to surmise that the 'softening' of these definitions, in effect, helped to remove the risk of stigmatisation for those who elected to send their children to school during this period.

As a result, during the second substantive lockdown running from 5 January 2021, many schools had significantly more students in school, while the local lockdowns of the bursting bubbles of the preceding terms had enabled the trialling of 'new' digital pedagogies and the development of new levels of digital literacy and confidence amongst many teachers and teaching assistants. In some cases, schools made a special effort to develop the digital literacy of parents, guardians and carers alongside that of staff. This US educator's comment is illustrative of such work, and also nudges technology suppliers to take their responsibilities in this respect more seriously:

> I've spent a lot of time teaching parents about technology – teaching them how to use Zoom, Microsoft Teams, etc. For parents who don't usually use technology in their work this has been a real learning curve. Technology providers are making lots of money but not offering training to the users.
>
> (Dr Vangie Aguilera, Coordinator, Centre for Educational Leadership, Trinity University, San Antonio, Texas, focus group – international educators, 12 May 2021)

As a result, many schools met the second national lockdown with a level of preparedness that they *could not* have brought to the first. We discuss this new level of connectivity, aided by greater levels of device access amongst children and young people in some settings, in detail in Chapters 8 and 9. Steve Mills is in no doubt that parents appreciated the efforts that teachers and schools were making, for instance, in facilitating the transfer from infant to junior school, something that begins as early as the Spring Term:

> Before COVID we would welcome Years 2 and 3 by a talk in the hall with the parents and pupils. Last year, instead, the SLT [Senior Leadership Team] would take a very small group on a 'walk and talk' of the school. The parents loved it, the kids loved it. They felt they knew someone from the SLT before they started at the school. We did that again this year because we were forced to [as a result of COVID], but we are going to keep that for next year.
>
> (Steve Mills, Headteacher, Whitehill Junior School, focus group – primary practitioners, 14 July 2021)

Another primary school leader, Daniel Kerbel, reflects on how the efforts to keep children based at home during this period also met with parental approval, citing a comment from a parent at the end of the Spring 2021 lockdown:

> When a teacher was saying goodbye to the children online, a parent said 'I am going to miss hearing your voice in my house every day.' When we stopped the online learning some of the parents felt a bit lost because they had been involved and now their children won't tell them what they have been doing at school.
>
> (Daniel Kerbel, Headteacher, Grange Primary School, Harrow, focus group – primary educators, 5 May 2021)

This connectedness worked at two levels: on the one hand, online 'live lessons' brought teachers into children's homes and parents into the class-room, albeit virtually, creating the new closeness to which Kerbel refers. On the other hand, the fact that schools remained open to the children of key workers and those deemed 'vulnerable' during the two substantive schooling lockdowns meant that these young people gained access to the kind of attention that they had not always had in 'standard' classes of thirty children. Thus, many of those participating in both the parent and teacher focus groups undertaken as part of the research for this book and for *Lessons from Lockdown* concurred with the observation in this teacher's comment to researchers working on the ImpactEd study, a major survey-based and case study-informed longitudinal study involving 62,254 young people across the primary and secondary age ranges:

> Most of our SEND [special educational needs and disabilities] pupils had continued attending school over lockdown, and our relationship with them strengthened as a result. They then required support with the transition back to 'normal' school life and interactions with peers.
> (ImpactEd, 2021: 30)

A class teacher in one of our focus groups made a similar point:

> Children who had been in [school] found it hard to adapt to all the other children coming back in, and the larger groups.
> (Alice Falkiner, Year 3 teacher, Crabtree Junior School, Harpenden, focus group – primary educators, 5 May 2021)

In some cases, this translated into children with particular needs and vulnerabilities making *greater* progress during periods when school opening was restricted, something that runs counter to the prevalent political and media narratives that we discuss elsewhere in these pages. This comment from a parent, who had participated in one of the *Lessons from Lockdown* focus groups, illustrates the point:

> My youngest is dyslexic. Because I teach, he was able to be in [primary] school through my 'key worker' status, and he has absolutely thrived during lockdown. He has loved the additional attention.
> (Parent (and secondary school teacher), in discussion with the author on condition of confidentiality, May 2021)

The stronger relationship between the home and the school had an additional consequence: it *exposed* vulnerabilities, in children and in families, that had not always been evident prior to lockdown, sometimes because lockdown had *produced* the vulnerability, for instance through pandemic-related job loss or income reduction. Thus, another teacher, who contributed to the ImpactEd research, commenting on students returning to school in Autumn Term 2021, noted the emergence of newly 'vulnerable' groups:

> … some of whom we didn't necessarily expect to be vulnerable, who had become vulnerable as a result of the initial lockdown.
> (ImpactEd, 2021: 24)

And sometimes because lockdown had *revealed* such vulnerability, for instance by drawing attention to domestic abuse that may have long-standing but was exposed through the closer relationship between the home and the school generated by the pandemic:

> We have had three families – families who, before all of this, had not ticked any kind of indicator – where a mother has opened up about domestic violence.
>
> (Primary school Senior Leader, in discussion with the author on condition of confidentiality, May 2021)

Against this background, it is difficult not to concur with one of the key conclusions from the ImpactEd study that:

> … those children who had struggled the most during lockdown were not always those previously identified as vulnerable.
>
> (ImpactEd, 2021: 24)

Or as David Miller puts it:

> Parents [do not want] their children labelled as vulnerable, [but] the definition of vulnerable has changed since March 2020.
>
> (David Miller, Headteacher, Pebble Brook School, Aylesbury, focus group – SEND practitioners and those based in alternative education settings, 30 June 2021)

And this was partly because Headteachers and other senior leaders were proactive, and generally successful, in seeking out vulnerability:

> I think we know the families much better than before, I think we know the children better. But I think, with some of the children and their families, we haven't made the connections in the usual way through school, through information sessions, through parents' evening.
>
> (Mary Ann Cooper, Federation Headteacher, Bushey Primary Education Federation, Hertfordshire, focus group – primary educators, 5 May 2021)

Instead, relationships have been built through a myriad of other conversations, some resulting from the work with the smaller groups that bubble schooling has facilitated. The downside of this is that the 'rhythm' of schooling is still an unknown tune to some children and families. Thus, Cooper continues:

> [Some] parents are now in the third year of their child's schooling and don't really understand the pattern, the rhythm, the expectations … or the normality of school life and how that translates into their expectations for the children's learning but also for the children's well-being – how do you balance that?

Against this background, the willingness of school leaders to take a more pragmatic and less bureaucratic approach to what is, essentially, inclusion during the second schooling lockdown is not to criticise their behaviour during the previous 'shutdown', a period that school leaders and the colleagues they led struggled to make sense of. By the time of the second schooling lockdown, a new confidence had emerged, as had an empathy borne of what were often closer, richer relationships between the home and the school – relationships that were better connected in a range of ways.

Summary

The 'new visibility' enabled by the circumstances created by the pandemic is a common theme that runs through many of the comments cited and points made in this chapter. In the first lockdown, schools struggled to connect with many of those that they had struggled to engage with in 'normal' times, the so-called 'hard to reach'. By the time of the emergence of the second schooling lockdown, fewer families faced technological barriers to access and teachers felt more comfortable with online learning and communications in various forms. In addition, relationships with some vulnerable families were characterised by a hitherto missing closeness, while 'softer' less bureaucratic and more pragmatic definitions of what constituted both a 'key' worker and a 'vulnerable' child contributed to these better relationships and those with parents in general. Understanding the factors that have underpinned these changes will be key if educators are to address these vulnerabilities – including those that have been rendered newly visible by the pandemic – and build on these relationships in the years ahead.

Recommendations

5.1 While practitioners and policymakers are right to be concerned about what children will have missed out on during lockdowns and other disruptions to schooling, both in curricular and developmental terms, it is important that schools capture, and are encouraged to capture, the learning that children and young people have undertaken during this period, seeing this as a resource on which to build.

5.2 Building on the positive experiences of those who thrived in the bubbles and smaller classes of lockdown ought to be a priority for schools as activities return to scale.

5.3 Where schools have formed richer relationships with parents, especially those hitherto defined as 'hard to reach', it is vital that senior leaders understand the precise and local factors that have generated this new closeness, such that this learning is applied to school-home relationship building post-lockdown.

5.4 School leaders, and all working at school level, ought to continue to address the needs of those newly revealed as vulnerable during lockdown, while bringing the needs of these cohorts to policymakers' attention.

5.5 Policymakers ought to pay particular attention to those hitherto unseen or lesser-seen cohorts who have been either rendered vulnerable by the virus, or who had pre-existing vulnerabilities exposed by it, so as to ensure that future policy reforms capture their needs.

'Examining' the class of 2021   6

Exploding the myths of 'teacher bias' and 'grade inflation'

The full extent of the grading crisis of 2020 is detailed in *Lessons from Lockdown* and revisited in Chapter 2 of this text. It is a story of error stacked upon error, u-turn upon u-turn, a story that started with the cancellation of written papers, proceeded through a delayed but rigorous teacher assessment progress, saw the late introduction of an algorithm to correct so-called 'grade inflation' (allegedly generated by this process), the subsequent withdrawal of the algorithm after an outcry from the profession, young people and their families, and the 're-awarding' of the earlier teacher-assessed grades, but not before some prospective university students had already missed out on their preferred place, and others had deferred for a year. And, in England's case, not before the Northern Irish, Scottish and Welsh governments had done so first.

As is pointed out in *Lessons from Lockdown*, the critical backdrop here is the culture of disdain that had been constructed around teacher assessment in any guise over a period stretching back for at least a decade and arguably for a quarter of a century. In *Lessons from Lockdown*, the position that we arrive at in the summer of 2020 is articulated thus:

> In the Gove reforms to GCSE and A level, teacher assessment is viewed as inherently subjective (because teachers are familiar with the students), and overly negotiable (because middle-class parents and students are thought of as being adept at pressurising teachers into

DOI: 10.4324/9781003204824-6

making favourable judgements), and because teachers are differentially experienced in marking work that contributes to public examination grades. There is some evidence for the first two of these risks when the discussion is about 'predicted' grades, and the third may have been accentuated by the removal of teacher-assessed coursework from the assessment mix by the Gove reforms, as this diminishes the opportunity for teachers to be involved in the assessment of public examinations.

(Breslin 2021a: 79)

An alternative analysis of teacher assessment to that implied in recent qualifications reforms, notably those introduced in England during Michael Gove's stewardship of the Department of Education, is provided by this experienced teacher, school governor and examiner:

Many years ago I taught courses for 'O' and 'A' Level and GCSE, all of which had a common element – a significant amount of coursework or teacher assessment. We used Cambridge 'O' Level English and English Literature syllabuses that were 50% coursework. The students thrived because they had more opportunity to show what they could achieve beyond a final exam; we conducted conscientious internal moderation and had a visiting external moderator too. We also used a Cambridge 'A' Level syllabus that included coursework and a long study, which was taxing but again proved far more about our students' abilities than an exam could have achieved. This too involved internal and external moderation. When GCSE arrived, I helped write 100% coursework syllabuses for English (Language) and Literature for one of the exam boards. Both involved timed, test-condition work as well as coursework, to ensure the students' ability to work alone and unaided. I also served as a Senior Moderator, so visited schools and was part of the national moderation (process) which set the ultimate grades. Throughout these experiences I found teachers, who were scrupulous in their approach, who showed no bias. Teachers are professionals and know how to be impartial. If any one individual strayed – a very rare occurrence, then the internal moderation processes dealt with this effectively and ensured a final impartial judgement.

(Judith Bennett, written submission (by email), 29 November 2021)

Critically, it was established in *Lessons from Lockdown* that the grades awarded in 2020 were, in no way, 'predicted', and, in no way comparable with a prediction-based process. Classically, the latter is used in the UK as an aspect of the university application process, which takes place prior to the sitting of examinations and the awarding of grades, through which teachers 'predict' the grades likely to be achieved by their students in the following summer's examinations. These predictions are social constructs designed to attract offers of university places from desired institutions and preferred courses which are, in turn, 'conditional' on the student subsequently achieving the grades set out in the 'offer'. Against this backdrop, there is some validity in the claim that middle-class students and their parents can prove adept at 'negotiating' these predictions upward, and teachers are sometimes open to such pressure, because mild 'overprediction', if it succeeds in attracting particular offers, can drive up student performance. Why? Because the receipt of an offer from a sought-after Higher Education destination can itself drive up student motivation, commitment and workrate, thus generating a grade in line with the initially 'inflated' prediction.

Much of the media and political narrative the previous year had been based around the false assumption that teachers were predicting grades. Rather, as we set out in *Lessons from Lockdown* and summarise below, the 2020 grades were the result of a precise and deliberate assessment process. The process, as we shall see, was different in 2021, but it was, again, one based on the assessment of actual work undertaken and not a prediction of potential performance in a future examination. Nonetheless, the narrative of teacher subjectivity remained heavy in the air, just as the presumption of teacher subjectivity had influenced qualification reform since the turn of the century, and notably the examination reforms developed under the auspices of former Education Secretary Michael Gove, and his Schools Minister, Nick Gibb, a role that Gibb remained in until September 2021. These had seen the removal of the internal, teacher-marked assessment (or 'coursework') components in examinations undertaken by young people in secondary (or 'high') schooling.

It is the central contention of the evidence-based argument advanced in this chapter that, although grades achieved by students in both 2020 and 2021 did rise, this was not a product of teacher subjectivity; further, it is contended that these enhanced achievements are improperly described as being examples of grade *inflation*. Rather, as was initially outlined in *Lessons from Lockdown*, they represent a grading 'spike' produced by a very particular set of circumstances – circumstances deriving directly from the unique context of COVID-19. Inflation is a trend over time; what we see during the COVID years is not a trend, but a system-shock directly attributable to the particular circumstances of the pandemic.

New school year: New start?

In a famous Conservative conference speech, Margaret Thatcher, who had begun her journey to the UK's political summit as the Secretary of State for Education who removed the entitlement of primary-school children to free milk during the morning break (earning the infamous title 'Margaret Thatcher, Milk Snatcher'), wowed the party faithful with the memorable phrase, 'You turn if you want to; the lady's not for turning.' Her successor, Gavin Williamson, consistently sought to emulate such stridency, but blinked at the first opportunity on each of several occasions: on the partial reopening of schools in June 2020, on the commitment to retain the algorithmically corrected Centre Assessed Grades later that Summer and, subsequently, on the removal of the algorithm from the process. It was a habit that he would sustain into the new academic year, most notably on the promised reopening of schools in January 2021, as we have discussed in Chapters 4 and 5.

Recall the optimism of September 2020 set out in Chapter 1, and how this was thwarted by the growing shadow of a range of 'local lockdowns', especially in disadvantaged towns and cities in the Midlands and the North, in particular those that had become home over several generations to those of Bangladeshi and Pakistani descent, many of which had retained a foothold in the textiles industries, and now found themselves competing to produce 'fast fashion' with outlets in the Far East and elsewhere.

As set out in Chapter 3, these local lockdowns were already proving disruptive to schooling in such areas, and with debates about a potential 'circuit breaker' that might coincide with the October half-term break (and be delivered through an extension of this break), attention was, again, turning to the prospect of cancelling conventional written examinations in 2021. The question was simply this: how might one deliver a fair, valid and reliable national examination system based mainly on written papers, given the growing reality of local lockdowns and bursting bubbles? The claimed fairness of a common examination system is at least partially based on the presumption of access to a common (some might say, *comprehensive*) schooling system as a precursor to the time spent in the exam hall, but this was clearly not the experience of many students. In any case, the argument is fatally flawed by the data, year on year, with or without the help of a pandemic. Examination outcomes across developed societies are socially patterned by a range of factors: social class, socio-economic status, area of residence, ethnicity, cultural background, gender, disability, and so on.

For now, though, let us accept the spurious claim of fairness and, in particular, the claim that the examination hall constitutes, at least metaphorically, a 'level playing field'. Lockdown laid this struggling meta-phor to rest. In fact, as has already been illustrated, it is reasonable to claim that no two schools, year groups, or classes experienced the same lockdown, the same level of disruption, the same kind of intensely local experience – not so much a level playing field as the bumpy bog of a non-league football team's pitch in the 1970s. By the close of the 2020–21 aca-demic year, Department for Education statistics revealed that 328 school days had been lost, 270 of these due to COVID-19 (Whittaker, 2022), with the vast majority of young people in primary, secondary, or Further Education colleges experiencing some form of school closure, albeit class-by-class, year group-by-year group, all this during what had been intended to be a 'back-to-normal' Autumn term. However, each – and this is crit-ical – had experienced something different. Recall that during the same period, towns and cities across the UK had experienced periods of local lockdown, albeit differentiated in its intensity by the tiers that different areas were placed in as Autumn progressed into Winter. Predictably, *Schools Week* reported that:

> In 2020–21 overall, pupils with special educational needs and disabil-ities (SEND) had higher rates of absence than other pupils.

And that:

> The overall absence rate for pupils eligible for free school meals was 7.8 per cent across the year, more than double the rate for pupils who were not eligible, at 3.7 per cent.

And that:

> Disadvantaged pupils were also more likely to be persistently absent than their non-disadvantaged peers – 24.4 per cent compared to 8.3 per cent.
>
> (Whittaker, 2022)

No matter this widespread but socially differentiated disruption, Gavin Willliamson, in the spirit of his illustrious predecessor, was not for turning, with the Department for Education conceding that, while some aspects of the examination process, examination scheduling and examination con-tent might be changed, the exams themselves, in the conventional form of written papers, would go ahead:

We expect exams to take place next year and continue to work with Ofqual and the exam boards on our approach, recognising that students will have experienced considerable disruption to their education in the last academic year.

There are a range of measures proposed by Ofqual following a public consultation, including a possible short delay to the exam timetable and subject-specific changes to reduce pressure on teaching time.

(Madeley, 2020)

In taking this position, Williamson was ignoring the advice of a range of influential commentators, most prominent amongst them, Kenneth Baker, the Conservative Education Secretary who, three decades earlier, had done so much to mould the current system through overseeing the introduction of both the National Curriculum and GCSEs and laying the foundations for a range of regulatory apparatus including the creation of Ofsted, the school inspectorate in England, and the establishment of publicly published school performance (or 'league') tables. In an article in *The Sunday Times* in the build-up to the new academic year (and as the grading crisis of 2020 swung into action), Baker, citing support from former Labour Education Secretary David Blunkett, wrote:

Next year will be challenging for pupils and teachers alike. Faced with this fact, I believe that for the 2020–21 school year, pupils should not sit GCSE or A-level exams. Lord Blunkett, a former education secretary like me, agrees. If the exams are not suspended, the gulf between the privileged and disadvantaged will never be narrowed. It will be set in stone in the form of unchangeable exam grades.

(Baker, 2020)

Once again, Williamson had adopted a position that was not credible in the eyes of the profession, or those of political friends and foes alike, and it was one which would ultimately prove untenable, as Christmas approached and the so-called 'Kent' variant, and subsequently the 'Indian' or 'Delta' variant, took hold. Reluctantly, days into the new calendar year, and accompanying the nationwide closure of schools the day *after* most pupils had returned, Williamson again succumbed to the inevitable. Thus, on the evening of 5 January, the Department for Education belatedly announced that:

The Government position is that we will not be asking students to sit GCSE and A-levels. Working alongside Ofqual, the department will consult on how to award all pupils a grade that reflects the hard work they've done and will continue to do.

(Cited in Jones, 2021)

In the build-up to this latest u-turn, Williamson had assured anyone that would listen that a Plan B was in place should such a reversal be forced. The Plan B, it seemed, was less of a 'plan' in itself, and more of a plan to commission Ofqual, the examination regulator, to draw one up – that is, a plan to plan. Ofqual duly published a strategy for consultation a fortnight later; the decision to consult may have signalled a change in tone and a willingness to work collaboratively with teachers, but one consequence of this was that the arrangements for 2021 were not confirmed until late in February.

Again, a decision that could have been taken at the start of the academic year, and which had appeared inevitable rather than optional by the close of October 2020, when the virus was enjoying its second surge, was delayed well into the new calendar year, by which time – as we have detailed in Chapter 4 – schools were already in lockdown. Back in March 2020, as the Education Secretary, school leaders, teachers, parents and pupils grappled with a completely new crisis, the delay in confirming examination arrangements may have been unfortunate but it was understandable. A year later, a determination to *ignore* the data until the last minute meant that vital preparation time – for teachers and examination candidates alike – was lost.

Moreover, the decision to not adopt the approach used the previous year (probably because Ofqual was fearful of a repeat of the events of Summer 2020, although the issues had, arguably, emerged not because of the assessments undertaken by teachers but by the application of a 'corrective' algorithm to these, and its subsequent removal), left teachers with the task of understanding and operationalising another assessment model – for a second successive year and, again, with only months to internalise it prior to implementation: Centre Assessed Grades (CAGs) would be replaced by Teacher Assessed Grades (TAGs), the detail of which will be explored later.

A lesson from lockdown (belatedly) learned: Examination plans for 2022

That initial arrangements for written examinations in 2022 were published twelve months in advance suggests that this particular lesson from lockdown may have been belatedly learned. In 2022, written examinations were scheduled to go ahead but with restricted specifications, such that a narrower range of content would be examined. However, as young people returned to school in January 2022, the details about the content and the timing of papers had yet to be announced. Students and teachers would have to wait for another month for this vital information.

Nonetheless, delaying papers, reducing content and giving some kind of 'heads-up' about content, would seem to be a sensible acknowledgement that students will have faced significant but different patterns of disruption in the build-up to the examinations, especially during the first year of what are usually delivered as two-year courses. However, these adaptions may have had the unintended consequence of further enhancing the advantages that accrue to middle-class candidates in the examination hall, whether or not lockdown is the prevailing context. Why? Three reasons are pertinent:

1. The virus has, as detailed throughout this text, been most keenly experienced in disadvantaged communities and in the areas in which these communities reside, such that it is these areas that have occupied the higher tiers, and schools in these areas that have found themselves struck hardest by the phenomenon of bursting bubbles.
2. Advantaged students, as detailed in Chapter 5, are more likely to have had a positive experience of home-learning, given their ability to draw on a home environment that is 'better connected' and richer in both cultural capital and physical space.
3. The proposed universal slimming of specification content in 2022 served to benefit most those who had benefitted from this combination of 'less but better' home-schooling and fewer 'burst' bubbles within their schools, simply because they will have had more time to study a shorter body of examined content, will have experienced more 'ordinary' school days in which to study it, and are likely to have had a more enhanced experience of home-learning where this has been necessary.

In this regard, it is important to recall and restate a key theme first identified in the research detailed in *Lessons from Lockdown*: that lockdown has not *caused* the educational and other inequalities that it has exposed, but it is likely to have *deepened* them. The proposed reforms to written examinations across the UK were well-intended and a step in the right direction that pupils and teachers welcomed. But they did little, if anything, to challenge inequalities as old as organised education and centralised, public assessment itself. This is not an argument against organised education or the public assessment of outcomes, but it does illustrate just how external inequalities are expressed in schooling outcomes.

The return of an annual ritual: The exam grading season

In the UK, the exam grading season is welcomed by two familiar but conflicting media images. The first is of joyous pictures of students receiving their results; the second is the inevitable charge of 'grade inflation', or where there has been some deliberate attempt to 'correct' this, hollers of protest from often well-heeled families that their children have missed out on a university place, or the equivalent, that is, they believe, rightly theirs.

As detailed in *Lessons from Lockdown*, the grading crisis of 2020 had all of these qualities: early shouts of grade inflation some weeks ahead of the results' publication (wrongly attributed on this occasion to the alleged inability of teachers to objectively assess their pupils' work in the wake of the pandemic-driven cancellation of written papers), the introduction of an algorithm to correct this, consequent protests from teachers, prospective university students and parents that the algorithm had 'stolen' university places that the young people concerned were entitled to take up and, subsequently, the reluctant, delayed, begrudging re-issuing of the earlier Centre Assessed Grades. At GCSE, the examination typically taken two years before A level, the experience had been similar, with the confusion impacting access to 'Sixth Form' courses and colleges and Further Education colleges.

2021 was slightly different but, as we shall see, the underlying themes remained consistent. As with the previous year, and as detailed elsewhere in these pages, written papers were replaced with the assessment of a range of activities carried out during the course and towards its close, but only after the Department for Education, the Secretary of State and the Prime Minister had protested that there would be no such cancellation. Thus, in September 2020, with the heat of that summer's grading crisis still thick in the air, the Prime Minister's spokesperson, was adamant:

> We do expect [GCSE and A level] exams to take place next year … We are working with the exam boards and Ofqual on our approach, recognising that students experienced considerable disruption to their education last year.
>
> (Cited in Sleigh, 2020)

It was a stance that Boris Johnson and his colleagues would maintain for the remainder of the calendar year. Speaking early in December 2020, as the Kent variant raged and with local lockdowns rife, and those schools planning to 'close' early for Christmas about to be threatened by legal action from the Department for Education, as detailed elsewhere in these pages, Johnson's Education Secretary confirmed the thinking behind the official position:

> Exams are the best way of giving young people the opportunity to show what they can do, which is why it's so important they take place next summer.
>
> (Cited in Sleigh and Davis, 2020)

But to others, the cancellation of the written papers remained likely, if not inevitable, and the Education Secretary, although he had committed to reintroducing written papers in Summer 2021 as late as the previous December, had left himself the option of a late change in direction, with talk of a 'Plan B' that was, we were told, ready to go, or, in one of the Prime Minister's favourite phrases, 'oven-ready'.

To reiterate, those at school level were acutely aware that the later any decision to cancel written papers, the harder it would be for schools and teachers – and young people and their families – to adjust to the changed plans. Again, stubbornly and with what appeared a false optimism, the Secretary of State delayed his announcement until 5 January, concurrent with the announcement of school 'closures' and a new lockdown; any sense of the proposed detail behind the 2021 arrangements did not emerge for another fortnight.

And when this detail did arrive, rather than a published Plan B, the Education Secretary informed a bemused profession and student body, that he would ask Ofqual, the examination regulator for England and Wales to consult on a set of proposed arrangements for the Summer 2021 assessments – less oven-ready, more a shopping bag of possibilities. Geoff Barton, the General Secretary at the Association of School and College Leaders spoke of his 'immense frustration' at the lack of clarity, adding:

> We have been calling for such a Plan B for many months, and offered to work with the DfE and Ofqual to help put together robust arrangements. There is now an almighty rush going on to try to cobble together a system of assessing students in lieu of exams, which will then have to be communicated and implemented in an increasingly short time frame.
>
> (Cited in Sleigh, 2020)

The soap opera of the previous summer is likely to enter into education policy folklore. Perhaps because of the tragic events in Afghanistan, perhaps because of the broader lockdown fatigue that was now so prevalent across various walks of British society, perhaps because the Education Secretary had broadly decided to stay out of the annual melee (opting instead, and probably wisely, to simply praise young people for their success), the outcomes in 2021 did not generate the multiple and daily pages of news copy or the level of television coverage seen twelve months earlier, although an off-the-cuff remark from Mr Williamson during results week guaranteed a morning of phone-in derision; incredulously, he had claimed that he had forgotten both his A-level grades, *and* the subjects he had studied.

Memory challenges were to arise, again, a matter of weeks later when, on 8 September, just as the new term was starting up, Mr Williamson, in an interview with the London *Evening Standard*, claimed to have met the school meals campaigner and Manchester United and England soccer star Marcus Rashford; he hadn't. He *had* met with another campaigning black sporting star, England rugby player Maro Itoje, who had focused on getting laptops into the hands of poorer children. Two black England stars but there the similarity ended: different heights, different accents, different sports, different campaigns. Mr Williamson had been almost invisible for the preceding academic year, with departmental colleagues and the Prime Minister making announcements that one would have expected to come from the Secretary of State; journalists, pundits and Members of Parliament of all parties were beginning to suggest why this had been the case. Like an untrusted child, he couldn't be let out alone.

Nonetheless, grades did rise, the charge of grade inflation duly emerged, and the finger was again pointed at teachers who, it was claimed, were incapable of marking their own students' work, a charge that the profession and its representatives took as a slur on their professional and personal integrity. It is worth unpicking these charges and the process through which the higher grades were generated.

The shift from Centre Assessed Grades (CAGs)

In 2020, the late cancellation of written papers and the broader novelty of the pandemic – for the profession, pupils and parents, the Education Ministry and politicians – forced the deployment of emergency arrangements at school level, namely the introduction of a system based on Centre Assessed Grades (CAGs). This is described in detail in *Lessons from Lockdown* but, in short, as set out there, involved three steps:

- The identification of specific items of work or internal assessment completed during the course, the marking of this work and the weighting of its contribution to the grading process;
- The allocation of students to categories based on levels of likely examination success;

- The ranking of students within these categories, both within their teaching groups and across year groups, subject-by-subject (Breslin 2021a: 63).

For one experienced teacher and examiner, this amounted to:

> The most demanding assessment process I can remember being part of in thirty years of teaching; at the end of it, as individuals and as a department, we had a very tricky balancing act but the load on Heads of Department has been especially onerous; they had to take all of this data from colleagues and generate not just a rank order across every teaching group but across the cohort, the year group, while deciding the weighting given to the assignments and pieces of work contributing to the process, in terms of the level of challenge involved and when they were carried out during the course, for instance during Year 10 or Year 11. In a subject like English; that's massive, especially at GCSE, because it's every pupil in the year.
>
> (Breslin 2021a: 65)

Throughout August 2020, the exam grading 'story' dominated social media, was splashed across newspaper front pages and feature items, and led news broadcasts, but this saturation coverage was shot through with one flaw. It persisted in describing the outcomes from this highly moderated ranking process as 'predicted grades'; as we have already outlined, they were, of course, anything but this:

> The routine use of this particular 'P-word', across print, broadcast and social media, was a disservice to all who had been involved in generating the grades and reinforced the suspicions of both government ministers – already sceptical about teacher assessment – and those members of the public without children in the system about teacher objectivity. The grades generated through teacher assessment were not estimates (or guess-timates) of the type sometimes entered on university application forms to indicate what a young person might get, on the best of days, in the examinations of a summer still months away, estimates sometimes adroitly nudged upwards by middle-class students and their parents. These were assessments based on work already completed during the course of the foregoing twenty-one months, by teachers who had set this work, and moderated by colleagues in their subject departments, where more than one teacher was involved in the assessment process. Critically, the process for generating these 'Centre Assessed Grades' had been set out by the

respective national exam regulators across the UK. Prediction, as such, played no part.

(Breslin 2021: 64)

Nonetheless, a retreat from teacher assessment and any form of centre assessment or 'coursework' that had its roots in the first suite of revisions to GCSEs in the early and mid-1990s and which had gathered pace with the reforms to GCSE and A level developed and introduced during Michael Gove's tenure as Education Secretary, and steered into place by Schools Minister Nick Gibb, had produced a public, an education department and a ministerial team that were sceptical about 'internal' (or teacher) assessment. Thus, ministers and their advisers were firm in the belief that the 2020 arrangements, devised in haste and rushed into place, could be improved upon in 2021. The result was a shift from Centre Assessed Grades (CAGs) to Teacher Assessed Grades (TAGs), but before we explore this, let us remind ourselves of the central case for a return to examination in the main through unseen, written papers delivered contemporaneously in sports and assembly halls across the land.

The case for returning to written papers, post-COVID

A more confident and sure-footed Education Department might have retained the Centre Assessed Grading model of 2020, building on the teacher expertise that it had begun to develop the previous year. This, as we have seen, engaged teachers – or certainly those involved in the upper phases of secondary or 'higher' education – in the process of formal assessment like never before. True, some teachers are examiners and many secondary departments boast one or more examiners in their ranks (almost invariably on examination specifications that their students are not sitting), but it is likely to shock parents and students alike to find that the examining work-force are a largely casualised group, engaged through zero-hours contracts, labouring late into the night on a pay-per-paper basis, while maintaining the day job throughout the marking season. For the most part, awarding organisations have long given up on requiring examiners to have a certain number of years of teaching experience (typically five or more and usually at least three), or on requiring examiners to be qualified teachers.

This well-kept secret has helped the examination system, at least across the UK, maintain an aura of objectivity and an image of scientific precision, in spite of periodic panics about the accuracy and consistency of marking in particular subjects, or about the comparability of marking between different subjects. Perhaps for this reason, the Education Secretary was not alone in making pronouncements about the fairness and accuracy of written examinations at various points during the pandemic:

> Exams provide us all with clarity: crucially, every pupil sits the same paper, and parents have no opportunity to try to convince teachers to be generous. Exams produce grades that are a fair reflection of how a child performs in comparison to his peers across the country, thus levelling the playing field.
>
> (Katie Ashord [Deputy Head, Michaela Community School, Brent], 2021)

> 'Exams are the fairest way to assess what students know and can do.'
>
> (Ofqual [Press release], 2020a)

The postponement of written papers has raised questions in some quarters about the need for examinations, or at least the current academically dominated suite of GCSEs and A levels in England, Wales and Northern Ireland, provoking a campaign for their removal: the Independent Assessment Commission. Professor Louise Hayward, who leads the Commission – which names a diverse range of supporters including the Chartered College of Teaching, the National Education Union, the EDGE Foundation and the Confederation of British Industry among its supporters – argues that:

> The current education and assessment system fails too many pupils, teachers and schools. Nor does it meet the needs of business. The time for change is now.
>
> Professor Louise Hayward, Chair, Independent Assessment Commission (Hayward, 2021)

Against this background, Hayward calls for a new 'ERA' of 'Equitable, Reliable Assessment' and:

> A national conversation around a new approach that radically overhauls the system, that is designed to realise the potential and life chances of all children, is kinder to teachers and students and benefits the whole country.

This has sparked an interesting debate in the profession and beyond, with the following letter to *The Times*, signed by over 300 educators, the majority working teachers, expressing concern about the timing *and* the substance of the proposal:

> Recently, a small number of people and groups have agitated for 'radical' assessment reform. One notable group, the Independent Assessment Commission, has been formed by the largest teaching union, the National Education Union, in the midst of the instability that the pandemic has brought to schools.
>
> These calls are untimely, opportunistic and wrong. As teachers, our experience of the instability of the past 18 months and the insecurity of the next academic year means that we need and crave normality. The rapid and under-resourced adaptation to new ways of working including changing assessments, means that the profession is on its knees.
>
> The last thing we need is an overhaul of exams and the additional workload that brings. Our pupils, their families and our colleagues need to be able to get back to some stability in schools, and this includes getting back to the certainty and fairness of the type of assessment that we had before the pandemic.
>
> All talk of exam and assessment reform is hugely unsettling. We are not against discussion of exam and assessment reform but those advocating such should try to be a little more responsible in the timing of their campaigns.
>
> Martin Busse
>
> Teacher, and colleagues
>
> (Busse, 2021)

The letter is important, not so much for its plea that change (and campaigns promoting change) are stalled as 'stability' is regained, but for one of the stated reasons for this, to repeat:

> As teachers, our experience of the instability of the past 18 months and the insecurity of the next academic year means that we need and crave normality.

This, of course, is one of the central conundrums of the whole COVID period: COVID has both exposed the shortcomings of long-standing practice and exhausted any appetite for change to address these shortcomings. The profession (and we might add parents and children to the list) are among those who 'crave normality', even where that normality (in this case the examination system) demonstrates its *unfairness* through the long-standing and embedded under-achievement of particular groups. The sequel to this book and the final text in this trilogy, *Reschooling Society After Lockdown* (Routledge,forthcoming) wrestles with this conundrum at greater length, but a recent *TES* editorial articulates the issue of professional exhaustion in the school (and doubtless college) workforce:

> In the running world, they talk a lot about 'hitting the wall': the moment in a race or run where there is a sudden onset of extreme fatigue and a loss of motivation. There is no warning. One moment, you are heading for a personal best; the next, you are collapsed in a heap of exhaustion, confusion and desperation ... The reason it happens is fuel: the body has used it all up and cannot find another drop in the system. As a result, the system stops working ... 'hitting the wall' seems a fitting description of what teachers are currently experiencing. They are suffering extreme tiredness, dissatisfaction and desperately need the 'water stop' of half term to be a few steps closer.

The editorial continues:

> It should come as no surprise that [teachers] have hit this point so early in the school year. The profession has been on high alert for 18 months, battling the various demands of the pandemic and running on adrenaline in the hope of that elusive point of 'normality' finally coming into view. They worked their holidays, they worked their evenings, they worked their weekends ... .
>
> (Severs, 2021)

In this context, it needs to be acknowledged that making the case for change is the easy bit, as the inequities of most modern pre-COVID schooling systems share these failings and they are clear in even a cursory analysis of the evidence; convincing exhausted professionals to embrace such change at a time when energies and appetites are so depleted presents the greater challenge, educationally and politically. Of this, the letter is a cogent, timely reminder. And the authors will be relieved that the then Education Secretary Williamson concurred with their analysis:

> We're absolutely going to be keeping GCSEs, I personally think it's really important to have examination and full assessment at the age of 16 (not least because approximately 50% of students) move to a new college or a new school (after Year 11) ... I think it's really important

that we have something that captures their attainment and their progress so far.

(Cited in Hazell, 2021)

Although we have already discounted claims about the 'objectivity' and 'neutrality' of written examinations (which is clearly not supported by the patterning of examination outcomes), continued references to the 'fairness' of such papers contributed to a narrative in which *any* examining arrangements put in place during the summers of 2020 and 2021 were judged as essentially 'necessary evils', suboptimal from the get-go, second-choice interim arrangements necessarily introduced in difficult and exceptional circumstances. This narrative, of course, stoked the fires against the very forms of teacher involvement upon which these arrangements had depended, albeit in different forms, in both 2020 and 2021. And it was this thinking that led to the switch from the so-called Centre Assessed Grades in 2020 to Teacher Assessed Grades in 2021; when in doubt, add apparent objectivity. However, if the desire was to rein-in grade 'inflation', the result was the opposite of this.

The switch to Teacher Assessed Grades (TAGs)

At the heart of the Centre Assessed Grade model used in 2020 was a comparative analysis of students, subject-by-subject across the year group, informed by performance in mock examinations and the analysis of class and homework assignments not originally intended for such use. The Teacher Assessed Grade model that Ofqual proposed for use in 2021 differed from its predecessor in several key ways:

- Assessment would take place during the period when examinations would have usually taken place, so as to reduce disruption to teaching programmes, with grades based on actual work carried out rather than on the place allocated to the student in a comparative, ranking process.
- Examination boards would make available a series of 'assignments' and 'papers' set by examiners that schools *could* choose to utilise during this assessment period, unless it was their preference to replace these with internally designed assignments or papers.
- Alongside these activities explicitly designed for the assessment process, it was suggested that teachers should 'take into account the standard of

a student's non-exam assessment' into coming to a conclusion about the grade to be awarded.

- Any activities or papers sat explicitly for the purpose of assessment could be completed at home or at school – in effect, a necessary insurance policy, given the ongoing threat of lockdown and the reality of bursting bubbles;
- The whole exercise would be 'standardised' through a three-pronged approach, involving:
  1 A package of advice on grading processes and the impact of localised disruptions to learning produced by the awarding organisations,
  2 The establishment of internal standardisation processes at school level, signed off by the school's leader, and
  3 A sampling process, not dissimilar to that which had long characterised the marking of coursework at GCSE, whereby awarding organisations would re-assess a sample of the school-assessed work, or that which examining teams use to 'standardise' their marking, whereby individual examiners send a sample of marked papers to the Chief Examiner or other identified senior examiners, early in the marking cycle, who re-mark these papers, a process much simplified by the advent of online assessment

> (adapted from 'The 2021 summer exams plan: everything
> you need to know': *Schools Week*, 2021)

As Gavin Williamson set out in a letter to Simon Lebus, the Chief Regulator at Ofqual, the objective of this shift was to:

> … give students confidence, maximise remaining teaching time and be flexible to accommodate changes to public health advice.

The switch to Teacher Assessed Grades, for which the Education Secretary claimed the support of a consultation that had brought 'over one hundred thousand replies from students, parents and carers, and teachers', also embodied a recognition of the different experiences of COVID-driven disruption that different learners, teachers and schools had encountered. Gavin Williamsn, in a letter to Simon Lebus, Ofqual's Chief Regulator, wrote:

> In this exceptional year, I recognise that schools and colleges will do all they can to cover the required subject content. It may not, however, be possible for students' evidence to be based on the assumption that all of the content was taught. Therefore, exceptionally, it is government policy that teachers' judgements this year should only be made on the

content areas that have been taught. Teachers should assess as much course content as possible to ensure in the teachers' judgement that there has been sufficient coverage of the curriculum to enable progression to further education, training, or employment, where relevant.

(Williamson, 2021a)

But Williamson was keen to underpin what amounted to a fairly 'open' approach to teacher assessment with a quality assurance process that operated not only at local level but which involved the awarding organisations, and ultimately granted them the ability to 'adjust or withhold' grades:

As well as the checks and balances that centres will employ themselves, it is right in the government's view, and that of over two thirds of consultation respondents, that the exam boards provide an additional layer of scrutiny to ensure centres adhere to the exam boards' requirements. These quality assurance arrangements should focus on making sure the process and evidence used by centres to award grades are reasonable. The exam boards should be required to undertake checks of all centres' internal quality assurance processes before grades are submitted to them.

It is the government's view that the exam boards' quality assurance should also include checks of samples of the evidence to support students' proposed grades. These checks of evidence will help ensure centres have undertaken an appropriate and robust process for determining grades and reviewing their judgements to promote fairness in the awarding of grades. Where robust investigation indicates that a centre's grades might not be justified, the exam board should ask the centre to investigate. If the exam board is not satisfied with the outcome of this investigation or malpractice is found, exam boards should reserve the right to adjust or withhold grades.

Deliberately or not, Williamson had, effectively, reverted to an approach to assessment that had characterised the then new GCSE examination introduced in 1988. Prior to this, young people had sat either the higher-status 'Ordinary' (or 'O') level examination or the lower-status Certificate of Secondary Education (or CSE), the dual track being a hangover of the bipartite system of Grammar and Secondary schooling that characterised post-war education in England, Wales and Northern Ireland. The GCSE, perhaps surprisingly developed and introduced under the Conservative governments of the 1980s, offered three distinctive characteristics:

- A single examination for all students and a broader range of grades,
- A significant internal assessment (or 'coursework') element, usually assessed by teachers, and
- Grading that was criteria, rather than norm, referenced.

The move from norm to criteria referencing may well have gone largely unnoticed to the untrained eye, but the switch from Centre Assessed Grades generated through a process of student ranking to Teacher Assessed Grades based on performance in specified activities – whether provided by the awarding organisation, developed specifically for the purpose of assessment developed by the teacher, or the retrospective assessment by the teacher of work completed across the duration of the course – amounted to a shift to a criterion-based model. In a norm-based system, standards are maintained through regulating the numbers achieving particular grades through reference to the distribution of grades in previous years. In a purely criterion-based system, grades are awarded for the achievement of identified goals, with no restriction on the numbers 'allowed' to pass or to achieve a certain grade. When first introduced, GCSE was a criterion-referenced examination but in a range of reforms in the three decades since its launch, examiners – largely driven by a concern about grade inflation – had reverted to a norm-based approach, and coursework (teacher assessment) had been removed from the assessment mix for the majority of subjects.

And behind this concern lay what some consider to be a very 'British' worry – that greater educational success is an indicator of declining standards; it may, of course, arise from other factors: improved teaching, a stronger teacher grasp of the examination specification (something that should be expected where the examination specification remains unchanged over a number of years), the mitigation of external factors with a known impact on educational performance (such as child poverty, domestic discord or childhood trauma), or an especially able student cohort. In this context, mild grade inflation over time ought to be welcomed and celebrated as an indicator of increased educational success, not derided as an indication of falling standards. To frame such improvements in negative terms is to presume that educational success ought to be preserved for an elite, that sharing such success more widely is to somehow diminish it; the reactions to the grading spikes of both 2020 and 2021 carried exactly these presumptions.

Imagine applying the same thinking to the driving test and dictating that only a fixed (or perhaps declining) number could pass each year. Such a move might prove to be an environmental saviour and reduce the number of cars on the roads, but it would not score highly on any 'fairness' barometer. And one senses that many of those who continue to argue in favour of a norm-referenced examination system – effectively a quota system that favours the socially advantaged – are also those who tend to argue fervently against affirmative action in other parts of the educational landscape, for instance, those programmes that seek to widen access to, and participation in, higher education for those from disadvantaged backgrounds – for example, through admitting young people to courses with lower grades to compensate for, and in acknowledgement of, their formally quantified social disadvantage.

Examination outcomes in 2021

As we outline in some detail in *Lessons from Lockdown*, the 2020 examination marking season was traumatic for all concerned. For Gavin Williamson, history is likely to conclude that much of the trauma was self-inflicted, in particular by the ill-conceived and subsequently abandoned algorithm discussed earlier. The algorithm may have been an attempt to 'correct' Centre Assessed Grades, so as to avoid the charges of both grade inflation and teacher subjectivity. In effect, and ironically, the cold, objective hand of science that the algorithm had attempted to bring to the table felt like an attempt to 'fix' outcomes, and once it became clear that young people from disadvantaged and minority backgrounds would suffer most from its application, it was, in the vernacular, 'dead in the water'.

Those with any role in examining – from ministers through to candidates – were desperate to avoid a repeat in 2021. Thus, the publication of results was brought forward to early August and truncated into a single week, such that GCSE and A-level results were published within 48 hours of each other so as to facilitate the space for both appeals and retakes, and the Education Secretary adopted a very different stance. This time round, Gavin Williamson adopted a much lower profile and, in spite of a second successive grading spike, resolved to abandon the usual 'falling standards' narrative and praise students for their success, arguing that they 'deserve to be rewarded' and that debates about grade inflation should not 'undermine or question the value' of students' results (Turner, 2021).

This lower profile appeared to be playing out well until, as noted earlier, the hapless and soon-to-be-replaced Minister claimed on A-level results day that he couldn't remember the grades he had achieved and he wasn't clear on the subjects that he had studied. He had hijacked his own good news story and the commentators made hay as the late summer sun shone. An appeal to listeners on the *Jeremy Vine Show*, a popular lunchtime programme in the UK on BBC Radio 2, could not identify a single listener who had forgotten their A-level grades, or their subjects.

The results achieved by students across the UK were, again, up on the previous year, and significantly ahead of those achieved in 2019, the year before the pandemic. Media reports had concentrated on the apparently growing ease with which students could gain a higher-grade pass.

The percentage of students achieving a GCSE grade 7 or above in English Language, English Literature and Mathematics in England in 2019, 2020 and 2021 is set out in Figure 6.1, while the percentage of those attaining an A or B grade at GCSE and A level in selected 'facilitating' subjects – those given a particular status by the UK's so-called 'Russell Group' of universities – over the same period is presented in Figure 6.2.

As we have seen, the Education Secretary had chosen not to dwell on the alleged 'grade inflation', or on 'teacher subjectivity'. School leaders were similarly reluctant to have their students' achievements diminished. Ian Cooksey, Head at Watford Grammar School for Boys (a partially selective state grammar school in Hertfordshire), whose letter to parents at the start of the 2020–21 we cited at length in *Lessons from Lockdown* (Breslin, 2021a: 133–135), reflected on the A-level results thus:

> The results at A level this year are considerably better than in previous years. This is true at Watford Grammar School for Boys and across the country, which has led to press reports of 'grade inflation.' In truth, this was anticipated by us and the educational establishment at large because the nationally devised system to replace the formal exam system was always going to favour motivated students.

Subject	2019	2020	2021
English	17.4%	23.5%	22.3%%
English Literature	20.7%	24.7%	26.0%
Mathematics	20.4%	24.3%	21.0%
All subjects	21.8%	27.5%	28.9%

Figure 6.1 Students (aged 16) achieving grade 7 or above in selected subjects at GCSE (Summer Examinations: 2019, 2020 and 2021).

Source: Results tables for GCSE, AS- and A-level results in England, 2020 (Ofqual, 2020b).

Subject	2019	2020	2021
English Literature	38.5%	50.5%	72.1%
Geography	37.8%	48.6%	66.1%
History	35%	46.3%	72.1%
Biology	29.6%	42.8%	69.0%
Chemistry	34.2%	47.4%	67.7%
Physics	34.9%	49.3%	72.1%
Mathematics	42.4%	51.3%	73.3%
Further Mathematics	65.7%	80.5%	88.1%
French	52.0%	66.9%	79.4%
German	50.6%	68.6%	82.4%
Spanish	49.6%	68.0%	80.9%

Figure 6.2 Students achieving grade B or above in 'facilitating' subjects at GCSE and A level (Summer Examinations: 2019, 2020 and 2021).

Source: Results tables for GCSE, AS- and A-level results in England, 2020 (Ofqual, 2020a; JCQ, 2021).

At Watford Grammar School for Boys, the assessment process was largely driven by a desire to generate 'high levels of control' for credible outcomes for each student. This involved a sequence of assessments conducted at the same time for each student in each subject. Additionally, the school used a range of questions including material which has never been in the public domain. However, adaptations were made, in line with the [Joint Council for Qualifications] guidance, to limit the volume of course content assessed as appropriate. Additionally, students were made aware of the topics that would be assessed on each occasion. This approach has largely favoured motivated and high attaining students who have been able to target their revision activity accordingly. Following a quality assurance process from the exam boards, I am pleased to report that none of our submitted grades were altered, so the judgements of our teachers were deemed to be accurate and fair.

So, rather than diminishing the achievements of these young men with discussion of 'grade inflation,' we should accept that these results are not directly comparable with previous years because the system of assessment was demonstrably different, and we should congratulate them on navigating this challenging period in their lives. They have shown remarkable tenacity, resilience and initiative. They deserve success in their lives ahead and we wish them well on their journeys onto university and beyond.

(Ian Cooksey, Headmaster, Watford Grammar School for Boys, Letter to parents, 10 August 2021, in Breslin, 2021a)

Cooksey found himself penning a very similar letter to parents a couple of days later, focused on GCSE outcomes. His analysis reveals the rigour with which school leaders and teachers brought to the examination process, but also exposes the folly of comparing the COVID cohorts with those who had faced examination in the preceding years without acknowledging the different assessment experiences of the students concerned. Young people leaving school during the first half of the 2020s have had a different educational and assessment experience but it is intellectually lazy to *assume* that they have had, in all respects, a lesser one. Rather, they have had a very different one.

Unfortunately, this may be lost on some of the young people themselves. Just ahead of the start of the Freshers' Week, the annual gathering of students, designed to help first-year undergraduates settle into university life, *The Observer* reported on a study by researchers at the University of Leeds, written up in the journal *Psychology Learning and Teaching*, which suggested that:

> Undergraduates arriving on campus this week may 'feel like a fraud' as they have not had the chance to 'earn' their grades in (traditional) public examinations.
>
> (Henry, 2021)

Quoting the study's researchers directly, the report continued:

> When students do not feel that their place at university is legitimately earned they may experience 'imposter syndrome' … however, academically-related imposter syndrome may be negated by pretertiary grades that serve as a testament to students' ability to perform academically.

The article concludes by citing the views of Jamie Halls, a first-year undergraduate about to embark on a Biology degree at the University of Essex, as he reflects on studying for A levels during the pandemic:

> I felt more confident about the A-level content that was taught before
> lockdown than during it. There was a lot of uncertainty about whether
> exams were going to happen or not, and that was unsettling. When it
> comes to comparing grades, it's hard to know if you are on the same
> page and have the same knowledge as other people.

Had part of the rationale for switching from Centre Assessed Grades to
Teacher Assessed Grades been to dampen down grade growth, it failed.
But, as with the use of Centre Assessed Grades the previous year, the introduction of a much more fluid and localised Teacher Assessed Grade model
in 2021 involved teachers in a rigorous and challenging assessment process,
albeit one that could not be standardised in the way that might have offered
reassurance to students like Jamie Halls. It would be an incredible waste to
discard, or fail to fully utilise, the professional development that teachers
had experienced through these forced innovations in assessment and examining process in the years ahead, especially if the motivation is just to get
back to (exam hall) normal.

Beyond COVID or beyond examinations?

Readers may recall that, throughout the research for both this text and
Lessons from Lockdown, focus groups and interviews have concluded with
an invitation to participants and interviewees to 'go back to February 2020,
just as the juggernaut of of the pandemic swung into view' and reflect on a
slightly clunky double question:

> What you can't wait to get back to, and what you can't wait to leave
> behind?
>
> (Breslin, 2021a, and this volume)

We have seen earlier how the advocates of traditional written examinations
have mourned their absence in 2020 and 2021, and we have explored the
annually recurrent theme of grade inflation, and its claimed accentuation
during the pandemic. Getting back to examinations, as they were, was a clear
aspiration for a significant number and range of stakeholders, including the
then newly named Secretary of State for Education in England, Nadhim
Zahawi, appointed in Boris Johnson's reshuffle in September 2021 (and subsequently moved to the post of Chancellor in July 2022). Announcing the
approach to be taken to examinations in Summer 2022, Zahawi echoed the
views of his predecessor, Gavin Williamson:

We are committed to rigorous standards being fairly applied, and exams are the fairest way to assess students, which is why they will take place next year.

(Cited in Weale, 2021)

We have also seen how the twin narratives of 'grade inflation' and 'teacher subjectivity' have led the charge-sheet waved by many of those seeking a 'return to normal' in terms of the place of conventional unseen written papers in the conduct of public examinations. The retort, offered in these pages, to their charge-sheet has been threefold:

1. The results in 2020 and 2021 are not evidence of 'grade inflation' but of a 'grading spike' driven by the very particular circumstances of the pandemic.
2. A modest amount of grade inflation over time ought to be a characteristic of an improving and effective education system and the growing familiarity of both teachers and students with specifications over time, as text books are published and a stock of 'past' papers builds up – as such, the inflation is not a cause for concern in itself.
3. Charges of teacher subjectivity are an affront to the professional integrity of teachers and to the rigour of the specific and quite different processes employed in 2020 and 2021.

In this context, the improved results generated at GCSE and A level, and in Scottish Highers, and across a range of professional, technical and vocational examinations during the pandemic years, may have a different explanation. True, this cohort of learners has not been 'tested' in the examination hall and this has been a concern to learners and to their teachers, to their parents and to system leaders, not least around what might be termed the 'currency' of grades and offers, as parent, teacher educator and Multi-Academy Trust Director, Lizana Oberholzer, makes clear:

With a sixth former in the house, the lack of clarity, how assessments would happen, what would be taken into account and how this would pan out for them in terms of university placements and offers. My daughter got some really good offers but can she accept those offers or not?

(Lizana Oberholzer, Senior Lecturer, Teacher Education, University of Wolverhampton, focus group – influencers and system leaders, 19 May 2021)

But this is to dwell on what young people may have missed out on because of the pandemic, rather than to reflect on what at least some of them might have gained during this period: enhanced skills of independent learning, exposure to a richer range of assessment activities and to new 'out-of-school' learning experiences, and, of course, new levels of resilience, such that the dismissive and never-fair description of this cohort of young people as a 'snowflake' generation can finally, and evidentially, be cast aside. Moreover, such a description, especially when applied to *all* young people, fails to acknowledge how hard some young people worked during this period. Oberholzer continues:

> As a parent I have a sixth former and she's doing her A levels and what we found there was the amount of work students got, to some extent it was very much a case of them getting so much work that the balance was out. She literally ended up doing homework and exam papers one after the other without having a balance, so I had to say to her 'look, sometimes it's ok not to be on screen all the time!'

This gives rise to a different take on the assessment outcomes generated during the pandemic and in its immediate aftermath, for while this cohort of learners have missed out on the exam-hall experience (and this has, clearly, become an established right of passage, especially for younger learners), they have been assessed in a multitude of other ways, a point finding perhaps surprising support from the government's leading adviser on examination standards, Simon Lebus of Ofqual:

> I think a good way to think of it is exams are a bit like a snapshot, a photograph – you capture an instant, it's a form of sampling – whereas teacher assessment allows teachers to observe student performance over a much longer period, in a rather more complex way, taking into account lots of different pieces of work and arriving at a holistic judgement.
>
> (Cited in Turner, 2021)

Lebus continues, perhaps unwittingly emphasising the limitations of conventional written examinations in a way that somebody leading an organisation charged with the responsibility of 'maintaining the integrity of the examination system' (Ofqual, 2021) might not be expected to:

> I think, from that point of view, we can feel satisfied that it's likely to give a much more accurate and substantial reflection of what their students are capable of achieving.

This, not grade inflation or the inability (or unwillingness) of teachers to be objective, might, of course, offer an explanation for the better grades achieved by students during the years of the pandemic, as does the motivational point raised by Ian Cooksey earlier: that any system drawing on performance across a (typically) two-year course of study will favour (and may *additionally* reward) the diligent and hard working. In short, higher grades might have been achieved because those being examined have worked hard and been assessed in a wider range of ways, thus providing – and through the much-derided vehicle of teacher assessment – to repeat the regulator's words, 'a *much* more *accurate* and *substantial* reflection of what their students are capable of achieving' (emphasis added).

According to this analysis, the higher grades are deserved and the product of a more sophisticated and broader assessment exercise; it is not the students of the pandemic, the so-called 'COVID generation', who have been cheated of their time in the exam hall. Rather, generations of students have had their achievements understated by a narrow, one-paced system, wholly dependent on a single assessment method: an exam in a hall on a set day after two years of study.

Assessment beyond lockdown

Against this background, the challenge beyond the 2020, 2021 and 2022 examination seasons (recall that written papers returned in 2022, but with reduced content) is to consider the exact place that written examination papers should have in the assessment of student (and school) performance.

If the longer-term presumption is that exams will return in much the same form as before the pandemic and that teacher assessment will depart the stage, the likely outcome is a significant downward adjustment in the grades that the young people will achieve over the next few years, and it seems, as this text edges towards publication, that this is the track that the English examination regulator is already embarked on, with 2022 outcomes at GCSE and A-level down on 2020 and 2021 but, for now, above those for 2019. In late Autumn 2021, the BBC had conveyed Ofqual's intention, reporting that:

> GCSE and A-level grades in England will be returned to pre-Covid levels over the next two years, the government has announced. Next summer's results will be wound back to a 'mid-point' between 2019 and 2021, after two years of unusually high grade inflation.
>
> (Richardson, 2021)

This notion of 'winding back' may conveniently confirm the pre-existing narrative about the allegedly 'soft' grades achieved during the pandemic years but it has two further consequences.

First, 'winding back' lays bare the process of norm referencing for all to see, revealing its central irony in so doing – it maintains 'standards' but it appears to do so at some cost to the contract at the heart of the examining process: that between the candidate and the examiner. This contract – the conditions of which for each paper are set out in a paper-specific marking scheme that examiners apply to ensure marker-consistency – lays down, as precisely as is practically possible, what marks will be awarded for. Marking schemes (and examination *marks*) are entirely criterion referenced; however examination *grades* are allocated on a normative basis in line with previous years, once marking totals have been confirmed. Marks arise from the contract with the examiner, but grades do not necessarily follow, and grades, not marks, are the individual student's take-away from the examination exercise. In short, grades trump marks, and are ultimately defined not by how well a particular cohort of students have done, but by the grading profile generated over previous years. For the influential teacher educator, Rachel Lofthouse, responding to the Ofqual decision on 'winding back', this serves as 'proof' that:

> It's not how hard you work if grades can be rationed before assessment even starts.
>
> (Professor Rachel Lofthouse, Professor of Teacher Education,
> Carnegie School of Education, Leeds Beckett University,
> via Twitter @DrRLofthouse, 30 September 2021)

Second, 'winding back' is likely to spark parental concern and may come at some political cost. If awarding organisations and the regulator, encouraged by the Department for Education, decide this cost is too high to bear, the grading spikes of this period will become baked into the system and translate into grade inflation over time, and doubtless, during the annual grading season, the same sterile debates will play out, year-on-year, on-year, on-year.

A more courageous government, and a more enterprising and progressive Education Secretary, could take another track; they could welcome back written papers to provide an element of the kind of system-wide and inter-school standardisation that has been difficult given the multitude of assessment tools used during the COVID period.

These would, though, sit *alongside* teacher assessment, drawing on a multitude of assessment activities and strategies that together provide the opportunity to make the kind of nuanced and holistic judgements available to teachers that Lebus identifies, and that the (Conservative but progressive) architects of GCSE envisaged the better part of four decades ago; this is exactly the sort of 'data' that conventional written examinations cannot hope to capture, especially where they are the sole means of assessment, or where they dominate the wider assessment (and, therefore, teaching and curricular) landscape with such omnipotence.

Summary

The shift from Centre Assessed Grades in 2020 to Teacher Assessed Grades in 2022 failed to rein in what we have described here as a 'grading spike' produced by very specific, COVID-driven circumstances, but which others persist in describing, inaccurately, as 'grade inflation' – something that they see as emerging from the inability of teachers to objectively assess their own students. Such an analysis devalues the achievements of students who have been subject to a multiplicity of assessment activities in extreme circumstances and insults the integrity of educational professionals.

Against this background, rather, than bemoaning the high grades achieved by students in 2020 and 2021, maybe we should ask: how many able, hard-working students have been denied the opportunity to fulfil their potential through the award of a place in Higher Education and the access to enhanced social networks and career destinations that this opens the way to, through an examination system based on a narrow and singular mode of assessment in the years before the pandemic? And how many of these young people are drawn from disadvantaged backgrounds and minority communities?

Asking questions such as this might pave the way to a rethinking of how we organise assessment in our schooling system, especially in secondary and Further Education. Such a rethink must not produce another rushed and botched attempt at qualifications reform, something that is likely to succeed only in further exhausting an already exhausted profession. Rather, it ought to produce a profession-driven model of assessment that retains a place for traditional written papers but rejects their utter domination of the assessment landscape, as was the case pre-lockdown. Re-establishing an expert agency, focused on the curriculum and its assessment, as proposed in *Lessons from Lockdown*, can be a major resource in this rethink, but its role is to support and enable the process, rather than to lead it.

Recommendations

6.1 Policymakers, policy influencers and senior education professionals ought to take responsibility for consciously leading a shift in mindset, such that increased educational success, however defined, is seen as something to be celebrated, without reservation, rather than rationed or claimed as evidence of falling standards; such a shift requires a re-commitment to an assessment and examination framework that is criterion rather than norm referenced.

6.2 The work undertaken by teachers in the development and application of assessment systems based on Centre Assessed Grades (CAGs) and Teacher Assessed Grades (TAGs) has made a significant contribution to their professional development; school and system leaders need to give serious consideration as to how to best utilise this as schools navigate the long road from lockdown.

6.3 The pandemic has opened a window on a much greater diversity of assessment practice; system leaders need to retain and build on this diversity and multiplicity of assessment methods, and to take the opportunity that it presents to begin to explore the potential of a much broader range of qualifications, especially in the professional and vocational domain.

6.4 As with other areas of educational reform, the approach taken in any reconsideration of educational assessment should be gradual, focused on clear objectives and driven by a profession, supported by expert agencies, including one focused on the curriculum and its assessment, themselves staffed by expert practitioners.

6.5 Systems and qualifications designed to measure student achievement have become mechanisms, through the aggregation of individual performance, for the assessment of teacher and school performance, and are likely to remain so post-pandemic, but they should never again be allowed to become seen, at least by some, as the sole measure of such performance.

Beyond lockdown 7

Building curricula for catch-up, recovery and much more

As already argued throughout these pages, lockdown, in spite of various universalities, was experienced differently by every child and every family. To suggest otherwise is to deny both the richness and the complexity of this experience. In *Lessons from Lockdown*, it was contended that most individuals passed through phases as 'lockdown strugglers', 'lockdown survivors' and 'lockdown thrivers', with some spending longer than others in any particular location. Thus, not only was there a diversity of experience at any one point in time but this experience varied *over* time, creating a myriad of fluid interactions between individuals and the multiple impacts of the virus. And nowhere was this diversity and fluidity of experience greater than in the sphere of educational provision. Wali, a student at a London comprehensive reveals this in a written submission that draws on his experiences across lockdown, submitted after a Student Council briefing session arranged as part of the research process for this book; it is reproduced in full:

> During lockdown, it was hard as we didn't get to see our friends and teachers. We were able to get distracted more often when having work set. The teachers called our parents at times to tell them about our progress and how we were doing. Lots of learning time was lost in the first lockdown. It was exciting at first as it was something new. Many were happy [at] first, thinking it would be fun but, as time went on, we realised the importance of school and missed talking to our friends in person. For me it was like a foreshadow of what could happen in the future with education. During lockdown two, the school introduced

DOI: 10.4324/9781003204824-7

Google Meets and these were more efficient [to] use as it felt like we were back in school. I was learning more than I was in the first lockdown. I was able to ask questions and even answer questions (which I normally don't do in class). However, I did miss speaking to friends and teachers in person. People were also able to get distracted. The teachers were constant[ly] in work (at the school) and helped us all through both lockdowns. When we came back to school there were 'Bubbles', I liked the Year Group Bubbles as we got our own breaks [and] lunch [times].

(Faizan-Wali Ahmed, Year 10, Student Council Leader, Newman Catholic College, Brent, written submission (by email), 13 October 2021 [name reproduced with permission])

And this was difficult for students *and* their families. Consider this note from an anxious and very active grandparent, and friend of the author, who has spent a lifetime in education, including headship in diverse and disadvantaged settings, and who remains an influential figure in the school improvement community; as with Wali's statement, it is reproduced virtually in full and is equally evocative:

I have a Year 11 grandson doing GCSE this year. He had a nightmare last year during lockdown, overcome with huge anxiety, never leaving the house and doing little or no school work. He attended school intermittently in the summer term once lockdown was over. Come September that was it. Complete school refusal. Huge anxiety. School has been so good however, allowing us authorised absence and curriculum materials. I have set up a home teaching programme between me, my daughter and his dad, dividing up the subjects between us and following, really, a catch up curriculum never mind learning new stuff. He is gradually calming down and has been able to go out of the house and walk the dog for a short time two or three times a week.

What is staggering to us is that we could never have predicted this fallout. We are shocked that we had no idea this is how he would react and suffer. He is a very bright student, quiet, reserved but not this! How could we have known? Can we get him back on the road to happiness and serenity [while] continuing the learning?

(Grandparent, email to the author [reproduced on request of the author and on the basis of confidentiality, with non-substantive details changed to ensure anonymity], 22 October 2021)

And the grandparent continues, in a subsequent email, bringing home not just how they have taken on their grandson's anxiety, but how they have their own concerns:

> I'm wrestling with genetics this [afternoon] for our biology lesson on Monday. I'm wondering if he'll face up to mocks in January. I haven't raised the matter. It's like egg shells with every interaction.
>
> (Grandparent, part of an email exchange with the author following the initial message reproduced above, 30 October 2021)

The grandparent's testimony is interesting partly because this child is not from a socio-economically disadvantaged background, has access to technology and family members professionally involved in education, and, prior to lockdown, had not presented any challenges to those responsible for his schooling. Indeed, he is described as 'a bright student, quiet, reserved'. As such, his case highlights that, while lockdown has undoubtedly, *in aggregate*, impacted on the most disadvantaged hardest, there are no catch-all universalities. Moreover, as young people return to their classrooms, schools will find that they are welcoming back pupils and staff members who variously display new vulnerabilities, new concerns, new strengths and new insights on, and attitudes to, schooling itself. Critically, some of those displaying changed behaviours and outlooks to learning will not fit the classic profiles of 'disadvantaged' or 'disaffected'; some of these young people will never before have appeared on any index of concern. Hence, the need, as has been argued throughout, for the primacy of nuance, and the pedagogies of personalisation, in every step along the long road from lockdown.

The need for curricular 'catch-up' and 'recovery'

While anxieties about 'falling behind' and 'catching-up' feature in the testimonies offered by both Wali and by the young man's concerned grandparent, the language of 'catch-up' and 'recovery' misses the complexity and diversity of experience expressed so evocatively by each of our email respondents.

Nonetheless, this language has dominated the political narrative and has featured strongly in the minds of educational researchers since the onset of the virus. It first entered the lockdown lexicon during the course of the first schools' lockdown in Spring 2020 and extended into the Summer months as the faltering return to school progressed. Specifically, it was about – and has remained largely focused on – *curriculum* catch-up, itself based on the presumption that absence from conventional classrooms is highly likely to translate into 'lost' learning. Elliot Major, Eyles and Machin are clear on the importance of the catch-up challenge and the future cost of the learning lost:

> Missing out on education from which they would otherwise have benefited is likely to have profound effects on life outcomes for what we have called the Covid generation. There are genuine concerns that the pandemic will exacerbate existing inequalities and reduce future levels of social mobility – the capacity of young people to transcend their background.
>
> (Elliot Major, Eyles and Machin, 2021)

And to underline the point, Elliot Major, Eyles and Machin remind us of the number of days lost between 23 March 2020 and 23 March 2021 in each of the four nations in the UK, pointing out that this amounts to more than 50 per cent of the days when pupils might have been in school, whatever the national setting. This data is reproduced in Figure 7.1.

The authors go on to assess the learning loss experienced by those in different socio-economic and national cohorts. Drawing on the data produced by the responses of parents to questions about home-learning during each of the substantive school lockdowns in the *Understanding Society* survey, Elliot Major, Eyles and Machin estimate the amount of study undertaken by students in different socio-economic and national settings. Again, the differences are stark and, unsurprisingly, of concern to a team of researchers substantially interested in social mobility. The data is reproduced in Figures 7.2 and 7.3.

That learning loss has taken place is indisputable, that the loss is greater in some nations than in others is clear, irrespective of socio-economic status, and that those growing up in the most disadvantaged groups have suffered

Days Lost	England	Northern Ireland	Scotland	Wales	UK Average
Number	110/190	119/190	119/190	124/190	118/190
Percentage	57.9%	62.6%	62.6%	65.3%	62.1%

Figure 7.1 Days lost during the first twelve months of COVID-related schooling disruption across the UK.

Days Lost	England	Northern Ireland	Scotland	Wales
Total Days Lost	61	61	64	66
Summer Term 2020	49	36	39	40
Autumn Term 2020	8	5	7	8
Spring Term 2021	13	21	18	18

Figure 7.2 Average learning loss across the UK.

	April 2000		November 2020		January 2021	
	England	Rest of UK	England	Rest of UK	England	Rest of UK
Bottom 20%	60.9	71.4	13.4	8.3	34.9	47.4
Middle 60%	56.4	62.7	11.6	9.1	27	38.3
Top 20%	47.5	59.7	5.9	6.7	24.4	38.6
Sample size	2,952	651	1,973	402	1,910	386

Figure 7.3 Inequality of learning loss across the UK.

greater learning loss than those in more advantaged groups in any setting is clear. Thus, there is merit in the conclusion that Elliot Major, Eyles and Machin reach:

> Home learning experiences differed enormously depending on the availability of a quiet place to study, internet connectivity and resources provided by schools.

In contrast:

> Children and young people from more affluent backgrounds – whether measured by parental income or type of schooling – received more instruction time during the first lockdown.

Such that:

> There were significant divides in learning loss across the year of the pandemic. Pupils from the bottom fifth of incomes experienced higher

learning loss than those from the top fifth. In England, for example, during the 2021 school closures, the poorest pupils missed out on a third of their learning (34.9%) while the richest pupils missed out on a quarter of their learning (24.4%).

Against the background of this kind of evidence, it is understandable that, by Spring 2021, the political hyperbole on catch-up was in full flow. In a speech to the Foundation for Education Development's National Education Summit, Gavin Williamson said:

> In order to head off a human and economic catastrophe we must double down on our efforts to enable children to catch-up.
>
> (Williamson, 2021d)

He continued:

> Catching up is the educational challenge of the decade … This is not going to be a quick fix. Even with the best of intentions you cannot make up [for] all this lost ground overnight, especially for those disadvantaged children who were already struggling to keep up. Which is why we are committed to providing a huge programme of catch up measures.
>
> This will include a new one-off £302 million Recovery Premium for state primary and secondary schools, building on the Pupil Premium, to further support pupils who need it most.
>
> We are expanding our successful tutoring programmes and there will also be an extension of the 16–19 Tuition Fund to support more students in English, maths and other vocational and academic subjects as well as funding to support language development in the early years.
>
> Finally we are making £200m available for secondary schools to deliver face-to-face summer schools to target individual pupils' needs.

To some degree, this focus on 'catching-up' and on 'lost learning' might have been anticipated, given the direction of education policy under former Secretary of State Michael Gove and his successors. It is to this that we now turn.

Cultural capital, curriculum 'catch-up' and the 'knowledge gap'

As outlined in *Lessons from Lockdown*, Gove was inspired by what some see as a particularly partial reading of the work of the American educationalist E.D. Hirsch. According to website *EdCentral*, Hirsch has two big ideas:

> We all need cultural literacy – certain facts, ideas and knowledge of literary works that people need to know in order to operate effectively as citizens of the country in which they live.
>
> Children need to learn facts in a highly organised and structured way – therefore creating the imperative to get back to the basics with a robust core curriculum.
>
> (Adapted from Ed Central, 2021)

In basic terms, this might be diagrammatically represented in the manner set out in Figure 7.4.

Hirsch appears to see this as a reductionist take on a lifetime's work (Severs, 2015), but it is essentially the interpretation that Michael Gove, encouraged by his then Special Adviser Dominic Cummings, applied in his reforms to both the National Curriculum and the qualifications infrastructure, and that continue to inform related reforms, for instance, to the inspection framework in England (Ofsted, 2019) and to the reforms to Initial Teacher Education in England (Department for Education, 2021a) under

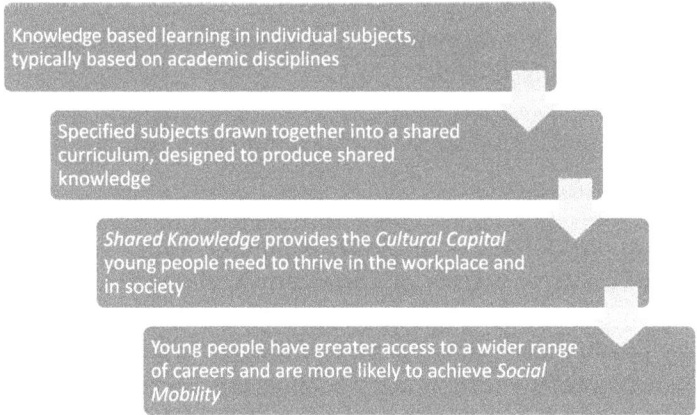

Figure 7.4 Knowledge acquisition and the enhancement of cultural capital.

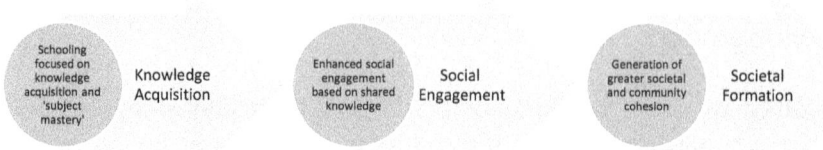

Figure 7.5 Cultural capital, social engagement and societal formation.

discussion as this book went to press. And, for Gove, this was not just an educational project but a societal one, as represented in Figure 7.5.

In this context, it is not difficult to understand the analysis that Gove's successors have brought to the table in terms of curriculum catch-up and lost learning. Very broadly, it might be presented thus:

1. The pandemic has caused children to miss out on the acquisition of knowledge.
2. This means that, in spite of the best efforts of schools to support their learning at home, they are sequentially behind where they ought to be at this point in their schooling, whatever point they are at.
3. The resultant knowledge deficit will produce a long-term deficit in cultural capital, because knowledge provides the building blocks for the development of such capital.
4. Therefore, the educational need is for a systematic, knowledge-focused, programme to address this deficit.
5. This will address the longer-term societal need to ensure that cultural capital is widely and consistently held across the population, such that social mobility is facilitated.

Figure 7.6 presents this analysis in diagrammatic form.

In *Lessons from Lockdown*, Chris Waller, the experienced teacher and respected former Professional Officer at the Association for Citizenship Teaching had bemoaned the apparent paucity of curriculum thinking behind the governmental response to the first lockdown, something that had prompted one of the fifty practice and policy recommendations in that text: that we re-establish a specialist curriculum and qualifications agency, in the mould of the former Qualifications and Curriculum Authority (latterly, until its abolition by the UK's Coalition Government, the Qualifications and Curriculum Development Agency), to bring such expertise into the discussion. There remains a need for such a body, but the focus on knowledge, and specifically

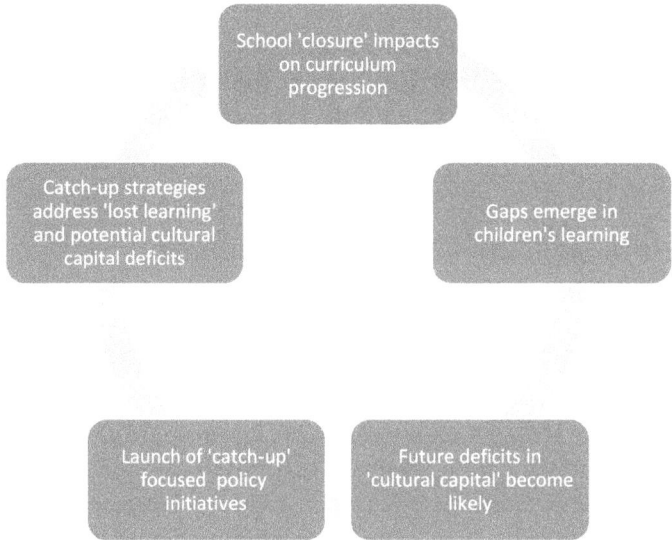

Figure 7.6 Curriculum catch-up and the restoration of cultural capital.

subject knowledge, that now pervades the educational infrastructure has made the UK Government's approach to curriculum catch-up inevitable. This focus is articulated by one senior Multi-Academy Trust figure, reflecting on his conversation with an Ofsted inspector during an Ofsted 'Monitoring Visit' carried out in July 2021, just before the annual summer break:

> I used the word 'skills' and he nearly jumped down my throat, saying words to the effect that 'We don't do skills; we're interested in knowledge, subject knowledge, that's what I want to see the focus of teaching on!', such that you'd think there was no relationship between the two.
>
> (Senior Multi-Academy Trust official, in conversation with the author, June 2021)

This focus on curriculum knowledge, on a body of identifiably 'lost' learning set out in examination specifications and in the National Curriculum, and therefore explicitly quantifiable, was to permeate government thinking throughout the pandemic, and to underpin its critical next step. For ministers and their advisers, addressing a quantifiable need is always more attractive than some 'fuzzier' alternative, even when the outcomes are largely superficial. For this cohort of ministers, though, lost learning was far from a superficial, if measurable, outcome. It represented a depletion in children's future cultural capital, a depletion most keenly felt by those with the least cultural capital in the first place, and a barrier to the promise of greater social mobility, of 'levelling-up', that had been at the core of the appeal to those constituents in disadvantaged 'red wall' seats who had voted Conservative, often for the first time, in December 2019.

Time for the appointment of an Educational 'Catch-up' Tzar?

On 3 February 2021, days after the publication of an Institute for Fiscal Studies report which suggested that the lost lifetime earnings attributable to COVID across the UK's 8.7 million school children could amount to £350bn (Sibieta, 2021), the Education Secretary had announced the appointment of Sir Kevan Collins as Education Recovery Commissioner, a role inevitably reframed by the media as 'Catch-up Tzar', adding that Sir Kevan:

> … brings a wealth of experience in education policy that I know will be invaluable in supporting all the young people who have been impacted by the pandemic.
> …
> He will be a tremendous asset to those young people, their families, and everyone working in education who have my lasting gratitude for their efforts to support young people throughout the pandemic.
> (Department for Education, 2021a)

For its part, in the statement announcing the appointment, the Department for Education used the opportunity to, again, force home a recurrent aspect of its lockdown messaging:

> The reopening of schools is a national priority. The Prime Minister recognises that school closures have had a huge impact on children's learning and has pledged to work with parents, teachers and schools to develop a long-term plan to make sure pupils have the chance to make up their learning over the course of this Parliament.
> (Department for Education, 2021a)

And, in the same press release, Boris Johnson added:

> I am absolutely determined that no child will be left behind as a result of the pandemic … Our top priority is to get schools open again and once

they are, we will make sure that teachers and students are equipped with the resources and the time they need to make up for lost learning … I am delighted that Sir Kevan has been appointed to lead this vital work – his experience and expertise will help ensure every young person is supported to catch-up on their education and gain the skills and knowledge they need to be able to seize opportunities in future.

Of course, the danger, as we have argued elsewhere in these pages, is that continual references to 'catch-up', in emphasising how far children are behind in formal curriculum terms, act as a demotivator and serve as a negative label that is all-pervasive and, ultimately, self-defeating. To define whole cohorts as constituting a 'lost generation' is to provide these young people with the opposite of a SMART (Specific, Measurable, Achievable, Relevant, Time-bound) target and to contribute to their isolation. For this reason, this experienced and successful academy school Principal has rejected the terminology in its entirety:

> We made a definite choice not to use the words 'lost learning' and 'catch up'. We didn't want the kids to come back thinking they were behind. We won't use that language with the children.
>
> (Kathleen McGillycuddy, Principal, Broadoak Academy, Weston-super-Mare, focus group – secondary educators, 13 May 2021)

Collins, it was to turn out, was more sympathetic to this analysis that his new employers had supposed. A teacher by profession and a former Director of Children's Services, he had been the driving force behind one of the Conservative Government's most favoured research organisations, the Educational Endowment Foundation (EEF) and was tasked with devising a plan to enable children and young people to recover the 'lost learning' that had resulted from the pandemic. Specifically, according to the Department for Education's Press Release as reported in *Schools Week*, he would:

> … work with [the] government to deliver measures that will support children who have missed out on face-to-face education due to extended school closures.
>
> (Dickens, 2021)

And the focus would be on:

> … addressing factors such as curriculum content and quantity of teaching time in the coming months, to ensure the impact the

pandemic has had on learning is addressed as quickly and comprehensively as possible.

The EEF had sometimes been criticised by the wider educational research community – both for the organisation's tendency to prefer certain approaches to educational research, and for what they (with some justification) see as an uncritical popularity amongst policymakers, something not granted to a wider educational research and teacher education community that one of Williamson's predecessors, Michael Gove, had infamously dubbed as 'the blob'. However, the EEF had built a significant following, especially amongst school leaders and other practice-shapers; therefore, the appointment of Collins had been broadly, if quietly, welcomed. Indeed, his appointment by an Education Secretary, long-ridiculed for his own apparent lack of educational expertise, drew little comment from either of the associations that represent Headteachers in England: the National Association of Head Teachers, which draws the bulk of its membership from those in primary (or elementary) schools, and the Association of School and College Leaders, which does likewise in secondary (or high) schools and Further Education colleges.

In any case, Collins' time as Catch-up Tzar was to be short-lived. Prime Minister Boris Johnson had personally and publicly pencilled in 21 June as the day on which society would 'reopen', a date coined by newspaper sub-editors as 'Freedom Day', one established when Johnson had set out his much vaunted 'route-map' to normality earlier in the Spring and a date that was to represent the culmination of the government's own long road from lockdown. Ministers had been encouraged by a glorious Whitsun Bank Holiday Weekend, one significant not only for the rarity of its sunshine or the novelty of its crowded – albeit mildly socially spaced – beaches, or the fact that it heralded the start of the Summer Term break, but for the fact that, for first time since the start of the COVID rollercoaster, zero deaths were attributed to the virus in England. Normality, and the (unfulfilled) promise of a decent Summer, lay ahead.

However, with the rise of the Delta variant, caution remained in the air and various print, online and broadcast media outlets reported on a long-standing debate about the wisdom of proceeding with such an aspiration. Most publicly, the discussion about whether or not to postpone Freedom Day raged between some occupants of the Conservative Parliamentary benches and the more vocal of the scientific community, but it also flourished across schools, workplaces, living rooms and phone-in shows the country over.

Later that week, the broadsheet newspapers announced the government's long-trumpeted plans for educational 'catch-up'. It is fair to say that the profession did not race to embrace these. And nor did the individual whom everyone assumed to be their architect, 'Catch-up Tzar' Sir Kevan Collins, who had been appointed barely four months previously; the evening news led with the news that he had resigned, and his resignation letter, published in the *TES* on 2 June, didn't pull any punches. It is worth reproducing in full:

Dear Prime Minister,

I am writing to offer my resignation as Education Recovery Commissioner.

The pandemic has caused a huge disruption to the lives of England's children. Since my appointment, I have spoken to hundreds of parents and over a thousand school leaders. Based on these meetings and my analysis of assessment data, I am in no doubt about the size of the recovery challenge we face. Without a comprehensive and urgent response, we risk failing hundreds of thousands of pupils.

Prior to my appointment, you announced the ambition that lost learning caused by the pandemic be recovered within this Parliament. I applauded this goal and viewed the responsibility of advising the Government on its approach to securing an effective recovery for all children as the most important task of my professional life.

When we met last week, I told you that I do not believe that it will be possible to deliver a successful recovery without significantly greater support than the Government has, to date, indicated it intends to provide. I am concerned that the apparent savings offered by an incremental approach to recovery represent a false economy, as learning losses that are not addressed quickly are likely to compound.

I believe our approach to recovery should also offer children opportunities to re-engage with sport, music and the rich range of activities that define a great education. I proposed extending school time as a way to provide this breadth, as well as to ensure that additional academic support does not cause existing enrichment activities to be squeezed out.

The package of measures announced today provides valuable support, including investment in teaching quality and tutoring. However, as I set out in my reports to you, I do not believe it is credible that a successful recovery can be achieved with a programme of support of this size.

I hope that you are able to allocate the additional resources that are likely to be needed for a successful recovery through the forthcoming Spending Review. I believe the settlement provided will define the international standing of England's education system for years to come.

Yours sincerely
Sir Kevan Collins

(Reproduced in Stewart and Clews, 2021)

Collins had proposed a package of activities reportedly costing £15bn. The Education Policy Institute had called for a slightly more modest investment of £13.5bn and, as noted earlier, the Institute for Fiscal Studies had estimated the value of the lost learning at a total of £30bn. Against this background, the government had proposed a programme valued at what many viewed as a paltry £1.4bn over three years, a figure said to amount to £50 per pupil per year. By way of comparison, this sum might have purchased an hour or two of private tuition, the kind of investment routinely made by better-off parents on a weekly basis to ensure effective preparation for a particular examination course or university entrance examination.

Perhaps for this reason, the comments attributed to Sir Kevan in subsequent interviews were more direct, variously describing the government's plans as:

> ... [falling] far short of what is needed.
>
> ... a half-hearted approach (that) risks failing hundreds of thousands of pupils.
>
> ... not [coming] close to meeting the scale of the challenge.
>
> (Coughlan, 2021)

Going further, Collins argued that:

> Not enough is being done to help vulnerable pupils, children in the early years or 16- to 19-year-olds. Above all, I am concerned that the package announced ... betrays an undervaluation of the importance of education, for individuals and as a driver of a more prosperous and healthy society.
>
> (Sandhu, 2021)

In this regard, Collins was echoing a central message from the research by Elliot Major, Eyles and Machin cited earlier:

> Our research indicates that any recovery programmes rolled out by the respective UK governments will need to be substantial to address

significant learning losses suffered by pupils across the four nations. They will also need to be highly targeted to help disadvantaged children and young people who, on average, missed out on more education than their more privileged peers.

(Elliot Major, Eyles and Machin, 2021)

And Collins' criticism of the proposed government package mirrored that of the professional association leaders representing both Heads and classroom teachers. Paul Whiteman, General Secretary at the National Association of Head Teachers was fulsome in his criticism:

> After weeks of talking big and building expectations for education recovery this announcement only confirms the government's lack of ambition for education. It's a damp squib – some focus in a couple of the right areas is simply not enough.
>
> The funding announced to back these plans is paltry compared to the amounts other countries have invested, or even compared to government spending on business recovery measures during the pandemic.
>
> Education recovery cannot be done on the cheap. The question about how much should be spent on recovery is best answered with 'whatever it costs', such is the importance of investing in the future wellbeing of our young people and the future prosperity of our nation.
>
> The government had the opportunity here to invest in the architecture of education; instead it has chosen to paper over the cracks. As is often the case, young people seem to be low on the government priority list.

(Whiteman, 2021a)

Dr Mary Bousted, Joint General Secretary at the National Education Union, which represents classroom teachers across primary and secondary education in English schools concurred:

> The government's plans for education recovery for the nation's pupils are inadequate and incomplete. Rarely has so much been promised and so little delivered. The 'new' money being offered amounts to £1.4bn – way below the £15bn sum which Kevan Collins, the Education Recovery Tzar, judged is needed to repair the damage done to the nation's pupils because of COVID.

(Bousted, 2021a)

In a further press release, issued the following day and devoted to Collins' resignation, Bousted added:

> Sir Kevan Collins understood the enormity of the task ahead to support children and young people to recover from the disruption of the pandemic. He also saw that there are no quick or cheap fixes if we are to build an education system that supports high standards and strong mental health for everyone. Unfortunately, the government which brought him in to provide solutions has totally disregarded his vision.
>
> (Bousted, 2021b)

Whether the backroom manoeuvres that had sparked his resignation arose from either their rejection by the Education Secretary who had trumpeted his appointment or the failure of Gavin Williamson's attempts to secure Cabinet, and notably Treasury, support for the investment involved is hard to determine, but, in any case, Collins' suggested package deserves scrutiny.

Beyond attainment: The Collins proposals

At the core of the Collins package were five key ideas:

1. A focus on the quality of teaching, and on the learning experienced by pupils;
2. Tutoring strategies that do not require withdrawal from regular lessons;
3. The protection of time for curricular enrichment, especially with regard to competitive sport, art and drama;
4. The distribution of funding directly and non-competitively to schools to enable swift and contextually appropriate activities, and
5. The extension of the school day to enable the programme to be delivered, especially where schools were teaching a 'short' day prior to the pandemic.

The initial proposal that a part of the mechanism for delivering the strategy would come from an extension to the school day by 30 minutes had brought both scepticism and concern, especially from the teaching unions, and support for Collins' proposals were not without qualification, Paul Whiteman conceding as much in his comments on the Catch-up Tzar's resignation:

We are relieved to see that some of the more headline-grabbing measures previously suggested have been shelved for now. Extending the school day in particular had the potential to negatively impact on pupils' mental health, reduce family time and leave less time for extra-curricular activities. Children's happiness and wellbeing should be prioritised as well as their education, or we risk doing more harm than good.

(Whiteman, 2021a)

Others were to point out that the extension to the school day was wholly insufficient compensation for the estimated 115 school days typically lost by children through the pandemic. In fairness to Collins, he had not proposed a blanket extension to the school day, about which, bizarrely, it appears that the Department for Education does not keep data:

I was shocked when I asked a question about time: what is the length of a day in the average school? We don't collect that data and we don't know. We had to start looking at websites and asking people, ringing them up.

(Sir Kevan Collins, Evidence to the Education Select Committee enquiry into Educational Recovery (HC452): Collins, 2021)

Instead, Collins, as best he could, had established that the average length of the school day was six-and-a-half hours, that ten thousand schools offered a shorter day and that a further cohort offered a longer day. Smartly, Collins had suggested extending the ten thousand schools offering a shorter day to the average (typically adding thirty minutes to their day), while effectively using those offering a longer day as a control group to assess the impact of an extended day, an approach that mirrored the focus on controlled experiments modelled by his former employer, the Education Endowment Foundation, albeit in the less controlled setting offered by schools across the country.

Thus, contrary to urban myth, Collins had not proposed a blanket extension of the school day and nor had he determined that any additional time should be devoted narrowly or solely to addressing deficits in *curriculum* content. This was not simply an attempt to compensate for lesson hours lost, but as the creation of a space in which both enrichment – notably focused around the arts and sport – and tutoring could take place without disrupting the re-establishment of the regular school day. As Collins was subsequently to outline, again, in his evidence to the Education Select Committee:

> I think there is an argument for increasing the amount of time children spend in school to do three things. One is to enable lots of other things to happen – to create the space for children to be involved in a broader range of experiences, the things they have missed such as competitive sport, drama and art, just for a limited amount of time. For three or four years, I wanted to increase the time to get those experiences.
>
> (Collins, 2021)

As noted earlier, the government narrative that greeted his appointment had been less about such enrichment and more about 'addressing factors such as curriculum content and quantity of teaching time' (Department for Education, 2021a). In such a framing of 'catch-up', as being substantively about *curriculum* recovery, policymakers overlooked a range of other losses incurred by many children and young people as a result of lockdown, such as those raised by the pupil and the grandparent cited in the opening pages of this chapter. Collins retained a focus on teaching quality but also acknowledged these broader losses, both in the breadth of his proposals and in his subsequent evidence to the Education Select Committee:

> As [with] everything in my work, I would try to work from the bottom up as well as the top down. The key thing is to connect with the families and the children. From my life previously as a director of children's services, I know you need to go and knock on the doors and engage with these families through different structures, whether that is the local authority, the faith groups, the community groups, and re-engage people and motivate them to be involved. That is why for me it is important that education is a broad and rich experience. I am not trying to excuse anybody but we need to find ways to motivate those young people to get back involved and stay involved in school.
>
> That is why I think the whole education experience in the day really matters. We know through the evidence that opportunities like, for example, free breakfast clubs are great motivators; they get more and more children involved and they achieve more. There is something about working from the bottom up with the schools and supporting the schools to reach out to these children, but also going beyond the schools with the other services, whether it is health, social care, the police … .
>
> (Collins, 2021)

This focus on broader concerns – on reaching not just children but their families, whether it be through the focus on building bridges with other services, or in providing access to breakfast clubs and after-school provision, which builds wellbeing and supports childcare needs – is routinely ignored by those who see themselves as responsible for *education* policy and, more specifically, *standards*. This blind spot explains the wrath that Amanda Spielman, Chief Executive at England's school inspectorate, Ofsted, incurred from many (though not all) school leaders for her comments, when she criticised their engagement in activities such as the organisation of school-based foodbanks, discussed both in this text and in *Lessons from Lockdown*. Fundamentally, it reads as the highlighting of social challenges as the proffering of excuses for under-performance, rather than as one part of an explanation for persistent underachievement, underachievement that demands affirmative interventions that engage not just the children concerned, but their wider family and social situation.

The case for family learning

In this context, it is perhaps surprising that the long-established methodologies around Family Learning have not been more widely discussed as part of the response to the pandemic, especially with regard to the pandemic's impact on the poorest communities and given the employment of home-schooling on a scale not previously seen in most modern education systems. Susannah Chambers, a UK-based consultant who has worked extensively in the Family Learning field, makes the case for such an approach in her evidence to a Parliamentary Inquiry held in the aftermath of the first schooling lockdown focused on the Summer 2020 grading crisis:

> The definition of Family Learning is any activity where there are learning outcomes for both the children/young people and parents/carers involved. This might be synchronous intergenerational learning between parents/carers and children/young people. Or it may be asynchronous intergenerational learning where, for example, parents/carers are learning strategies from tutors about techniques their children are taught via school in order to better be able to support learning in the home environment/support with homework. It directly supports and works well with the efforts of education providers.
> (Chambers, 2020)

She goes on to make the case for such an approach in her evidence, drawing on the example of work undertaken by one local authority cited in an inquiry into the impact of such approaches, 'Family Learning Works: The Inquiry into Family Learning', led by the National Institute of Adult Continuing Education (NIACE):

> Looking at pupils deemed to be achieving a good level of overall development at the end of the foundation stage, Sheffield City Council's analysis shows that the difference between those pupils involved in a family learning programme is as much as 15 percentage points higher for some groups compared with those that have not been involved in family learning programmes.
>
> (NIACE, 2013)

Thus, Chambers contends, in her evidence to the Committee, that:

> Family Learning is a high impact yet cost effective approach to improving outcomes for children and young people.

And the NIACE inquiry makes the association with raising attainment, so often ignored by those with a narrower focus on educational standards, the focus of the first of six recommendations:

> Family learning should be integral to school strategies to raise children's attainment and to narrow the gap between the lowest and highest achievers.

It is to these broader concerns and approaches that we now turn; they amount to much more than curriculum 'catch-up' or 'recovery'. The core of Collins' message seems blunt: without addressing these contextual, and not necessarily *overtly* educational, factors, and without recourse to long-marginalised strategies such as those delivered through a Family Learning model, there will be no catch-up, curricular or otherwise.

Recapturing the water-cooler moments of childhood

As we have learned with the decline of traditional 'smoke-stack' (or, in the US, 'rust-belt') industries throughout the 1980s and 1990s and, more recently, the decline of the high street and the shopping mall, large industrial plants and vibrant town centres are important for much more than the primary purpose for which they were originally established. A steelworks or coal mine provides a meeting place and social space for a community, a source of employment and community identity, and a hub for a much broader supply and consumption chain. Likewise, the closure of shops, banks and restaurants, which accelerated during the pandemic, has left former high streets barren, with recently glitzy shopping malls standing as empty temples to a consumerism now satisfied with the click of a mouse and delivery direct from warehouse to front door. With this change, the social by-product of 'going to the shops' and the busy throng of the town centre or high street is lost. So it is with schools.

In *Lessons from Lockdown*, which sought to curate the story of the first lockdown through the voices of pupils, parents and educational professionals in the way that this text seeks to with subsequent lockdowns across 2020–21, the case was made for recognising the broader, and not necessarily *explicitly* educative role of schools, with the question framed thus:

> Might our experience of lockdown serve as a positive reminder of the social value of schools – as hubs of education, yes, but also as places for children to meet and interact, and as childcare facilities that enable parents to work and society to function? And if we're going to acknowledge these multiple purposes of schooling, can, beyond COVID-19, we begin to judge school performance (not unreasonable in such an important publicly funded service), across a wider scorecard, one that engages educators in the process, and one that has greater empathy for these educators?
>
> (Breslin, 2021a: 32)

Taking account of the wider social purpose of schools, both as centres in which children and young people *learn* how to socialise and as hubs through which families connect and network, is vital to understanding the limitations of a 'catch-up' analysis obsessed with content and coverage but which pays less attention to children's wellbeing and personal development; school leaders and their colleagues were acutely aware of this:

> I don't think their GCSEs and A levels in the future will be affected. I do think though we'll have to do a lot of work on the social and emotional side – considering a change in attitude and a change in the way they play. Do we define their behaviour as bullying or just being unkind? It's that aspect which will need work. I'm upset with the Government rhetoric of a 'lost generation' – their opportunities have just been different and that's what we're going to focus our energy on from September.
>
> (Steve Mills, Headteacher, Whitehill Junior School, Hitchin, focus group – primary educators, 14 July 2021)

> With the Year 5 boys, we're seeing multiple issues with wrong choices
> of games at break time which end up with kids getting physically or
> emotionally hurt. They've forgotten how to play.
>
> (Jill Allen, Headteacher, St. Wilifred's Catholic Primary School,
> Ripon, focus group – primary educators, 14 July 2021)

The importance of the social dynamic provided by the school as a physical
space, and the sense in which COVID caused this to be compromised, is
even more profound in special schools and in various alternative settings,
as this parent and Headteacher's Personal Assistant, Shelley Bray, who has
transcribed most of the focus groups and interviews reported on in these
pages, makes clear:

> There has definitely been a social and emotional impact. Our Deputy
> Headteacher made a comment that our Year 8s are only half-baked
> Year 7s. I would like to get the dining room back – a lot of kids
> with Special Needs don't have friends outside of school because the
> neighbours' kids go to mainstream schools, so they are more isolated
> and need that social interaction at school. They used to sit six round
> a table chattering, swapping things out of their lunchboxes, throwing
> chips at each other – just being children and making friends. Now it's
> two to a table facing the front – too far away from each other to have
> a proper conversation and staring at people's backs.
>
> (Shelley Bray, Headteacher's PA, Pebble Mill School, Aylesbury,
> focus group – primary educators, 14 July 2021)

The Chief Inspector of Schools in England, Amanda Spielman, who had
been vocal on the need for curricular catch-up, acknowledged the social
impact of lockdowns and bursting bubbles, and the interplay between the
two, in a speech to school leaders in March 2021:

> Of course, [catch-up is] not just about academic learning, as you'll
> be acutely aware. Being cooped up for weeks and months on end
> has piled on the misery for otherwise sociable and active children. So
> many have been bored and lonely – and getting very little exercise.
> Teachers have even reported to us that younger children have lost very
> basic skills, such as using a pencil, having lost the daily practice that
> comes from being in school.
>
> (Spielman, 2021c)

Sir Kevan Collins' proposals recognised these non-curricular losses, although
those who have spent a professional lifetime arguing for the centrality of

inclusion-first approaches and a strong social curriculum are likely to have mixed feelings about the location of this work in a time slot added on to the school day, and for a limited period.

Thus, and to reiterate, like the workplace and the town centre, the school is a social space. Indeed, for children and young people it is *primarily* a social space, rather than an educational one. The authors of detailed analyses of miscreant behaviour, especially in secondary schools, often ruminate about 'disaffection'. Arguably, more often this is as much about young people 'having a laugh' as it is about some deep unhappiness with the system (Breslin, 2001), reflecting a central but possibly healthy tension at the heart of school life: for teachers and school leaders, the primary purpose of schools is educational, while for children and young people, the *primary* purpose of schools is social. As children prepared to return to school after the UK's second substantive lockdown in March 2021, it was not the joy of the English, Geography, or Science class that many looked forward to; it was the joy of *seeing* each other, sitting next to each other in person, and not through a computer screen. But there were also anxieties that accompanied the reopening of school. For these P6 and P7 children in a Scottish primary school, the formal educational purpose of schooling was, certainly, not the key concern that emerged in a classroom discussion about the reopening of their school after the first schools lockdown and recorded in a blog post by their teacher, Jennifer Kirkwood, for the Children's Parliament:

> 'I was nervous because it was our first time back in months'
> 'I was happy because I got to see my friends'
> 'I am worried in case I get the virus'
> 'I'm nervous about Covid-19 now that schools are open'
> 'I am sad because I have to wake up early'
> (Jennifer Kirkwood, P6 and P7 teacher, Dailly Primary School and
> Early Years Centre, South Ayrshire: Kirkwood, 2020)

And catching-up on this area of school life is, arguably, much more complex than in-filling the gaps in a disrupted but published curriculum. A gap in the coverage of a specific element of the National Curriculum at, say, Key Stage 2, or in a GCSE or A-level specification is both identifiable and quantifiable. This is not to be complacent about the importance of curriculum coverage, or to suggest that it is 'easy' or inexpensive; it needs, as Collins rightly identified, both time and resourcing, but it is within the wherewithal of the profession and of schools to deliver such 'catch-up', as he clearly believed. Indeed, prevailing school improvement strategies with their utilisation of 'booster' classes, revision guides and a plethora of in-school and out-of-school 'interventions' – developed and embedded over the past thirty years – have helped to enhance this capacity.

However, figuring out how a 6-year-old might make up for a year's missed playdates, or how a 14-year-old might recover the kind of social development that flows from a year of corridor and staircase jostling and schoolyard banter is much harder to quantify and, therefore, address. For Margaret Mulholland, who participated in the focus group research for *Lessons from Lockdown* and who leads on Special Educational Needs and Inclusion for the Association of School and College Leaders, this requires a much more nuanced approach than the presumption of near-universal curriculum gaps:

> We need a shift in focus: from learning loss to learning disruption. Recovery has to move beyond the inane calculator of 'gaps' to instead capture the lived experiences of the past few months, upon which teachers, parents, schools and their communities can build.
>
> (Mulholland, 2021)

We pick up on this theme in our discussion of personalisation and the place of SEND pedagogies and inclusion-first teaching strategies in Chapter 9, but for now, it is worth remembering a mantra that runs throughout these pages, that no two children and no two families have had the same lockdown, and that nuance is everything, a point captured adeptly in the following statement from an experienced child psychologist:

> It's important to remember that children have had hugely different experiences during lockdown. Some children who experience anxiety normally, may have found a break from going to school, a break from triggers for their anxiety. For them going back to school is going to be very anxiety provoking. There are other children who have had a great time with [their] families and don't want to return to school. And then, of course, there are many children who have been in family situations with lots of arguing, and possibly violence and neglect who will find getting back to school a refuge. Do not assume that you know how children feel.
>
> (Dr Jessica Richardson, Principal Clinical Psychologist, NHS South London and Maudsley NHS Foundation Trust: Richardson, 2021)

Richardson's warning about assuming that 'we' know how children feel strikes a cautionary note that policymakers and practitioners would be wise to heed.

Student wellbeing and disruptions to Further and Higher Education

A similar challenge is replicated for those moving on to Further and Higher Education, a theme earlier addressed in Chapter 2, in our exploration of the initial experiences of university life gathered by those at the heart of the 2020 marking crisis. Drawing on a study conducted amongst those who sat A-level examinations twelve months later, during the early Summer of 2021, a report in *The Observer* noted that:

> Students' sense of disconnect could be exacerbated by the reduced opportunities to mix because of online teaching. Most UK institutions are retaining some online teaching, despite students' preference for in-person learning and government directives to offer a normal student experience.
>
> (Cited in Henry, 2021)

Thus, the researchers, based at the University of Leeds, observe that:

> Given that [some] online teaching may last into the next academic year, students in the incoming cohort may also not have the affordances of frequent in-person peer-to-peer social interaction during the transition to university ... the social networks of students are an important factor in buffering stress and improving academic performance.

And they recommend that, as Julie Henry puts it:

> Universities take measures to foster a sense of belonging, particularly with under-represented groups of students, through peer-to-peer support schemes and measures to boost the academic confidence of a cohort that has missed out on substantial amounts of schooling.

Whether we are referring to the pre-school playgroup, the primary school classroom, the secondary school corridor, or the university lecture theatre, these essentially *social* events and experiences – events and experiences that are so vital in the development of character, resilience and self-esteem – might be termed the 'water-cooler moments' of childhood and early adulthood. Granted the phraseology is occupationally limited and middle class, but this is exactly the kind of thing that Zoom-fatigued and keyboard-weary adults tell us that they are missing too: the unscheduled, unscripted conversations of the lunch queue, the car park, the walk from the station and, of course, the water cooler and the coffee machine. Nobody Zoom-calls a friend to have an incidental conversation about something they haven't thought of yet.

How one identifies and addresses these profoundly *social* gaps ought to be a much more urgent concern of policymakers. Again, it is worth outlining the parallels with other areas of everyday life, notably the workplace, not least because our models of schooling draw so much from the industrial age that emerged in the nineteenth and early twentieth century.

During the first third of the twentieth century, the way that employees were organised and managed in the workplace (or in most workplaces) went through a quiet revolution. The 'hard' division of labour of scientific management (epitomised in the noisy and isolating 'Fordism' of the car production line) increasingly gave way to processes and strategies that acknowledged and built on the reality of humans as social and pro-social beings, articulated initially through a body of practice referred to as the 'human relations school'. Moreover, as the twentieth century progressed, it became obvious that not only was it smart for business leaders to utilise the social skills of workers in designing production and administration processes, but that work had a vital social purpose for employees and their communities, whatever its productive output. Work was a part of the social fabric of life. As the traditional industries of western economies wound down their activities, they left workless communities bereft of purpose and identity, and the arenas that so often brought them together – that is, workplaces.

Something similar is true of schools. COVID-19 has underlined that, whatever the merits of the dash for grades that is such a characteristic of our current education systems (not just in the UK, but internationally), and whatever the curricular loss of lockdown, the social purpose of the school has been underlined by the pandemic. Children don't just collect knowledge and grades as they progress through school; they develop as individuals and, critically, as citizens. Moreover, as schools have become more and more effective and efficient at delivering learning to remote learners across digital platforms – a point that we pick up in Chapter 8 – attention has rightly turned to the social deficits of an entirely online existence, to the mental and physical health of young people, and to the learning that rarely features (or features sufficiently) on the timetable, the learning that derives from the multiple unscripted interactions of a school day – to reiterate, the water-cooler moments of childhood.

And for those in school during lockdown, the water cooler was barely accessible, with children necessarily operating in the much more controlled settings provided by bubbles, group work (which had emerged as a key element of pedagogy for much the same reasons that had spurred the industrial changes spurred by the humans relations school) largely off limits, one-way corridors displaying the kind of order that, as teachers and school leaders, we once dreamed of, and whole school breaks and lunchtimes – for many – a thing of the past.

Summary

Post-lockdown, there is both a challenge and an opportunity for all who work in education. On the one hand, how, in-school, do we rebuild the kind of collaborative pedagogies and recreate the kind of social spaces that enable young people to practice and develop all manner of social skills? On the other, especially amongst those who have enjoyed and thrived on the autonomy of learning online, how do we remake the case for onsite learning, especially when some children's memories of this might not have been great? In all of this, the social curriculum, and the skills, knowledge and expertise of those engaged in its delivery, ought to take on the status and profile that it should always have had. For all of Sir Kevan Collins' good intentions and smart analysis, cramming learning of this importance into thirty minutes added to the tail end of a stretched school day is unlikely to cut it.

Recommendations

7.1 At school level, education professionals should be encouraged and enabled to move away from the deficit language of 'catch-up' and 'recovery' and towards approaches that are diagnostic, personalised and proportionate.

7.2 Both at the level of classroom practice and in the national narrative, the social and emotional wellbeing of children and young people should be given at least as much prominence as matters of curriculum content.

7.3 Policymakers, system leaders and educational researchers should be encouraged to draw on the literature of 'learning disruption' rather than just that focused on 'learning loss' in framing responses to the challenges now facing school leaders, curriculum managers and classroom practitioners.

7.4 School-based professionals should be encouraged to utilise the principles and practice of family learning as they navigate the long road from lockdown, building on the positive relationships developed during this period with families that had sometimes previously been defined as 'hard to reach'.

7.5 Practical policy responses need to be developed to meet the needs of young people who have transitioned from schooling into either Further and Higher Education, or into training programmes or employment during this period, such that their experience is as positive as it can be, and education and training providers and employers ought to be prepared to demonstrate how they have done this.

Leadership and governance in a hybrid world

8

The long road to genuinely blended provision

Throughout this text, and in the final book in this trilogy, *Re-schooling Society After Lockdown*, reference is continually made to a 'blended' future – to repeat the mantra: the future isn't online or offline, it's blended – whether we are talking about schooling, the world of work, retailing, leisure, or any other field of human endeavour in mature, modern societies.

However, the road *to* a 'blended' tomorrow is at least as long as any road *from* lockdown. The reason for this is simple: a genuinely 'blended' system, whatever it is designed to deliver, is not simply 'introduced' with an accompanying manual or the help of a software engineer; it evolves over time, generating a new working culture that is nuanced and personalised but which finds coherence around a shared ethos, agreement on working arrangements and a set of objectives. And before any system emerges as genuinely 'blended', the form it takes is *hybrid*. The bubbles, and the bursting bubbles and the associated home-schooling, of Autumn Term 2020 and the second full schooling lockdown of Spring 2021 are a case in point.

Thus, hybrid models bring together and *bolt together* quite different approaches, often requiring professionals to work across two or more approaches, rather than with a unified blended approach. Thus, teachers delivered a taught curriculum to those in front of them, sometimes in sessions that were contemporaneously open to students learning at home,

DOI: 10.4324/9781003204824-8

and prepared additional (usually and increasingly online) content, whether teacher-produced or drawn from another source, such as that provided by the Oak National Academy or BBC Education, for use when 'live' online lessons were not available. These activities, while designed to deliver curriculum coverage (and, in England, coverage of the National Curriculum) and to impart particular 'blocks' of curriculum content – especially during the first schooling lockdown discussed in *Lessons from Lockdown* – were not typically developed as part of a holistic exercise in curriculum design. Rather, they were *assembled* (necessarily hastily during that first schooling lockdown) from a multitude of sources, and brought together so as to meet student needs – whether these students were in school, out of school but connected, or out of school and less connected or unconnected, and whether they had particular needs or talents.

Nonetheless, and almost accidentally, these COVID-driven hybrids opened up possibilities and provoked conversations: might digitally connected home learning negate some of the impact of the casual, regular absence that is a feature of some children's attendance patterns? Might it support the child who is forced to be out of school for a considerable period of time or periodically because of a medical condition or an injury? Might it open up a communication channel with a family hitherto thought of as 'hard to reach'? Might it provide a model for much greater curriculum enrichment with the virtual worlds to which it offers access? Might it help remould parent-school liaison, partly through the widely unexpected success of that popular COVID-Keep – the online parents' evening – and partly because of the instancy of contact now offered, at least to those families who are both connected and device-rich (because one is little use without the other)? For the optimists, the answer to each of these questions was, and remains, 'yes':

> We had a SEND meeting … with the Local Authority, all done online, we got all the professionals there whose diaries are always a nightmare and they all have to travel, but you could find an hour slot really easily to have that conversation. It's also very accessible for people who don't particularly want to be in a room full of other people.
>
> (Dan Hall, Director of Information Technology Systems, Girls' Day School Trust, focus group – Ed Tech experts and advocates, 20 June 2021)

And, as if to emphasise the potential of a post-lockdown educational landscape infused with online practice, one member of the Focus Group of EdTech experts convened in the researching of this text noted:

It helps when you're isolating, like me today – I've got COVID but I'm alright. I can't go anywhere for the next ten days so luckily we can do this online.

> (Sam Shellcross, Teacher of Computing, Bromley High
> Junior School, focus group – Ed Tech Experts
> and Advocates, 20 June 2021)

Dan Hall pointed to the student-friendliness of specific online conduits now emerging, such as the 'chat' function, and that have not featured in 'classroom' practice before:

It's the medium they're happy with and that they're chatting to each other in. The teachers have dropped into a medium where the students are really comfortable. These students were never using email before.

Of course, the co-use of spaces like 'chat' by teachers and students, and the use of student-owned mobile phones to inform learning in the classroom give rise to appropriate and real concerns about both safeguarding and about concentration and focus during lessons. Simply denying a role for the technology hardly seems an option, even if denial has a superficial and populist appeal in some quarters. Thus, the position on mobile phones taken by England's Secretary of State for Education, Gavin Williamson, at the heart of the lockdown crisis attracted incredulity from one longstanding Northern Ireland-based Ed-Tech advocate:

What the flip is your Education Minister over there doing trying to ban mobile phones? Thank goodness for devolution at times!
> (Research participant, speaking on condition of confidentiality,
> focus group – Ed Tech experts and advocates,
> 20 June 2021)

At particular points in history, particular groups of specialists come to the fore. The lockdowns and bursting bubbles of the pandemic brought a surge in interest in online learning and shone a light on those who had been (often quiet) enthusiasts for all things digital, whatever their formal job titles. The experience of this senior leader is illustrative:

For the last year I've had people knocking on the door, as the Ed Tech person, looking for assistance, so it's been a great year for that – it's

not officially on my duty list but certainly [it's] something that I'm
passionate about and that I'm keen to assist others with.

> (Denny Tennyson, Senior Teacher, St. Joseph's Grammar
> School, Donaghmore, focus group – Northern
> Ireland-based educators, 8 June 2021)

For those involved in curriculum leadership or on school leadership teams,
this optimism, while genuine, was sometimes more guarded. On the one
hand, long-established classroom practices were no longer an option, as
these experienced senior leaders make clear:

> I felt like a beginning teacher again because all of the strategies you
> had used before in the classroom, none of them quite worked. Group
> work, group tables – no, we were in rows! Circulating around – no!.
> Anything I tried to implement I got pulled up short, oh no, that's
> not going to work! How am I going to do that? I'm going to have to
> approach it in a slightly different way … .

> (Alistair Hamill, Senior Leader and Head of Geography,
> Lurgan College, Armagh, focus group – Northern
> Ireland-based educators, 8 June 2021)

> You kept getting caught out. It's like when the electrics go off in your
> house and you try every switch, and you realise 'I can't do this.'

> (James McClintock, Director of Evaluation and Development,
> Dunclug College, Ballymena, focus group – Northern Ireland-based
> educators, 8 June 2021

On the other, this kind of hybrid-practice was also proving demanding:

> We were streaming to our pupils at home as well as catering for the
> pupils in front of us … [Teachers] were having to upload everything,
> make little videos after school time and it just wasn't going to be
> practical for teachers to maintain that amount of work so we had
> to be flexible. We had to ensure the pupils at home could answer
> questions and work collaboratively with those pupils in the class-
> room, so [that those at home] could keep up with everyone else in
> the classroom.

> (Jacqueline Gray, Head of Biology and School Governor,
> Strathearn School, Belfast, focus group – Northern
> Ireland-based educators, 8 June 2021)

In part, these challenges about rolling out initially hybrid practice arose from an incomplete understanding of what 'going online' or the greater use of technology in the classroom (or both in tandem, during periods of lock-down) meant for teaching and learning. Here, the challenge was not just to shift teaching from classroom or textbook to screen, but to understand how teaching through the screen required different approaches, opening up new options but ruling out some aspects of long-standing practice:

> We had one secondary school that was thinking about a 'bring your own device' scenario … you've got this great plan [for sourcing] the laptops to run it all but, actually, are the teachers clear about what the teaching will be like in the classroom if you're going to have that set-up? Just because you have an electronic device [doesn't mean] you have the same approaches to teaching.
>
> (Sheila McKenzie, Chief Operating Officer, Anthem Schools Trust, focus group – influencers and system leaders, 19 May 2021)

And this experienced provider of educational resources, previously through a traditional publisher and latterly through a well-established online portal focused on supporting school leaders, concurred:

> If I could call out one area for development [it's this]: you can have all the systems set up but if you're not actually delivering the teaching and learning appropriate to that technology, maximising that different medium. I got the sense, and certainly from the feedback I got, that [some teachers] were trying to replicate face-to face teaching with the technology, but it just wasn't really landing with a lot of the student community.
>
> (Michael McGarvey, Managing Director, *The Key for School Leaders* website, focus group – influencers and system leaders. 19 May 2021)

However, traffic to sites like *The Key for School Leaders* reflected both the extent to which COVID-related matters dominated both the thinking and headspace of Heads and senior leaders, and their desire to get this right. McGarvey continues:

> *The Key* gives advice [across] the whole range: staffing, recruitment, admin, finance, school improvement, school inspection; there's a whole gamut of advice and information [and] case studies. The remarkable thing was the core 'bread and butter' content dropped and the whole

COVID thing took over. It was all about digital learning, frameworks [to support online activity], ensuring compliance; it was all [about] interpreting the ridiculous amount of Department for Education updates – I think there were 150 in the Summer Term alone. My team described it as COVID just dominating. It almost suggested that regular school activity [had to be] put on pause during those months.

And, of course, embracing this hybrid world en route to a blended nirvana had to be done *alongside* the daily stuff of school leadership and governance. It is to the day-to-day stuff of leadership and governance that we now turn.

COVID governance: Oversight from a distance, and up close

In *Lessons from Lockdown*, we began to explore the way in which school and trust governing boards were approaching their responsibilities in a much-changed environment. The Department for Education's *Governance Handbook* (DFE, 2020a) is the periodically updated go-to manual for those involved in the governance of schools in England, as well as the majority of supporting resources produced by organisations such as the National Governance Association, the membership body for school governors and trustees in schools in England, Wales and Northern Ireland, and online portals such as *Governor Hub*, *The Key for School Governors* and *Modern Governor*, and underlined in the framework that guides the cadre of newly appointed 'National Leaders of Governance', established by the Department for Education in England in October 2021, and those involved in the preparation and training of school governors. According to the Governance Handbook, the core responsibilities of those who serve as school governors are focused around three themes:

1. Setting the vision, ethos and strategic direction of the school (or group of schools) and overseeing practice and progress in line with these aspirations;
2. Appointing and supporting the Head or Principal, and holding them to account for outcomes, and
3. Ensuring financial and resource probity.

Figure 8.1 sets out these responsibilities in more detail and adds three additional responsibilities that the particular official guidance cited here tends to underplay but which is prominent in that from other agencies, notably the school inspectorate, Ofsted (Ofsted, 2019).

Responsibilities set out by the Department for Education in the Governance Handbook (DfE, 2021)	What this means in terms of Governing Board actions and obligations	Additional legal responsibilities applying to all of those who are members of governing boards
Setting vision, ethos and strategic direction	• Agreeing objectives over defined time-scales • Establishing a shared sense of what success looks like • Setting the tone around how the school goes about achieving these objectives	**Ensuring that safeguarding is effective and embedded across *all* aspects of school life**
Appointing and supporting the Head or Principal, and holding them to account for outcomes	• Appointing the Head or Principal and ensuring that he or she is appropriately *supported* to succeed in the role • Holding the Head to account for the performance of the school through a *formal* performance management process • Ensuring that the Head has such a process in place for the performance management of staff, and maintaining *oversight* of this	**Ensuring that *all* statutory or legal responsibilities are fulfilled (for example, under equalities, employment and health and safety legislation)**
Ensuring financial and resource probity	• Ensuring that the principles and processes that underpin financial decision making and resource allocation are *understood* and *embedded*	**Maintaining connections with stakeholders, in particular, parents and the immediate school community**

Figure 8.1 Governance responsibilities in summary.

Source: Adapted from governing board training materials produced by the author for HFL Governance Services (Herts for Learning, 2021).

The challenge for those involved in school governance was to deliver on these responsibilities but, as with school leaders, in a hitherto entirely unfamiliar context, that was generated by the pandemic.

In *Lessons From London*, we talked about emergent governance practices, spurred by the pandemic and the first lockdown, practices had attempted to both lighten the load on school leaders while remaining sufficiently agile to react to a fast-changing landscape, with directives and guidance from the official agencies, such as the Department for Education and Ofqual, Local Authorities or Multi-Academy Trusts, and teachers' and school leaders' professional associations being published on what felt like, for Heads, a daily basis. For both senior leaders and school governors, the manner in which these directives arrived was not always helpful:

> One of the trickiest things for us was that … all of the announcements were so public and that nothing ever came to school leaders before the public knew about it. And that caused quite a lot [of pressure] in terms of a workload … quite a lot of additional work … barrages of emails from parents, from teachers just [asking] 'What's going to happen?'
>
> (Donna Hubbard-Young, Senior Deputy Head, Chesterton Community College, research interview for Breslin, 2021a: 137)

This left governors similarly feeling as if they were 'behind the curve' and required approaches that were more agile and adaptable than the traditional routine of termly or half-termly meetings. Why? First, because of the speed with which the landscape was changing. Second, because the decisions that Heads were being asked to take were either profoundly strategic (therefore, falling rightly into the domain that would normally spur discussion with governors, or at least with the Board's Chair or the individual charged with convening the relevant sub-committee), or involved the kind of substantive change in operational practice that, again, would be of legitimate interest to governors. Third, because Boards were acutely aware of their responsibility, laid bare in England in a new inspection framework that we discuss later in this chapter, to attend to the wellbeing of the school leaders charged with delivering the school improvement plans that they had at the least signed-off and, more likely, played some role in co-producing.

Thus, the first lockdown had often served to strengthen and deepen relationships between governors and school leaders, something that Emma Knights, Chief Executive at the National Governance Association, discussed in a blog post cited at extended length in *Lessons from Lockdown*:

Without a doubt, the last few months has strengthened the relationships between most senior leaders and their boards: each appreciating the other's role and the effort and care with which it is carried out … These discussions between boards and senior leaders should be liberating.

(Knights, 2020 – cited in Breslin, 2021a: 139)

In part, this strengthening of the relationship between the Board and Senior Leaders derived from a deliberate attempt to increase accessibility to the Board in the way that the Department for Education, who had helpfully suspended a number of administrative responsibilities, had suggested at the time:

School leaders should stay in touch with the governing board in a proportionate way, including providing information on the welfare of staff and pupils, so that they can retain a strategic overview of the situation and the school.

(Cited in Department for Education, 2020)

And, in practical terms, as was reported in *Lessons from Lockdown*, this need to be proportionate and accessible – that is, to be in some sense both 'closer' and *less* demanding – meant that:

We [had to be] very much more agile. You know, [that we] could respond quickly. If I wanted to get an answer out of the Board, I could just issue a request. I could have a Board meeting in two days, [on] Zoom, with a single subject on the [agenda] you know: 'Are we going to open or aren't we?' … And we were very focused at the time on supporting the school in terms of making sure they had the resources, whether that was risk assessments, Board time, [access to] simple, practical advice … And I think that made a huge difference for us.

(Colin Platt, Chair of Governors, Monks Risborough Church of England Primary School, focus group – school governors. 21 July 2020, in Breslin, 2021a: 144)

This new mode of operation was sustained through the local lockdowns and bursting bubbles of the Summer and Autumn terms in 2020, and across the second schooling lockdown in Spring Term 2021, but governors returned after the Summer 2020 break with the same trepidation that was held by many school leaders and educational professionals:

> I think last Autumn, well that term, before the summer we were scrambling around, working out what to do, and when we came back in the Autumn we thought 'We have to get on with this, this thing is sticking around and we have to reinvent ourselves.' How do we manage this going forward? What if it goes on for two years? We need some structure that works.
>
> (Rosemary Hoyle, Foundation Governor and Committee Chair, The Winterton Federation, focus group – school governors and trustees, 17 April 2021)

> I've been looking at emails from that time to remind me. When it [lockdown] started we thought, by Autumn, we will be back to normal, we were fire-fighting, but then it got to Autumn and we realised it was not going to be anywhere near normal.
>
> (Kathryn Wilkinson, School Governor, Hardy Mill Primary School, Bolton and Manager, City of Leeds Governor Support Service, focus group – school governors and trustees, 17 April 2021)

> I was apprehensive – waiting for our first positive test.
>
> (Tracey Price, Chair of Governing Board, Moulsham High School, Chelmsford, focus group – school governors and trustees, 17 April 2021)

This apprehension was altruistic rather than selfish, with governors, especially Governing Board Chairs, acutely aware of the need to support the Head and the professional team. Thus, Price continues:

> The weight of responsibility to support the Headteacher, the exams fiasco, I felt this weight on my shoulders, trying to support but feeling helpless – are we going to have to close bubbles? We started getting positive cases towards Christmas and it was 'how sustainable is this?'

Governors missed the onsite dimension to their role – visits to observe practice in specified areas, meetings with the Head, working group meetings with staff, and sometimes the non-governance support that a number of school governors routinely provide:

> I used to volunteer in school once a week and I really miss that. Some things you can't pick up on screen. [The Chair] was still having

face-to-face meetings with the Headteacher so we relied on him to know how the Head and the staff were doing. He was our eyes and thermometer.

> (Sarah Morgan, School Governor, Bushey Primary Education
> Federation, focus group – school governors and trustees,
> 17 April 2021)

Tracey Price underlines the sense of 'missing' the kind of contact with the school that engagement as a governor routinely and necessarily involves:

> I have been in school. I wanted to see the Headteacher physically to see how she was. We can't see the whole picture on Zoom. I used to talk to the staff a lot but really missed talking to them and seeing how they are. I did go in at Christmas – it's all a bit of a blur. I missed being there, whereas I used to be in [school] once a week.

And, the new governance is not without other pitfalls, not least in the way that it blurs what have traditionally (simplistically and probably wrongly) been presented as the separate domains of 'strategic' and 'operational' activity, but there has been an attractiveness to aspects of lockdown governance that many will hope to retain in years to come:

> We need to keep the rapidness of decision-making [developed during lockdown], this fantastic ability to move at speed. If governing bodies can deliver that in normal times, I think governance of schools will be far better for it.
>
> > (Dan Hall, Parent Governor, Bushey Primary Education
> > Federation, focus group – school governors, 21 July 2020)

In all of this, technology has been key: online meetings held early in the first lockdown often began with a regretful refrain, accompanied by nodding heads, that it was a shame colleagues could not get together onsite in the traditional way. Eighteen months on, as Boards confirmed their meeting arrangements for the new academic year, most found themselves setting a 'mixed economy' of meetings, encouraged by a membership now more comfortable with the technology, and clear about the benefits of online meetings – meetings that they can enjoy in the comfort of their home, meetings that are often better attended, something that appears to be increasing levels of accessibility to governance in the short term and which may increase the diversity of the governance community in the longer term.

Those involved in governor training, including the author, have identified a similar trend. To take one example, across the 2018–19 academic year, HFL Education, the school and local authority-owned educational services company that supports schools in Hertfordshire, Buckinghamshire and elsewhere, delivered virtually all of its governance training courses in person. In 2021–22, the vast majority of its courses were delivered online, and early bookings for the 2022-23 academic year are suggesting that, for many, online delivery remains a preference. If there is to be a post-pandemic world, there is likely to be some further rebalancing of these figures as on-site practice is re-established. Nonetheless, as a part of the mix, online governance, and online governance training, is here to stay.

Leadership beyond lockdown: Navigating a re-emergent compliance culture

Heads and other school-based senior leaders who have contributed to the research both for *Lessons from Lockdown* and for this text have spoken at some length on the unexpected freedoms that the first lockdown (in Spring 2020) conferred.

Fifteen months later, school leaders, and their colleagues in school governance, were beginning to express concern about the re-emergence of a pre-lockdown compliance culture that, in English schools, saw their work scrutinised and their performance held up to public gaze from four different anchorage points:

- The publication of performance (or 'league') tables detailing the attainment of children in reading, writing and mathematics at the close of primary schooling and at the two points at which young people might exit secondary schooling: at age 16 through GCSE examinations in all, or virtually all, subjects, and at age 18, through the Advanced Level examinations that govern access to university or, alternatively, various professional (or vocational) courses;
- Periodic inspections, typically every four years, carried out by the school inspectorates in England, Wales, Northern Ireland and Scotland;
- Regular visits from school improvement specialists, on behalf of either the Local Authority or the Multi-Academy Trust within which the school sits, and
- An annual Performance Management exercise delivered either through the Governing Board (in Local Authority Maintained schools) or by school improvement professionals (in Multi-Academy Trusts).

During lockdown, there was a significant relaxation of these pressures. As we detail and discuss elsewhere in these pages, the standardised assessments in the final year of primary education did not take place, and most written examination papers (other than those relating to some vocational courses) for pupils aged 16 and 18 were cancelled and, with this cancellation, the performance (or 'league') tables that usually detail and, critically in terms of claimed school performance, *aggregate* examination results, were suspended. In addition, most involved in the delivery of Headteachers' performance management processes had the good sense to stand aside objectives (or 'targets') that had been set in a very different climate. Meantime, with some notable exceptions, Local Authority and Multi-Academy Trust-based school improvement specialists tended towards empathy rather than judgement in the typically termly 'visits' that usually underpinned their relationship with schools. Finally, school inspections were stood down for the majority of UK schools, although the inspectorate for schools in England did conduct a range of 'information-gathering' visits during Autumn Term 2020 and Spring Term 2021, and they resumed the 'Monitoring Visits' made to schools recorded at their most recent inspection as 'Requires Improvement' or 'Inadequate' in the subsequent Summer Term.

The removal or relaxation of these pressures during these phases of the pandemic had been welcomed by Heads, as had been the decision, noted above, by many school governing boards to err towards the 'support' end of the 'support and challenge' continuum that informs day-to-day governance practice. Taken together, these 'relaxations' had helped to create a space for the innovation demanded by the circumstances. The concern that the re-emergence of these instruments of compliance and measures of perform-ance sparked amongst those in leadership and governance was essentially three-fold, that:

1. A re-emerging compliance infrastructure would stifle the culture of innovation that had emerged in a range of schools.
2. It would take insufficient account of the challenges that schools had faced during the intervening period.
3. It would strengthen a 'back to the future' narrative that painted pre-lockdown schooling as a 'golden age' without acknowledging the fault lines – for instance, around socially patterned attainment gaps – of that period, fault lines that, as we have argued throughout, COVID had given a new visibility to, notably around the impact of poverty on edu-cational attainment, wellbeing and the quality of a child's schooling experience.

In any case, for many Heads, this was all too soon: the system-shock had been traumatic and the after-shocks were still emerging. Indeed, as the opening term of the 2021–22 academic year edged into the winter months, print and broadcast media were again focused on rising COVID numbers (especially in Continental Europe), the emergence of the Omicron strand and associated travel restrictions and, in the UK, the threat to the NHS. Weeks earlier, as the half-term break in UK schools approached – in mid-October in Scotland and in the final week of the month elsewhere – newspaper headlines carried a certain familiarity:

> 'NHS chiefs urge "plan B plus" amid COVID surge'
> (Andrew Gregory, Heather Stewart and Ian Sample,
> *The Guardian*, 20 October 2021)

> 'Javid warns of 100,000 daily cases and urges MPs to lead by example'
> (Heather Stewart, Peter Walker and and Andrew
> Gregory, *The Guardian*, 21 October 2021)

> 'Javid warns daily COVID cases could hit 100,000: public urged to get booster jab and wear masks'
> (Chris Smyth, *The Times*, 21 October 2021)

However, for the first time since the virus had emerged early the previous year, infection rates appeared to be rising fastest amongst school age children, the majority of whom remained unvaccinated. Figure 8.2 illustrates the prevalence of the virus among children and young people from August 2020 through to October 2021 and shows the sharp rise in childhood infection rates during the autumn months of 2021, with the charity Long Covid Kids reporting that, by early October, one in 35 primary school pupils and one in 14 secondary school students were infected.

Against this background of rising child infection rates, let us spend a little more time on the most prominent of the compliance-related pressures identified earlier: the public inspection of schools, a feature of schooling systems across the UK and in many other settings.

Same old pressures: Brand new inspection framework

For those leading schools in what has become known as the 'inspection window' (those due an imminent inspection), the post-lockdown return of such inspections for all schools posed the greatest anxiety. The English

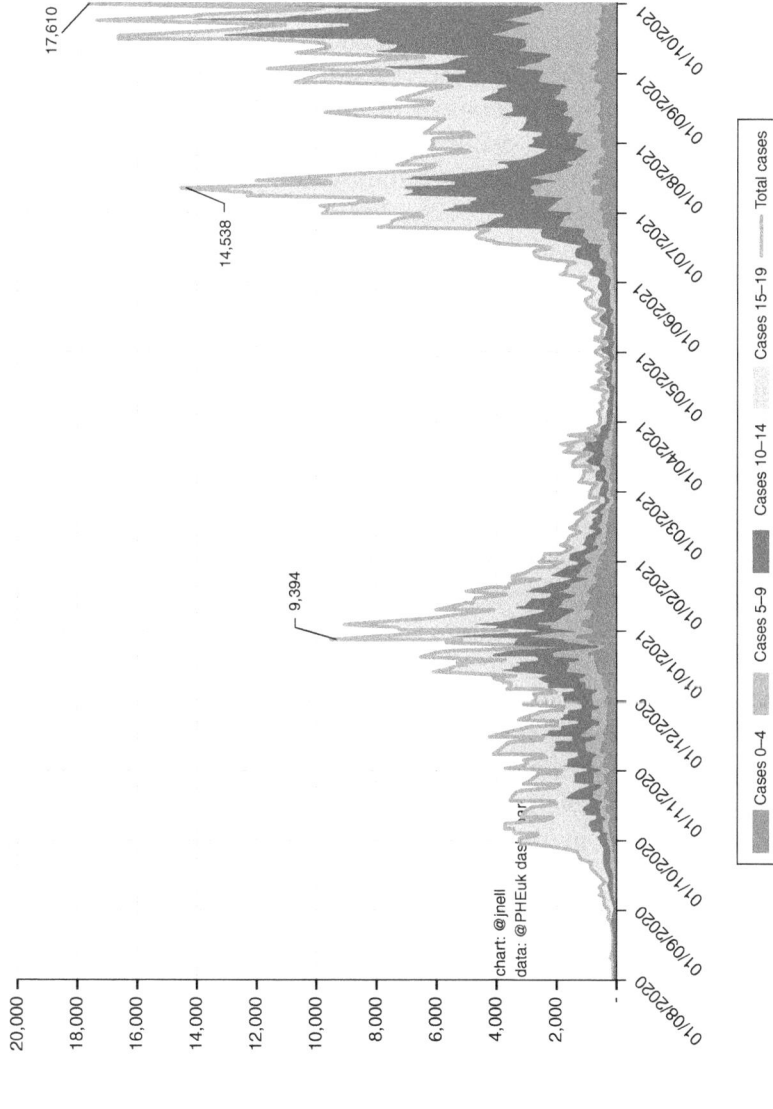

Figure 8.2 Children and young people's COVID-19 infection rates in England (August 2020–October 2021).
Source: Long Covid Kids www.longcovidkids.org/post/graphs-statistics-children-covid-19-updated-10th-october-2021

inspectorate, Ofsted, reintroduced full onsite inspections for all schools in September 2021. English schools were contending with a new inspection framework – launched in September 2019 – at the start of the academic year that was then to see the arrival of the pandemic. Thus, for schools in England, the concern was not simply the relaunch of inspections, but in 'getting to know' an inspection framework that was still 'new' to practitioners two years after its original launch and, in particular, the promise to inspect matters relating to curriculum content and sequencing, subject knowledge and the development of cultural capital, a departure from practice over the past two decades. Many in the teaching profession had welcomed the change of emphasis promised by the new framework and much of the thinking behind it, re-articulated by the Chief Inspector for schools at the annual Festival of Education conference in June 2021:

> I would never argue against the life-changing impact of good exam results – and of course all schools and colleges should aim to make the most of every student's potential. But grades aren't education in themselves; they should be a mirror of good education – and it's the education that we want to look at.
>
> I was also determined that inspection should not be predicated on a narrowly utilitarian view of education. We do children a great disservice if we see them only as economic units, with education as the path to work-readiness, important as that is.
>
> (Spielman, 2021a)

Many teachers and school leaders welcomed the greater prominence it gave to student and staff wellbeing, matters of inclusion, and a greater concern for what was taught, coupled with an apparent shift away from what had come to be seen as an obsession with performance data.

However, any change in the ways in which school performance is measured is likely to prompt anxiety amongst staff in general and school leaders in particular. For primary school leaders, the new focus not just on the curriculum but on curriculum *subjects* was a particular cause for concern, given that most primary specialists teach *across* the curriculum, delivering the majority of subjects through an integrated day to a single class. The new focus on wellbeing may have worked well for primary practitioners, given the overtly pastoral relationship between the teacher and each child, but the focus on curriculum, and especially on subject knowledge, seemed to favour their secondary colleagues. Perhaps predictably, early inspection reports of primary schools based on the new framework seemed to justify these reservations, especially in comments about subjects other than

English and Mathematics. The following extracts are taken from inspection reports published just before the first lockdown and are typical of those pertaining to schools judged to be 'Good' under the 'new' framework:

> Leadership of English and mathematics is strong. Monitoring procedures are well established. Leaders have successfully designed and implemented a curriculum offer for other subjects. However, not all subject leaders are clear about their role in developing this work further. Senior leaders should now clarify the role of these new leaders and provide training to enable them to better monitor and review the effectiveness of the curriculum in their subjects.
>
> (Ofsted Inspection Report, Primary School, Manchester, January 2020)

> In some foundation subjects, such as art and design, teachers attempt to cover too much content in the time available. This means that pupils move on too quickly and do not develop a real depth of understanding. Leaders need to make some refinements to curriculum plans to ensure that pupils have enough time to study some topics in more depth.
>
> (Ofsted Inspection Report, Primary School, Birmingham, December 2019)

> Teachers' expertise in the curriculum is underdeveloped in some subjects. Pupils do not learn well enough. Curriculum leaders need to develop their plans, so that pupils' learning is well sequenced in every subject. Leaders should ensure that teachers know how to teach the curriculum successfully.
>
> (Ofsted Inspection Report, Primary School, Hertfordshire, February 2020)

In fairness to the English inspectorate, schools had been given a year's grace to 'get curriculum right' after the introduction of the new framework in September 2019, and on the re-launch of a full schedule of inspections in September 2021, this was reinstated and extended 'at least until March 2022' (Ofsted, 2021) but, given the 'high stakes' nature of school inspection, the anxiety among school leaders did not dissipate, even when the transition period was subsequently extended to cover the full academic year:

> This term teachers are stressed and pressured. They haven't been able to process, to seek to reconnect with children over the last two years. To bring back children a little bit stronger. They've been told to get

back to normal, to get back now. 'We're coming in to check, we shall be monitoring you, there will be visits and Ofsted' and that's an awful lot … .

(Helen Shirley, Pastoral Lead, Bushey Primary Education Federation, research interview, 15 October 2021)

And, for some, the threat of inspection took schools away from what they needed and wanted to focus on in the aftermath of the previous 18 months:

Our CPD staff sessions are focused on our curriculum [but] we'd much rather just focus … on the social and emotional aspects [of learning] and how we can help families and see where they're at after this. We know … we are in the Ofsted window and we know we have to respond to [their] demands for the curriculum [but] that's the priority the system is placing on us.

(Primary Headteacher, speaking to the author on condition of confidentiality, October 2021)

Nor was the concern about inspection limited to those in the primary sector. Schools deemed at their previous inspection to be 'Requires Improvement' were the subject of monitoring visits and inspections during Summer Term 2021. The Headteacher at a large secondary school was blunt about what he thought of this process:

You might be aware that we're RI [Requires Improvement] at the moment and don't even get me started on that.

(Secondary Headteacher, speaking to the author on condition of confidentiality, 18 October 2021)

School leaders in Scotland had been granted a little more 'recovery' time than their English peers, with the relaunch of school inspections in Scotland scheduled for January 2022; they were, though, were no more relaxed than their English peers about the return of their inspectorate:

[Scottish inspectors] have said they will go back into schools in January and I think that is absolutely wrong … There is a school … just up the road from us … they were due to have an inspection just before the first lockdown so they've been told they'll be first on the 'hit list' for January. I was out with a very good friend who's a Deputy at the school on Monday. They have approximately seventy full-time equivalent teaching staff and on Monday 14 of them were off [with]

COVID-related absences … I just think it's shocking. I think it's absolutely shocking that [this] is happening. I think it's grossly unfair.
(Secondary school Head, speaking on condition of confidentiality, research interview, October 2021)

In the event, voices such as this struck a chord with Education Scotland, the government department responsible for all aspects of schooling and its inspection. Thus, school inspections in Scotland did not resume until the start of the 2022–23 academic year, just as this book went to press.

As noted, there was to be no such reprieve in England. Indeed, speaking to English Heads in Spring 2021, the Chief Inspector for Schools had implored schools to take the upcoming resumption of 'normal' inspections in their stride:

I want Ofsted to play its part in helping schools and colleges get back on track – through inspection and professional dialogue that contributes to development. I want us to help, not hinder. And I certainly don't want hard-pressed teachers spending time on fruitless exercises to 'prepare for Ofsted'. That's true in normal times and it's vital right now. So please: don't run mocksteds, don't bring in inspection consultants, don't ask your staff to document their activity over the last few months, on the off-chance the inspector will call.
(Spielman, 2021c)

Given, though, the very public nature of UK school inspections – that is, inspection reports are published in the public domain and can have a dramatic impact on a school's standing in its community and on the career prospects of those reported on – it is perhaps unsurprising that Spielman's advice gained short shrift from this school leader:

Let's face it, it's about putting on a show isn't it? All of this 'Don't plan for an inspection' – it's like 'Don't tidy up when your friends are coming round to your house!' No, of course you want your best show!
(Secondary school Head, speaking on condition of confidentiality, research interview, October 2021)

Interestingly, none of the Heads who contributed to the research process for this book, or for *Lessons from Lockdown*, called for the abolition of inspection. Rather, they are questioning two things: whether inspections can be fairly delivered in what they (reasonably) see as extreme circumstances, and whether 're-starting' a full schedule of inspections so soon 'after' the pandemic shuts down what might be a period when school-based education professionals are encouraged and enabled to reflect on their experiences, apply lessons and select 'COVID-Keeps' so that, in education terms, 'building back better' (the phrase beloved of former UK Prime Minister Boris Johnson) translates from a political slogan to an educational reality.

Thus, it was unsurprising that Amanda Spielman's warning – that many who had been previously judged as 'Outstanding' (Carr, 2021) would lose this status under the Ofsted framework launched in September 2019 – did not go down well with the profession. By the middle of what was already proving an exhausting Autumn Term, a Headteachers' support group, Headrest, was calling for the postponement of inspections (Roberts, 2021).

In due course, professional associations representing Heads in England added their voices to the calls for postponement in special circumstances (Lough, 2021) and the main teaching unions were to subsequently advocate a similar course of action, going further and demanding inspections be halted until the February 2022 half-term (NEU, 2021). The English inspectorate did not respond to the calls, other than postponement where COVID-related absence was especially high, but they did cancel those inspections scheduled for the final week of term before Christmas, no doubt influenced by the surge of infections that followed the emergence of the Omicron variant of the virus that had emerged at the beginning of December.

Lockdown starters: A resource for next-generation schooling?

For the most part, lockdown is discussed as an interruption to 'normality', the normality of the school run or school yard, the normality of the chaos of the playdate or the bustle of the school corridor or staircase, the normality of teaching in groups, the normality of onsite Governing Board and staff meetings, the normality of the field trip or the parents' meeting, the normality of the assembly or the teaching practice placement.

Such an analysis risks missing a set of key cohorts – the 'lockdown starters': the children who entered pre-school provision or started at primary or secondary school in September 2020 or 2021, the undergraduates and trainees (including those headed for a career in teaching) who started college or university courses at this point, those appointed to their first teaching or leadership roles during the 2019–20, 2020–21 or 2021–22 academic years, those becoming school governors or academy trustees during the same period, and those becoming parents during lockdown. Untrammelled by the practices of the past – and often any knowledge of these practices – these individuals ought to be a fantastic resource for school and system leaders, and a key constituency for educational researchers and for all those framing education policy and practice for the post-lockdown age. Why? Because they offer not only the fresh eyes that always come with the new parent, the new pupil or student, or the newly qualified teacher, but also a freshness untainted by the baggage of what things used to be like. As with the kind of deficit analysis that frames the commitment to 'catch-up' and 'recovery' discussed in Chapter 7, the tendency is to focus on what this group has missed; maybe we should turn the lens around and ask also what they may have gained. For any of these lockdown starters, lockdown isn't the 'new' normal – it is the *only* normal: parenthood without parent and toddler groups or nursery provision, classrooms (for children and young people alike) with the false order of social spacing, school governorship and governor visits, parents' evenings and school induction tours online and remote rather than in person and onsite, university life without the lecture hall, seminar room, or student bar, teacher training without teaching placements, or at least with placements of a very different nature, and so on. As the new academic year beckoned ahead of the summer 'break' of 2021, this leading teacher educator was resigned to the fact that 'normality' (howsoever defined), and a bubble-free and lockdown-free future, remained some way off:

> I think there was an intention that our programmes at the University would just go back to normal in September although it doesn't look like that can happen, we're still going to be social distancing, we're still going to be doing a lot of work online. People in those management roles thinking through next year's programmes will be pretty tentative about what they can actually return to normal over.
>
> (Professor Rachel Lofthouse, Carnegie School of Education, Leeds Beckett University, focus group – teacher education, 30 June 2021)

And across the teacher education community, the approaches taken were necessarily diverse, as a result of the variety of contexts and conduits through which teachers' initial and continuing education is delivered. Lofthouse continues:

> The year has been a long slog, I think, for a lot of people in teacher education. I think the adaptations that programmes have made have been pretty varied across the sector because, essentially, despite the fact we're all working towards common aims, [with the] same standards, [the] same kind of core requirements, the nature of the provision,

whether you're a big university provider with just postgraduates or whether you've twenty or thirty people as opposed to five hundred students. In the end, the way that IT [Initial Teacher Education] provision is arranged means there has had to be an awful lot of individualised decision making at programme level … What I would say is that everybody that I know worked phenomenally hard – having to make arrangements that suited them – their programme, their partnership, their students – and that has resulted in a fair degree of diversity in the practice.

As with the nature of children's and young people's experience, one might judge the subsequent intake of new 'lockdown generation' of teachers in deficit. Certainly, they have not had the kind of broad similarity of educational experience that they might have expected to have had in 'normal' pre-lockdown times (even if the reality has always been more diverse). Again, though, one might turn the lens around: these Early Career Teachers (as they are now defined in English schools) will arrive in staff rooms and classrooms with very differing skill sets, some of which might not have been developed in 'normal' times – Lofthouse again:

> I think a lot of the students have gained an enormously broad skill set, they will have had their eyes opened to an awful lot of the trauma that is involved with being a teacher and serving communities, particularly serving the more deprived communities, that perhaps they wouldn't always see.

It will be as important to build on these gains in order to address any gaps in the expertise of new entrants to the profession, which will have arisen from the unique period during which they have trained. This beginning teacher – who participated in a focus-group discussion from a ferry in the Irish Sea as she returned from Scotland after a successful interview for her first teaching post – is certainly keen to embrace the lessons from her period in teacher education:

> What am I going to expect, what have I got to come? I think this year has prepared me more than any other PGCE year that has gone before. This year has been a challenging one but has stood me in good stead for my future career. I think my learning curve has been steep but has stood me in good stead for using technology in the classroom … .
>
> (Zoe White, trainee teacher, Lurgan College, Lurgan, focus group – Northern Ireland-based educators, 8 June 2021)

And, of course, this beginning teacher will be entering a profession that may either be pushed, by a mix of policy intention and practice nostalgia, to look back to a pre-lockdown tradition, or forward to a new range of approaches that have their origins in the lockdown years. It will be recalled that each of the focus groups and interviews conducted as part of the research for this text and for *Lessons from Lockdown* concluded with an invitation for participants to reflect on educational life prior to lockdown, before considering the question 'What can't you wait to get back to, and what can't you wait to leave behind?' However, this school leader, speaking after the second schools' lockdown, suggests that the 'pull' to revert to previous practice was already being felt:

> I'm sensing we are already going back to default – that's what the system does to us. I think we should get back to the forward thinking [that the national and local lockdowns and the bursting bubbles of the period had spurred]. It was exciting when we came back, but now we're 'back on track' with more of the same.
>
> (Mary Ann Cooper, Federation Headteacher, Bushey Primary Education Federation, focus group – primary educators, 5 May 2021)

And she was supported, some months later, by an experienced inclusion-focused educational professional, who works across Cooper's two-school federation:

> This term teachers are stressed and pressured. They haven't been able to process, to seek to reconnect with children over the last two years. To bring back children a little bit stronger. They've been told to 'get back to normal', and get back now. 'We're coming in to check, we shall be monitoring you, there will be visits and Ofsted' and that's an awful lot. We haven't had the time and the space to decide on our 'COVID-Keeps'.
>
> (Helen Shirley, Pastoral Lead, Bushey Primary Education Federation, research interview, October 2021)

In part, this reversion was driven by a political and public desire to illustrate, sometimes in spite of the evidence, that 'things' were returning to normal, that the long road from lockdown was nearing completion; illustrating that all was back to normal in schools played a key part in this narrative. This, though, did not necessarily help school leaders on the ground:

I don't think it's been helpful for people outside of the system to think we're back to normal, because we're not back to normal.

(Allyson Dobson, Headteacher, Dalkeith High School, Dalkeith and President, School Leaders Scotland, research interview, 13 October 2021)

But, of course, there was no 'back to normal' for our new starters. Those starting out in lockdown did not have the anchorage point of previous practice to be pulled towards. The freshness of perspective that this gives this particular cadre of parents, education professionals and governance volunteers ought to be a resource on which schooling systems draw, whatever their particular circumstances, as they navigate the long road from lockdown.

System and school leadership in light of lockdown: A sustainable challenge?

It is something of an understatement, albeit an understatement of the blindingly obvious, to say that COVID-19 has been a chastening and traumatising experience for school leaders, not just in the UK but the world over. In England, this has impacted on both Headship retention and Headship recruitment, as is illustrated in Figure 8.3, Figure 8.4 and Figure 8.5, which draw on a recent study of Headteachers' wellbeing and aspirations by the National Association of Headteachers (NAHT, 2021).

Virtually all of the school leaders involved in the research undertaken for this book and for *Lessons from Lockdown* describe the responsibility of leadership during the pandemic as the most challenging experience they have faced. It has been in varying degrees disorienting, exciting and exhausting. The sheer complexity of the multiple challenges that revealed themselves on a day-to-day basis are crystallised in the following statements from these Headteachers who have participated in the focus groups convened for each book:

	'Likely or very likely to recommend Headship as a career goal'	'Unlikely or very unlikely to recommend Headship as a career goal'	'Neutral'
2020	47%	32%	21%
2021	30%	47%	23%

Figure 8.3 Recommending headship as a career choice (2020–21).

	Those not aspiring to Headship
2016	40%
2020	46%
2021	53%

Figure 8.4 Those not aspiring to headship (2016–21).

Health and wellbeing indicator	2020	2021
Impact on the quality and / or quantity of sleep	83%	88%
Increased worry, fear or stress about my job	72%	83%
Negative impact on the quality of my family life or personal life	77%	80%
Inadequate time for exercise / physical activity	69%	75%
Negative impact on my mental health	62%	75%
Reduction in time spent with family / friends	72%	74%
Negative impact on my physical health	46%	59%

Figure 8.5 Percentage of school leaders reporting negative health or wellbeing indicators as a direct result of their role (2020–21).

There was no break from the March lockdown until the summer GCSEs. We had health and safety, track and trace, bubbles, anxious students, anxious staff, anxious parents – not a bright term. Government directives, media information … .

(Kathleen McGillycuddy, Principal, Broadoak Academy, Weston-super-Mare, focus group – secondary educators, 13 May 2021)

We went from being strategic to [being] very operational, tactical sometimes, day-by-day. Each day we were faced with 'What today?', 'How do we carry on planning?'. [How do we] keep everyone enthusiastic?' One of the other things that was really important was to really work on communication with parents – that confidence had to be there.

(Steve Mills, Headteacher, Whitehill Junior School, Hertfordshire, focus group – primary educators, 5 May 2021)

Coming back in September, [we'd done] lots of work in August and September – lessons from the first lockdown. We thought we were back on track, then we had five members of staff that had contracted COVID. We started to have an understanding of a future lockdown happening. It really stretched our capacity and we didn't have enough staff cover, so the Senior Leadership Team were doing a lot of the teaching. We were being cautious about [who] should come in – everyone felt a bit reactionary. We had to make decisions very quickly. We had to look at the scenario of bubbles closing down, so [that] we were ready for the next lockdown. We had [to have] a plan about remote learning … .

> (Mary Ann Cooper, Federation Headteacher, Bushey
> Primary Education Federation, focus group – primary
> educators, 5 May 2021)

As school leaders, the mental health side of supporting staff is a real challenge and you can never do enough for them. I would like more guidance for leaders at the sharp end with staff to get that right.

> (David Miller, Headteacher, Pebble Brook School,
> Buckinghamshire, focus group – SEND and
> inclusion specialists, 30 June 2021)

For me it became very important to really think about purpose, more than ever. Why are we doing what we are doing? Then, whatever happens [as] guidance changes, there will be a core value driving us. I asked the leadership team to see the humanity in everything – we were going through trauma. We had difficult conversations – what if somebody didn't want to come into school? We didn't judge, we accommodated. These were the things that kept me focused.

> (Daniel Kerbel, Headteacher, Grange Primary School,
> Harrow, focus group – primary educators, 5 April 2021)

During the course of the pandemic, school leaders have been much more than simply the leaders of their schools; they have been community leaders, advisers to parents, information hubs, technological innovators, bereavement counsellors, social workers and much more. And every responsibility that they have had to fulfil 'externally', to pupils and to parents and carers, has had to be performed internally, supporting staff with their own vulnerabilities and anxieties, many of them parents or the carers of parents, while managing staff rooms that often sprung vacancies as another bubble burst, another test returned a 'positive' result, or, during Spring and Summer 2021, another phone pinged during the so-called 'ping-demic' of that period.

Of course, it might be reasonably contended that Heads and their senior colleagues always carry these multiple loads – that the ability to carry these burdens, and to do so over a number of years, day in and day out, while retaining a dignified smile, whatever the circumstance, and to do so while navigating the range of compliance pressures detailed earlier – defines whether an individual has the intellect, adaptability, emotional literacy, physical capacity and personal resilience for the role.

But history will reveal how different the nature of leadership has necessarily been during this period; different not because of its substance but because of its intensity and because the pre-pandemic certainties (about what constitutes a vulnerable student, a disadvantaged family, or an anxious staff member) no longer hold. In bringing long-hidden disparities and inequalities into plain sight, COVID has not just rendered these issues visible. It has reminded us of the scale of the schooling challenge, and just how much we expect of our school leaders.

Summary

Given the statistics on Headship recruitment and retention set out above, we need urgently to ponder how sustainable current models of school leadership are, and to ask whether the solution lies merely in the provision of better support networks (as, in the short term, it surely must) or in a more substantive re-design of the role itself, something that we begin to suggest in our discussion of 'Next Steps' at the close of this book, and which we explore substantively with school leaders in the final text in this trilogy, *Reschooling Society After Lockdown* (Routledge, forthcoming).

Recommendations

8.1 Policymakers and system leaders ought to pivot the range of educational agencies that they oversee or lead away from compliance and towards development, such that the creativity sparked by the pandemic is captured and developed in post-lockdown landscapes.

8.2 With specific regard to the inspectorate in England, policymakers ought to explore the kind of developmental focus discussed in *Lessons from Lockdown*, possibly reframing and rebranding Ofsted as an 'Office for School Development'.

8.3 The Department for Education in England, and equivalent departments and agencies elsewhere, ought to commission research with 'lockdown starters' – those in the school workforce, governors, parents and pupils who have started in education, or in a new educational phase during lockdown – so as to reveal the specifics of their experience and insights.

8.4 At every level, the potential impact on the retention of education professionals in general, and school leaders in particular, ought to be guiding consideration in the framing of schooling policy.

8.5 System leaders, school leaders, those involved in school governance and educational researchers need to collaborate so as to provide a much richer understanding of leadership and governance in multi-school settings, identifying how and where this works well, and where it does not.

Personalising learning for all   9

Utilising E-tech and bringing SEND strategies into the mainstream

We have been here before: in English schools, the language of personalising learning first came to the fore in the early New Labour years, years founded on Prime Minister Tony Blair's promise to focus on three policy priorities: 'Education, Education, Education' and much championed by one of New Labour's then-rising stars, David Miliband.

UK-based readers of a certain age – a significant number of whom now occupy key roles in school and system leadership – will remember a plethora of initiatives that emerged during this period, some more successful than others and some more enduring, although – as in other areas of public policy – it is not always the successful initiatives that endure. Sure Start (and the associated network of Children's Centres), the National Literacy and Numeracy Strategies (and the daily Literacy and Numeracy Hours that accompanied these strategies in the primary classroom), Excellence in Cities, Extended and 'Full-Service' Schools, Citizenship Education, Lifelong Learning, Every Child Matters, Specialist Schools and Academies, and a range of reforms to the curriculum and qualifications infrastructure (not all pulling in the same direction) emerged, or enjoyed a particular prominence, during this period, as did the idea of 'personalised learning'.

At the time the author was privy to a joke circulating in policy circles that nobody at the Department for Education (or the Department for Education

DOI: 10.4324/9781003204824-9

and Skills as it then was and the Department for Children, Schools and Families as it was shortly to become) knew what personalised learning was, but everybody knew that it was expected to feature in every policy paper or presentation. With the experience of lockdown in hand, the concept may now be more widely understood and definitions agreed upon, but for a number of figures involved in the UK's Teaching and Learning Research Programme, it remained ambiguous, in spite of its political popularity, leading them to speculate that:

> Perhaps Personalised Learning can satisfy the aspiration of both political parties to provide more 'choice' in public services? Perhaps it can galvanise professional energies in schools through its focus on learners and learning, and produce a step change in the quality of educational provision? Perhaps it can help to transform the experience of disadvantaged children, as suggested in 'Every Child Matters' (DfES, 2003). Perhaps it is one of the new 'evidence-based' government initiatives? Perhaps it strikes a chord with the electorate in terms of what they want from a modern education service, and from public services more widely?
>
> (Pollard and James, 2004)

Today, aided by the lockdown-assisted maturation of Ed-Tech, a range of emergent pedagogies and the effective use of Teaching Assistants, we are beginning to see the re-emergence of personalisation and its growing influence on teaching and learning in mainstream schools. For one group of often marginalised practitioners, though, personalisation has long been at the heart of their practice.

SEND strategies and pedagogies, and the personalisation of learning

SEND (Special Educational Needs and Disabilities) practitioners have always used the kind of methodologies that are increasingly being framed around a narrative of personalisation. The work of the SEND Coordinator – and their team where they are sufficiently resourced to have one – is intrinsically personal in its nature; it is focused around, or mindful of, a particular (or 'special') learning need or a cluster of these, sometimes involving withdrawal from a class but increasingly delivered in a mainstream classroom and often through a Teaching Assistant working with a specific pupil or a small group of pupils.

One reason for giving greater status and time to SEND methodologies is, of course, the profound impact that the pandemic is likely to have had on the most vulnerable children, whatever the original source of this vulnerability, and whether this vulnerability has preceded, been deepened by, or been caused by the pandemic:

> The whole issue of our more vulnerable children, whether that is through special educational needs or whatever, in the pandemic, is a story we have not really told. Those children have had a really difficult time and we need to be ready to give them every support we can as soon as we can when they get back, because many of them have suffered more than most.
>
> (Collins, 2021)

Perhaps, given the need to understand the stories of these children and young people – and in spite of the concurrent social spacing-driven move to teaching in rows – some elements of the pedagogical pendulum swung significantly towards SEND-informed and SEND-inspired practice during lockdown. For this reason, we offer, at the close of this chapter, a specific recommendation that:

> At every level, policymakers and shapers, system, school, curriculum and pastoral leaders, and those involved in initial and continuing teacher education need to give far more attention to SEND pedagogies, if the aspiration of a more personalised schooling experience is to be delivered for all.

To some degree, this might be at odds with some fashions in current educational practice, notably those that focus on the utilisation of so-called 'zero-tolerance' behaviour strategies and those that give a central place to the development of subject knowledge, as epitomised in the examination reforms developed during Michael Gove's tenure as England's Secretary of State for Education, and articulated in subsequent reforms to the inspection framework for English schools introduced in September 2019, and updated in July 2021 and 2022.

Zero-tolerance behaviour strategies have never sat easily with those who work most closely with the young people on whom such strategies are enacted – the young people who make up the exclusion statistics periodically issued by schools – or amongst those educational leaders who favour the kind of attachment-aware and trauma-informed approaches discussed at some length in *Lessons from Lockdown*, and now coming to the fore as schools grapple with the challenges of addressing the wellbeing needs of students. For critics, the problem with zero-tolerance approaches might be summarised thus:

> The behaviourist approach – zero tolerance and rewards and sanctions – only looks at behaviour, rather than deeper causes. We chucked it out of the window ten years ago and began to look at underlying emotions, rather than symptoms. Kindness, restorative practice and strong relationships underpin the culture of everything we do.
> (Dave Whitaker, Director of Learning, Wellspring Academy Trust: Whitaker, 2021)

Zero-tolerance approaches are especially unpopular with those who work with a particular subset who are significantly over-represented in these statistics: those young people with particular histories of early childhood trauma, and those young people who reside, or who have resided in the care system, young people whose vulnerabilities are often masked by behaviours that schools can, understandably, find challenging:

> Young people with physical disabilities are easy to see and understand. When young people have suffered from trauma and inconsistent care at a young age, they have strong emotional needs that are not so obvious to the eye. They don't trust adults well because their needs have not met by the care-giver. For them, life is like being in shark-infested waters. We can't see anything, but the smallest trigger could see their bodies go into crisis and automatic fight-or-flight mode.
> (Ann Marie Oliver, Associate Principal, Springwell Leeds: Cited in Whitaker, 2021)

Research by the charity Adoption UK (Adoption UK, 2017, 2019; 2021) reveals just how disproportionately one cohort of children – those adopted from care – are likely to feel one consequence of zero-tolerance approaches: exclusion from school, something that, doubtless, contributes to the comparatively poor qualification outcomes achieved by these young people at age 16. These children are twenty times more likely to be excluded from school and, at both primary (elementary) and secondary (high school) level, do approximately half as well as their non-adoptive, non-care-experienced peers.

Likewise, the rise of the focus on subject knowledge in current educational practice in English schools poses particular challenges for those who work with those young people with special educational needs or disabilities, or who are otherwise vulnerable. However, the same framework, with its new focus on matters of student and staff wellbeing might offer a rebalancing that can be of benefit not just to those somehow defined as 'vulnerable' but to all learners, because it requires a new level of personalisation if it is to be delivered, and one often underused or misused component in the school workforce might have a key role to play.

Teaching Assistants and curriculum personalisation

Over the past thirty or so years, Teaching Assistants (TAs) have become one of the mainstays of staffing structures in English schools. However, the roles ascribed to TAs have at times aroused the suspicions of some in the profession, and the teaching unions in particular, one prominent teachers' leader earning a furious backlash from within and beyond the profession after being quoted in the *TES* as equating Teaching Assistants with 'pig-ignorant peasants' (Slater and Dean, 2001). Nigel de Gruchy, the NASUWT General Secretary, denied that this was his intention, asserting that he had legitimately been concerned at the potential of substituting professionally qualified teachers with less qualified and underpaid colleagues, but his clarification hardly corrected the initial impression:

> I said you could not have pig-ignorant peasants supervising classes, but you needed people of good education with appropriate training.
>
> (Cited in Garner, 2002)

Teaching Assistants (the appointment of which gathered pace during the New Labour years, notably during the tenure of Estelle Morris as Education Secretary whose focus on 'workforce remodelling' so concerned de Gruchy) now make up 28 per cent of the school workforce in England and 35 per cent in primary settings (Webster, 2021). In primary schools, classes often have an 'attached' TA, but they are also used extensively (and increasingly) to support identified students with particular needs across all phases.

However, the impact of the employment of Teaching Assistants on educational outcomes remains contested, and the effectiveness of their use, and their productive input to the teaching process, is a frequent source of interest for the school inspectorate. In this regard, a recent study funded by the Education Endowment Foundation led by Rob Webster at the University College London Institute of Education (Webster, 2021) sheds new light on how to, and how not to, best use Teaching Assistants, with Webster contending that:

The lack of agreement and clarity about their specific purpose in the education machine means that teachers and school leaders often overlook and undervalue their contributions. It also leads to this vital part of the school system not being utilised in the most effective ways.

(Webster, 2021)

Claiming that Teaching Assistants are 'virtually invisible' to policymakers, Webster cites the current drive to overhaul initial and continuing teacher education and the introduction of the Early Career Framework for those starting out in the profession, and asks:

Where do TAs fit into this drive? Where is the comparable professional development and progression for them?

Pointing (critically) to the recent suggestion from the school inspectorate that TAs, in his words, 'need subject-specific training in order to be useful in the classroom', Webster rejects the notion of the Teaching Assistant as 'proxy teacher' (the very role that had originally sparked the suspicion of the teaching unions), especially when used to 'support children who have the greatest difficulty in accessing learning'; this, he contends is 'understandable but it has become problematic'. Instead, Webster and his team suggest that the answer lies in:

… repurposing the everyday opportunities TAs have for extended interaction with pupils. Instead of replacing the teacher in an instructional capacity, we recast them as scaffolding experts, supporting pupils to engage in learning and develop the skills to manage their own learning.

In such an approach, Webster is proposing a methodology that amounts to personalisation, defined by a form of supported autonomy which gives dignity to the learner and fosters independence, rather than a dependency that risks contributing to the visible and social exclusion of those in receipt of the support. For him, the prize is clear:

It's the build-up of this independence that underpins better learning. You cannot teach independence but you can provide small, safe opportunities in which pupils can experience it and be in full control of their learning. And TAs are key to taking this practice to scale.

Rather than being attached to specific learners 'like velcro', the vision presented is of a mobile TA triaging need and supplementing rather than replacing (or impersonating) the teacher in the process. For Webster, such an approach is focused on 'the development of pupils' "non-academic skills"', rather than on the reiteration of subject knowledge introduced by the teacher. In short, it is about building these young people's preparedness to learn and their sense of individual wellbeing. And, as they become reacquainted with classrooms and navigate their personally distinctive long roads from lockdown, 'these young people' are likely to constitute a larger and more diverse component of the population of each school and every class. In this context, attaching particular TAs, velcro-like, to particular children, often defined as having some kind of 'special' educational need – less than effective and socially excluding, according to Webster – is likely to become impractical in the post-COVID classroom, as the numbers needing this kind of support grow.

This growth is not, in the main, because more children are returning to school with newly recognised, COVID-induced 'Special Needs'; it is because their very different experiences of the pandemic and their journeys through varying periods as 'lockdown strugglers', 'lockdown survivors' and 'lockdown thrivers', to use the typology outlined in *Lessons from Lockdown*, will need a swathe of intensely personalised pedagogies. One size probably never did fit all – witness the socially patterned disparities that characterised developed education systems in the UK, the US, across Europe and elsewhere pre-pandemic – post-lockdown, it certainly will not.

The lost children of lockdown?

A month after most students in schools in England, Wales and Northern Ireland returned to school in September 2021, the launch of a Commission on Young Lives was announced. Hosted by the Oasis Charitable Trust (established by Baptist Minister Steve Chalke and which houses one of the UK's larger academy school groups) and led by the former Children's Commissioner for England, Anne Longfield, one of its first acts was to draw attention to the 'disappearance' of approximately 135,000 children from school rolls – children who had simply not returned for the Autumn Term, variously described as the 'lost children' or the 'ghost children' of COVID (Griffiths and Das, 2021).

The Commission had initially focused on the involvement of young people in gang culture and 'county lines' activity, the practice whereby vulnerable young people are recruited by those involved in the distribution of drugs in major cities to act as carriers of supplies destined for those overseeing subsequent distribution in market towns and rural and coastal areas. Perhaps unsurprisingly, Longfield concentrated on the potential role of these 'lost' or 'ghost' children in such networks. Traditionally, there

Experience	Percentage
Prisoners who had regularly played truant or 'skipped' school	59
Prisoners who had been suspended or temporarily excluded from school	63
Prisoners who had been expelled or temporarily excluded from school	42
Prisoners who reported that they had left full-time education by age 14	25
Prisoners who stated that they had been taken into care at some point in their childhood or who had lived with foster parents for a period	24
Prisoners who stated they had experienced emotional, physical, or sexual abuse as a child	29
Prisoners who stated they had observed violence as a child	41
Prisoners who reported having family members who were convicted of a non-motoring criminal offence	37
Prisoners who reported having a family member with an alcohol problem	18
Prisoners who reported having a family member with a drug problem	14

Figure 9.1 Educational participation, childhood experience, family background and incarceration.
Source: Williams, Papadopoulou and Booth, 2012.

has been a strong association between those young people excluded from school and engagement in criminal activity and, as Figure 9.1 illustrates, an appraisal of the prison population reveals the commonality of back stories characterised by exclusion from school, the early curtailment of schooling and a troubled family background, or some combination of these factors.

Chalke and Longfield were concerned that lockdown would provide a fertile ground for the accentuation of such trends, with increasing numbers of those newly rendered 'vulnerable' through their experience of lockdown drawn into criminal activity. Unsurprisingly, the level of 'disappearance' seemed to confirm their hypothesis, with Chalke commenting:

> We are not just risking a lost generation. We are watching it happen.
>
> (Griffiths and Shanti, 2021)

Longfield added:

> These are kids who, if we don't get them back to school, will have diminished life chances and job opportunities.

The comments were attributed to Chalke and Longfield in an article that included references to proposals for a longer school day and Saturday opening and cited the recently appointed Education Secretary, Nadhim Zahawi, calling for a return to pre-pandemic practice, but suggesting the picture might not be as bleak as Longfield and her colleagues suggest:

> My priority is to make sure children are in school and back to face-to-face learning. That's the best place for them and so it's fantastic to see more than 91 per cent of them back in the classroom with their teachers and friends, compared to 87 per cent this time last year.

This 'back to the future' analysis is one we have been critical of throughout these pages and in *Lessons from Lockdown*; as such, it uncritically romanticises the success of such schooling prior to the pandemic. The children that Chalke and Longfield (both of whom have dedicated much of their professional lives to seeking to improve educational outcomes for children from disadvantaged settings) are most concerned about, and who are most likely to figure highly amongst the 'disappeared', are those who were routinely amongst the least successful in pre-pandemic schooling against any plausible measure – attendance, exclusion, attainment, participation in extracurricular or student voice activity – and in almost any modern mass-schooling system, as the data offered in Chapter 1 makes clear. To reiterate, this is not a call for deschooling or a criticism of educational professionals, nor is it to ignore the very real safeguarding concerns that must emerge when children 'disappear' from the landscape. Rather, it is a call to think differently about an education system and, in particular, a system of secondary (or high) schooling designed in the nineteenth and early and mid-twentieth century, and struggling to meet the challenges it is now facing as we move towards the middle decades of the twenty-first century, challenges made visible and accentuated by the pandemic, but not *caused* by it. To get children into schools, which will continue to have a key socialisation role whatever their educational impact, is vital, but it remains wholly insufficient.

For most children, attendance at school may be a prerequisite for much of their learning, but attendance alone is not a guarantee that learning *will* take place, nor is absence from the school site a guarantee that learning *will not* take place. As Scottish Headteacher Campbell Hornell puts it:

> The students haven't learned what they would have learned but they've learned different things and they've learned a lot in terms of their ability to use Google Classroom and Google Meet … There's a myth that just because students are present physically in the building, they're engaged – they're actually actively listening and thinking and considering. We've all had, as leaders in schools, teachers that we were more worried about than others – although they maybe had thirty kids in their class, they didn't necessarily have thirty kids that were learning. It's the kind of simplistic approach of folk that haven't been involved in the system – that just because kids haven't physically been there, they've not been learning. They've just been learning and taking their learning forward in different ways and that's certainly the way that we've approached and I know a lot of my peers have approached it in that way. We need to build on the good things that have happened and the positive things.
>
> (Campbell Hornell, Headteacher, Lasswade High School, Bonnyrigg, research interview, 19 October 2021)

Against this background – given the variety of learning experiences that children have had across the period ushered in by the pandemic – to refer to these young people as forming a 'lost', 'ghost', or 'disappeared' generation, as Chalke and Longfield do, is to add to the language of deficit that we have been so critical of in these pages.

Shifting the lens from 'lost learning' to 'learning disruption'

In this context, we need a paradigm shift – a shift that might be framed as one that takes us from 'lost learning' to one of 'learning disruption'.

Sinead Harmey and Gemma Moss and their colleagues at University College London Institute of Education (Harmey and Moss, 2021) have done much to highlight the utility of approaches based around learning disruption rather than lost learning, not just in the rapidly emergent sphere of Lockdown Studies but in areas such as the use of Teaching Assistants and in the provision of support for those with Special Educational Needs and

Disabilities. As such, the analysis that they offer has much to contribute to approaches that place personalisation and SEND pedagogies at their core, as we do here. For Harmey and Moss:

> In an attempt to anticipate and mitigate the effect of school closures, researchers and policymakers have turned to the learning loss literature, research that estimates the effect of summer holidays on academic achievement. However, school closures due to COVID-19 have taken place under very different conditions, making the utility of such a literature debateable.
>
> (Harmey and Moss, 2021)

Thus, while they acknowledge that learning loss is likely to have taken place, and that 'children of higher-income parents are more likely to have better access to technology and spend more time on home learning', they are more cautious than authors wedded to the 'lost learning' analysis epitomised by contemporaneous commentators such as Chalke and Longfield (cited above), and Elliot Major, Eyles and Machin (cited in our earlier discussion of 'catch-up' in Chapter 7); Harmey and Moss remind us that while:

> There is evidence to suggest that academic achievement has been impacted (Blainey and Hannay, 2021; Educational Endowment Foundation, 2021) … losses equated to less than two months and reduced over time. Other researchers have found that the impact is not as detrimental as was predicted earlier in the pandemic (Johnson, Kuhfeld and Tarasawa, 2021).

For this reason, they argue that:

> A methodology used to quantify learning losses, while attractive to policymakers seeking to allocate funds for recovery (DfE, 2020a), is of far less direct use to schools, and may indeed lead to an overemphasis on the need to 'catch-up fast' that a closer look at the research evidence does not warrant.

Thus, Harmey and Moss contend that an analysis of the literature on learning disruption is more useful because of the focus on 'how systems have responded to other unprecedented events like natural disasters'. Within this paradigm, rather than that offered by 'lost learning', there is surely value in their observation that:

During the COVID-19 pandemic, the circumstances under which schools closed and subsequently reopened are more akin to the conditions under which education had to operate during other pandemics (e.g. SARS) or weather-related events, such as Hurricane Katrina or the Christchurch earthquakes (see Harmey and Moss, 2021). As with COVID-19, these closures were sudden and unplanned; communities were put under immense pressure by the events themselves, and the return to school was characterised by further 'aftershocks' in the form of ongoing local outbreaks and public health restrictions.

In other words, they call for a focus on how learning is impacted when schooling systems encounter a system-shock, such as that delivered by COVID-19, and use the evidence from previous system-shocks to illustrate that the impact cannot simply be extrapolated from a measurement of the number of days out of school. Why? Perhaps there are three reasons. First, learning 'lost' during school holidays is lost during a period when there is no expectation that, or provision for, most students to continue learning during this period. Second, learning is not, in any case, linear in the way that formal curriculum structures (which have many advantages) like the National Curriculum in England tend to suggest. Third, and critically, different learners learn in different ways and make different rates of progress at different points in time. In terms of 'lost' learning, each student's experience is different, and some may not have experienced loss at all. Underlying the broader analysis offered by those committed to the 'lost learning' analysis is the assumption that pre-lockdown schooling worked for every young person and was enjoyed by every young person. To reiterate, it is no criticism of teachers, school leaders, or educational professionals, or the concept of mass schooling itself, to concede that it doesn't work as well for some as for others, or to point out that it works with greater (or lesser) effectiveness for particular learners at particular points in time.

The challenge for teachers is to support and manage the progress for each individual student over time, whether or not they are struggling at a particular point in time and whether they are somebody who makes the kind of steady, linear progress set out in the textbook or programme of study, somebody who appears to struggle earlier in a course but then submits (later than is good for their teacher's nerves), an assignment that demonstrates that they 'get it', or somebody who appears to 'drift' through the course, and then puts in incredible 'shift' in the terms leading up to the examination. Such variety amounts to a clarion call for personalisation. One size does not fit all and, in terms of COVID-19, one loss has not been experienced by all.

In their analysis, Harmey and Moss make a further vital point. They argue that if the curriculum, rather than being used as a body of content to be 'covered', is seen as a therapeutic vehicle that enables young people to explore their multiple and different experiences of the pandemic, it can play a positive role in *pastoral* terms. Thus, if the curriculum is utilised in this way, it can support the social and emotional recovery of both children and educational professionals. However, if it is seen as (just) a body of content to be caught up, it is likely to add to the stresses on the mental wellbeing of at least some teachers and students.

Personalisation, blended provision and 'Next Generation Schooling'

Absence from school during the pandemic, either as a result of enforced closures through lockdowns, be these local or national, as a result of the need to 'shield', because of infection, through the bursting of classroom and year-group bubbles, or because of the anxiety that the pandemic has imbued in some parents and children, ought always to be a cause for concern. As detailed in the preceding section, the reality that a significant number of children are somehow 'lost' to the system (or, at least, invisible to it) ought to ring a series of alarm bells: about safeguarding, about equity, about access to other children and the vital socialisation role that this plays, and, of course, about the effectiveness of the education system itself, and the experience that it offers certain children and young people. Indeed, if significant numbers of young people and their families are 'opting out' of schooling as a means of education, this ought to concern us as much as the drifting of others into the kinds of criminal activity that Longfield and Chalke point to.

For this reason, we need to turn our attention to why they might be doing so, what might lure them back, and what post-COVID schooling might look like or rather, given the exhaustion of the profession and the craving for stability identified in Chapter 6, what schooling could look like if some of the often teacher-driven innovations of this tumultuous period were to weave their way, gradually yet strategically over the course of the second quarter of this century into our schooling. In no small part, the technology we now have access to – and which, during the pandemic, a significant proportion of teachers became increasingly adept and confident at using – is likely to play a major role in the evolution of what we might call 'Next Generation Schooling'.

As detailed in *Lessons from Lockdown*, the first national lockdown was especially challenging for school leaders, steering their schools and communities through wholly uncharted waters, whatever the sector; it is worth recalling the words of these heads cited earlier:

> Back in the middle of March, in that final week, my overriding feeling was that people were voting with their feet. We lost control of the situation; we are trying to get ahead of situations constantly, because we're leaders. That's what leaders do. We anticipate. We study. We plan ... but for the first time, really, and I've been teaching for 32 years now in London, we weren't ahead of the game.
>
> (Daniel Coyle, Headteacher, Newman Catholic College, Brent,
> research interview, 17 August 2020)

> It was kind of ... just step-by-step. Have we talked about this? Have we looked at this aspect of it, or that? [What about children] moving around the fields? How are we going to sanitise and clean? What does a deep-clean really look like? I was also looking at other schools. So there [were] ... conversations with other heads ... I don't think any school has got a piece of work that they can say that's all their own; you know, I've taken bits and pieces from other schools.
>
> (Mary Ann Cooper, Federation Headteacher, Bushey Primary
> Education Federation, research interview, 27 August 2020)

> This is all completely new. We're all making it up as we go along but, because of this, we've lost the fear of getting it wrong. That's liberating.
>
> (Dave Miller, Headteacher, Pebble Brook School,
> Buckinghamshire, focus group – special education
> and alternative provision, 8 July 2020)

The presumption, though, in the late Spring and early Summer of 2020, was that this was an essentially temporary affair, with a common refrain about yearning for a return to less digital days, or to put it in the words of one school leader cited in *Lessons from Lockdown*, a desire to 'put the computers back in the cupboard'. We have seen how politicians and other key influencers have clung to these kind of sentiments throughout the pandemic, and it was a sentiment that, in some classrooms, sustained into the academic year that followed:

> There was at least a proportion of teachers who were a little bit 'head in the sand' coming back to school in September – 'Phew, thank God that's over, we're done with the pandemic.' Part of my role [at this

stage] was [to say to] people 'Let's get ready, whatever it looks like now it's not going to look like this in November.'

(Alistair Hamill, Senior Leader and Head of Geography,
Lurgan College, Armagh, focus group – EdTech
experts and ambassadors, 20 June 2021)

And, of course, it didn't, but Hamill won't feel his work is complete until digital practice is embraced alongside established classroom pedagogies, on its own merit:

> Eventually there will come a point where teachers will say thank goodness we're past that, we'll pack that technology away, we don't need it anymore, unless we convince them the technology adds value.

The local lockdowns and bursting bubbles of Autumn and early Winter 2020, with the arrival of a vaccine (never mind its roll-out in the UK, the US and across the EU) still some weeks off, put paid to the aspirations of those who had assumed the pandemic would gradually disappear in the rear-view mirror, with the realisation that COVID was no temporary blip, and that laptops, tablets and phones (and access to them) would remain as important as exercise books had been, for the foreseeable future, and maybe beyond. It was during Autumn Term that a far greater number of schools began to embrace technology and capture a glimpse of its potential for the longer term, enabled in part by the emergence of a new staffroom hero: the sometimes self-proclaimed, geek:

> I'm an English teacher by trade but when lockdown happened my geek and nerd side came in handy and I got qualified as an Apple educator, Google educator and a Microsoft educator for staff.

(Ciara Hunter, Head of English and Integration Coordinator,
Fort Hill Integrated College, Lisburn, focus group – Northern
Ireland-based educators, 8 June 2021)

> I'm a Biology teacher in a girls' grammar school in East Belfast. I've been there for over 20 years now. I was made Head of Biology this time last year and I'm a timetabler and [school] governor and it's nice to be here with fellow geeks. I wouldn't say I was enthusiastic about what has happened over the last year but I think the geeks have come into their own.

(Jacqueline Gray, Head of Biology and School Governor,
Strathearn School, East Belfast, focus group –
Northern Ireland-based educators, 8 June 2021)

Just as another sometimes marginalised group, UK-based physical education teachers, had enjoyed and embraced their enhanced status in the run-up to the London Olympic and Paralympic Games, the 'geeks' were ready for their long-awaited (and long-overdue) moment in the sun (and it ought to be more than that), and the parallel was worth sharing with participants in one especially digitally literate community of teachers:

> One thing that you're drawing my attention to that I haven't picked up to this degree before is the way that events like this change the status of particular groups of staff in schools. I did a lot of work in London 2012 and I don't know if there are any PE teachers in the room but PE teachers have often felt that they are not accorded the status that they ought to be and suddenly, with the advent of London 2012, they became the most important people in the school and we did a CPD session for them – the only session I've ever been to where the last person to arrive was 45 minutes early – they were so keen to be part of it and also to kind of grab the moment.
>
> (Tony Breslin, author and focus group facilitator, focus group – Northern Ireland-based educators, 8 June 2021)

Unfortunately, within months of the London Games, and in one of the political own goals of the period, the then Secretary of State for Education, Michael Gove, announced the removal of funding for locally based School Sport Partnerships. Harnessing the energy of a newly digital-friendly community of education professionals will be vital if digitally enabled 'Next Generation Schooling' is to become a reality and, in so doing, become a vehicle for the personalisation of learning. The progress made in this area during the course and immediate aftermath of the pandemic must amount to more than a 'place in the sun' for the group of staffroom innovators who have done so much to provide the merest glimpse of what one aspect of Next Generation Schooling might look like. One digital learning leader articulates the extent of this progress at her own school:

> I'm the Digital Learning Lead and a part of the senior team at a school in County Tyrone and just like the others it's been a fantastic year for us to really build on the IT skills across the whole school and what I found is, as staff, we have experienced what it's like to teach with basically no technology, but also to teach fully with technology – with all the online learning. It brings a great perspective, because now we can see the best of both worlds going forward. I think all staff in the

school now have a greater appreciation of where technology works and where it is most effective and it's a really strong base for our school going forwards now.

> (Danielle McKirnan, Digital Learning and Communication Lead, St Patrick's Academy, Dungannon, County Tyrone, focus group – Northern Ireland-based educators, 8 June 2021)

McKirnan's emphasis about the 'best of both worlds' is key to finding agreement on the proper role for technology in the classrooms of the future, and in Next Generation Schooling. It is to this that we now turn.

The second school lockdown: EdTech comes of age

Sweeping generalisations about the need to 'get back into the classroom' did not abate during the second substantive lockdown, and often these were coupled with similar generalisations about the limitations of on-screen learning. Let's be clear, a key tenet of the analysis offered in these pages is the vital social role of schools and the importance of sociability to the learning process, whether this takes the form of the structured group work of the collaborative classroom, the intense personal competition of the 100-metre race, one-to-one and small group tutoring, whether this be of the child with a Special Educational Need or the young person being coached through the university application process, or the bustle of the corridor, staircase and dining hall queue. In bringing young people together on a particular site with education professionals, schools perform the core aspect of their educational function, informally and formally. But this does not mean that any form of teaching that does not take this form is either necessarily poorer or a lesser alternative. Such binaries are unhelpful and deny the multiple ways in which online and onsite learning can *complement* each other, the former enhancing rather than displacing the latter.

They are also unhelpful because they assume that learners will always choose onsite over online learning. However, as we have illustrated elsewhere in these pages, classroom learning – the most common form of onsite learning – does not work for a significant number of students, and does not work in every subject for most students, and this is as much the case for adult learners as for school students. The experience of actor Agnes O'Casey, who burst, fresh from drama school, onto UK television screens in the BBC series *Ridley Road* as the research for this book was been undertaken in Autumn 2021, is a case in point:

> In my third (final) year, I really lost confidence. I was daydreaming about getting on a plane and leaving. Then came the pandemic and our graduation showcase was cancelled. In some ways, that saved me, because I think I was spiralling … I didn't have to go into a big, strange, intimidating building and wait in reception. I just opened my laptop in my own student bedroom.
>
> (Hastings, 2021)

The point is that for some learners – some defined as having Special Educational Needs, and some not – and some families, classrooms and schools amount to environments that are 'big, strange (and) intimidating'.

In terms of 'COVID-Keeps', one technologically enabled, pandemic-inspired innovation is the online parents' evening, something that has proved as popular with parents as with teachers and school leaders, as this experienced Head notes:

> I guess if you spoke to people about parents evenings – I was amazed, the feedback from parents was overwhelmingly that they want to keep remote parents evenings.
>
> (Richard Lord, Headteacher, The Deepings School, Peterborough, research interview, 7 October 2021)

And their reasoning is not difficult to understand. Consider the pre-pandemic reality, especially in secondary settings: parents of Year 7 students (the first year of secondary schooling in England), arrive, hurriedly from a working day for their first parents' evening on a school site that they often feel is as daunting in its size and scale as it was to their children a term or so earlier. They are typically armed with a sheet listing a series of back-to-back five- or ten-minute appointments, and either make their way around a series of desks in a drafty hall, or set out around the school campus, dashing from one appointment to another in departmentally based rooms, inevitably running late, not because of their own time-keeping but because the parent three spaces ahead in the queue for English or Maths or Spanish overruns their allotted time. If their child has settled well to secondary school, the succession of good news stories make up for the pain of the delayed appointments; if they have not, the misery of one meeting piled upon another builds up and, too often, after Year Eight, these parents are the least likely to return, with teachers lamenting 'We never see the parents we need to see!'

During lockdown, parents had no such woes; they got home, made a cup of tea and switched on their laptop, clicking into five- or six-minute meetings (much like Agnes O'Casey in her Zoom audition), governed by the kind of 'countdown' timer that features in TV quiz shows, and embarked on a conversation with each of their child's teachers that was short, focused (because of the limited time) and sometimes cut a little short. Apparently, some parents were even able to participate during their commute home from work:

> [On 'COVID-Keeps'] I would say virtual parent evenings – mum on the train on the way home from work, dad at home, ten minutes, no delay because someone's running late with a 'book look' … that will definitely stay. I think parents and teachers will be up for that.
> (Steve Mills, Headteacher, Whitehill Junior School, Hitchin, Hertfordshire, focus group – primary educators, 14 July 2021)

There are, of course, two objections to the online model: first, by definition, it excludes the unconnected and the disconnected, and second, the clipped, time-limited conversation does not allow the depth that particular pupils, parents, or circumstances will need. The counter is straightforward: either through their absence or through the demonstrable inability to explore key issues in the time allocated in the online session, the need for a replacement or supplementary and longer, deeper exploratory discussion is identified. Again, the mantra is clear, for parents' meetings and so many other aspects of schooling post-lockdown: the future is not online or onsite – it is blended, it is both. The online parents' evening becomes a kind of maintenance check that all who have an internet connection are expected to undertake; the onsite session becomes an occasional supplementary to address a behavioural concern, a special need, or a particular choice, perhaps of a course or focused around progression to college or university, or a particular career.

The growth in digital literacy, between the first and second lockdowns in particular, has also opened up other opportunities for blended practice in other contexts. On the one hand, the child who has the misfortune of an enforced absence because of, for instance, a lack of mobility arising from a sporting injury, may have their learning supported through online provision. On the other hand, shorter absences, arising from a bug or a sprain, might be supported in the same way. Of course, the optimal choice here is to 'get into school', but absence from school no longer has to mean absence from *schooling*, and that ought to be celebrated and utilised as a benefit.

Finally, and to return to the reality that conventional pre-pandemic schooling never has worked for every young person and, for far more, there are periods during their school careers when it is less than optimal, the growth of digital literacy across and beyond the teaching profession and

	2017–18	2018–19
Overall absence	4.8%	4.7%
Authorised absence	3.5%	3.3%
Unauthorised absence	1.4%	1.4%
Persistent absence	10.9%	11.2%

Figure 9.2 Absence from school in England in the immediate pre-pandemic years.
Source: Department for Education, 2020c.

the emergence of a plethora of learning-focused online platforms opens up the possibility of a significantly or substantively digitally delivered education as an option for these young people and their families. That there is a cohort of children and young people – some of whom are controversially defined as 'school refusers' – who might benefit from such an option is undeniable, given the ongoing challenge of persistent absence, a challenge that has declined marginally but not significantly in spite of a range of policy initiatives to address this, many of which have taken an essentially penal approach to parents and guardians. Assessing the level of absence during the pandemic is incredibly difficult, but the immediate pre-pandemic picture is set out in Figure 9.2.

And when these statistics are combined with those relating to the year-on-year (and sharply accelerating) growth in the popularity in home-schooling (or 'elective home education' as it is more formally termed), as set out in Figure 9.3, the need to support part- or full-time schooling outside of school becomes clear.

Moreover, given the expectation that the post-lockdown landscape is likely to feature increased levels of home-schooling, as some parents and some students opt for it because of their *positive* experience during lockdown, the possibility of home-based schooling that is less isolated and better connected to the mainstream emerges.

In the long term, the further development, maturation and popularity of both support networks for those educating their children at home, and of EdTech in its various manifestations is likely to generate a plethora of varied and differently focused models, where some learners mix home-based learning, workplace-based learning (in the upper secondary or high school years) and 'conventional' school-based learning. Again, the future is not online or onsite, but blended – an environment in which, for most teachers and learners, schooling remains a substantial

	Number of home-educated children
2018	52, 770 *Based on the annual survey conducted by the Office of the Schools Adjudicator*
2019	60, 544 (an increase of 15% on 2018 but less than 1% of the school population) *Based on the annual survey conducted by the Office of the Schools Adjudicator*
2021	81,200 *Based on an estimate by the Association of Directors of Children's Services*

Figure 9.3 The growing popularity of home-schooling in the UK.
Source: Long and Danechi, 2022.

part of the mix, and probably the core and substantive element, but not the sole one.

Technology, curricular breadth and school leadership

Of course, in the short term, these initially hybrid and increasingly blended models for the delivery of schooling are likely to send a shiver down the spine of some more traditionally minded school leaders and governors.

But the efficiencies that might derive from such approaches are already becoming evident for some school leaders. Richard Lord, Headteacher at the Deepings School in Peterborough, reflects on a range of COVID-inspired changes that are, for him, potential COVID-Keeps, a number of which relate to movement around school and efficiencies in the use of curriculum time:

> We've kept [the new] double lessons – we can't call them 'bubbles' but we've now got a Key Stage 3 and a Key Stage 4 zone. I'm a language teacher and I've worked in a German school and the tutor group pretty much stays in that room and the teacher moves, they'll go out for practical subjects and that's what we've done here. So general purpose classrooms, by year group, English, History, PSHE, [where] the teacher moves to the pupils … and like lots of schools, and lots of primary schools anyway, when the students come in, if they have PE, they wear their PE kit – we'll maintain that. If we have issues in PE they're probably in the changing rooms, the lost time of changing … .
>
> (Richard Lord, Headteacher, The Deepings School,
> Peterborough, research interview, 7 October 2021)

Lord sees comparable advantages with the delivery of a broad and balanced curriculum, especially for students in the upper years of secondary (or 'high') school, where 'minority' subjects might be delivered to online groups drawn from various schools across a Multi-Academy Trust or a Local Authority by expert teachers based at specific schools within the group.

This kind of inter-school collaboration has always enabled the delivery of curriculum breadth in the upper years of the secondary phase and notably the sixth form, with various locally based networks of schools forming consortia to facilitate this, but pupil movement between schools is often a complex matter and inevitably raises safeguarding concerns, even when the schools and colleges concerned are located within walking distance or a short bus ride of each other. In addition, it has never been an option for those in rural schools, single-school communities, or the kind of geographically dispersed Multi-Academy Trust in which Lord's school sits.

Technological connectivity offers the opportunity to address these concerns, and introducing teachers and learners to their peers in comparable settings opens up opportunities not just for students' learning but for the further professional development of the schools workforce. The digital upskilling of this workforce during lockdown has the potential to be an enduring and enriching legacy of the virus, but only if two conditions are fulfilled: first, that this new digital literacy is nurtured and developed for the long term by school and system leaders, and second, that internet connectivity is elevated to a level of priority by political leaders that places it on the same level as the supply of electricity, fuel, gas and water, and ensures that families have access to the devices that enable them to make use of this.

Summary

The increasing range of options presented by EdTech – as technology and educator confidence in this technology develop alongside each other – and the broader shift towards personalised and cohort-specific pedagogies that draw heavily on long-established and emergent practice amongst SEND specialists and those working in alternative provision settings – provides a glimpse into what the post-lockdown classroom, and 'Next Generation Schooling' more broadly, could look like.

A consequence of these developments ought to be a much more bespoke, less clunky approach to the identification of need, and so-called 'special' needs in particular, such that these are seen as much more fluid definitions that do not generate the fixed labels that so often 'land' on students least equipped to carry them. 'Vulnerability' is a case in point: in the first schooling lockdown, the term acted as a barrier to the engagement of exactly those children and young people that teachers and school and system leaders were seeking to attract into schools that had remained partially open, and for whom lockdown *often* posed the greatest challenge. As we have seen, for some, to send one's child or children into school during this period amounted to a public declaration of vulnerability, one that rested not with the child but *on* the family as a whole. Not for the first time, a clumsy attempt at inclusion, initiated by national policymakers served to reinforce the very exclusion that it had sought to address.

However, during the course of the emergence of the local lockdowns and bursting bubbles of Summer and Autumn 2020 and thereafter, this 'fixed' definition became much more fluid and nuanced in its application. Why? Because many school leaders began to take greater ownership of the definition of 'vulnerability'; because a significant number of parents and guardians, perhaps fearful of the challenges posed by another bout of home-schooling, were more accepting of this wider, more fluid definition; because of the revealing of a whole range of 'new' vulnerabilities – sometimes prompted by the pandemic and sometimes long-standing but exposed by it. Together, these factors served to increase the number of students in schooling during the second schooling lockdown in the early months of 2021.

The pandemic has undoubtedly driven anxiety and generated needs amongst those of school age, but it has also revealed anxieties and needs that pre-pandemic schooling had inadvertently conspired to conceal. For this reason, catastrophising the educational impact of the pandemic and assuming the universality of this impact on any one cohort, as those focused entirely on models of 'lost learning' have tended to, lets pre-pandemic schooling off the hook and is likely to generate policy and practice responses focused on narrow notions of *curricular* catch-up that compound some of these anxieties amongst those they are seeking to help. It also burdens those who have had their schooling impacted by lockdown with a series of deficit labels that are likely to contribute to their exclusion.

In contrast, a focus on the lessons emerging from the 'learning disruption' literature may offer a better starting point for post-lockdown responses, especially at the level of the classroom. If this is combined with the kind of personalisation outlined in this chapter, facilitated in part by greater digital literacy amongst educators, by SEND-inspired practice, by curriculum content that enables children and young people to process their multiple and often profound experiences of the pandemic, and by the more effective use of Teaching Assistants, the result is likely to be better outcomes for the children and young people that sit at the heart of our concerns.

Recommendations

9.1 At every level, policymakers and shapers, system, school, curriculum and pastoral leaders, and those involved in initial and continuing teacher education need to give far more attention to SEND pedagogies, if the aspiration of a more personalised schooling experience is to be delivered for all.

9.2 Policymakers, system and school leaders, and classroom practitioners and all who support them should seek to make sense of the educational impact of COVID-19 less in terms of 'lost learning' and more in terms of 'learning disruption', a lens that enables practitioners to escape a deficit narrative that risks generating negative self-fulfilling prophecies, system-wide, but which will weigh heaviest on the shoulders of those already suffering the greatest disadvantage.

9.3 Urgent attention ought to be given by policymakers as to how excellence in digital pedagogy is identified and shared system-wide, where possible on a peer-to-peer basis, and supported by national efforts to develop and accredit the growing digital literacy of educational professionals.

9.4 Partnerships formed during lockdown with technology suppliers and those in related industries need to be developed as part of a national Every Child Connected initiative, possibly part-funded through a levy on the profits of the so-called 'tech-giants'.

9.5 Policymakers, at national, regional and local level, need to elevate Internet connectivity and device access to the same level as that pertaining to access to electricity, fuel, gas and water.

Autumn's return

10

A testing time (and term) for all

As educational professionals, parents and pupils in England, Wales, and Northern Ireland enjoyed the Bank Holiday weekend at the close of August 2021, their thoughts began to turn to the school year ahead. Pupils in Scotland had already returned to their classrooms the best part of a couple of weeks earlier.

Of course, there was the ordinary stuff of a new school year: the newly polished classroom and assembly hall floors, the tidied lawns of the school site, the checking and renewal of uniforms and PE kit and the last-minute parental name-tagging of these, the purchase of core texts – especially for those about to embark on the run-up to public examinations – and the annual family talks, invariably stressing the importance of the particular year ahead. But, for the second September in a row, there were also the procedures and protocols of COVID; many of the practices around spacing and bubbles were thankfully either cast aside or scaled back, but testing, and its quasi-industrial delivery, was to remain a feature of the Autumn return, a reality that had already brought the following reactions from Scottish school leaders:

> I think, when we came back in August, what we noticed immediately was the kids were probably a wee bit more fed up from the point of view that Scottish students had been wearing face coverings for quite a while … We were bringing in three times as many as we [had been the previous term] and that kind of indicated immediately that these kids were less switched on, for want of a better word. In the

DOI: 10.4324/9781003204824-10

classes, once they get [the masks] they comply, [and] they're still good at sanitising and wiping things down. They're less good at the minor things like one-way systems … .

(Campbell Hornell, Headteacher, Lasswade High School, Bonnyrigg, research interview, 22 October 2021)

The year has been a real rollercoaster. I think looking back on it – it was a year of underlying anxiety of what the next thing was we were going to have to face. We faced lots of different things … from coming back in and all of the mitigations that had to be in place [to the] uncertainty of the exam systems, whether or not the exams were going to take place; then that switch during [the second] lockdown to online learning, and to then coming back into school, having the senior pupils back in, then finding out the Scottish Government wanted the [younger secondary] pupils back in education – we hadn't anticipated that. That was 'gee whizz, don't know how we're going to do that!', but we did … .

(Allyson Dobson, Headteacher, Dalkeith High School, Midlothian, research interview, 14 October 2021)

Dobson, who is also a recent past president of School Leaders Scotland, continues:

I think it's only now that school leaders are really realising just what that was like. I'm referencing school leaders, I don't think it was just school leaders that had that underlying anxiety, families experienced that and of course young people and we're now seeing that manifest itself in terms of really high levels of mental health concerns with young people in a way that we anticipated was going to happen … .

The testing, and an ongoing debate about the vaccination of children and young people, ensued against a background of the remaining shadow of the virus. By this stage, two-thirds of UK adults had been 'double-jabbed' (the vaccine had been delivered through two injections, applied approximately two months apart), but vaccination rates varied significantly between different demographics, as illustrated in Figure 10.1, which draws on a study led by Charlotte Hannagh Gaughan and colleagues (Gaughan et al., 2022), and published in the *Journal of Public Health* in early 2022.

The tragedy of the human exodus from Afghanistan had largely kept COVID off the front pages in the preceding weeks, but the August Bank Holiday weekend's newspapers still managed to convey concerns about

Age standardised vaccination rate by ethnicity and sex

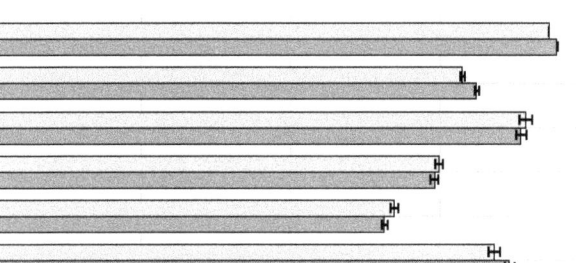
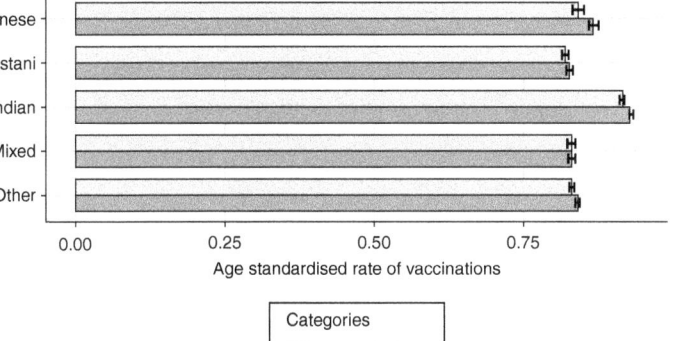

Age standardised vaccination rate by ethnicity and country of birth

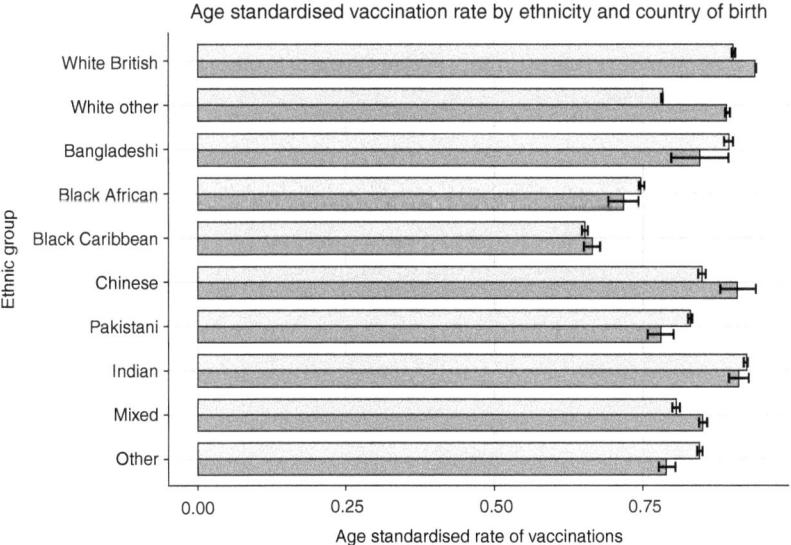

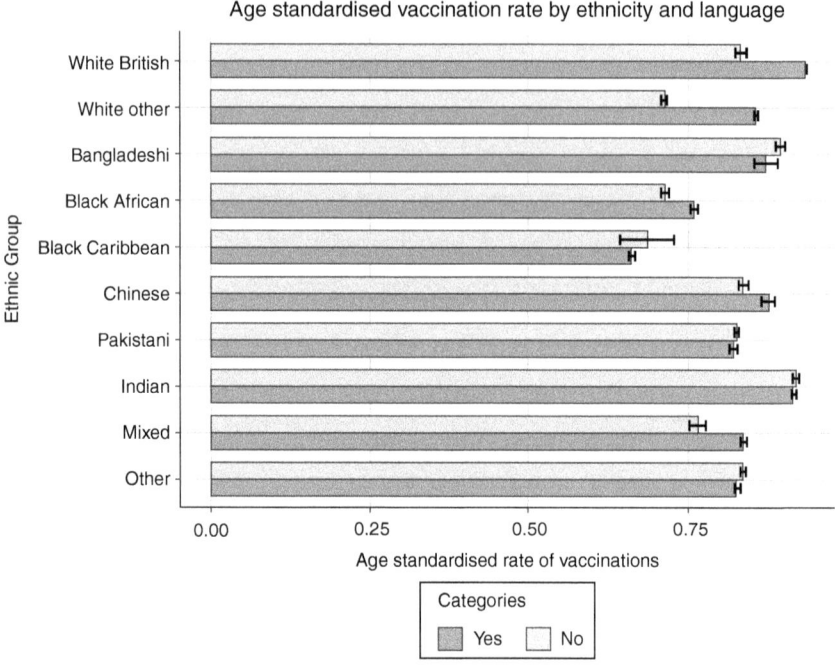

Figure 10.1 Comparative vaccination rates amongst those from minority ethnic groups by gender, country of birth and language spoken.
Source: Gaughan et al., 2022.

the prevalence of the virus. Thus, citing data from the Office for National Statistics, *The Observer* reported that:

> Coronavirus infections in England are now 26 times the levels that were experienced this time last year (and) the reopening of schools in England this week (is) likely to trigger further rises in COVID cases – with more to follow when students return to colleges and universities.
>
> (McKie, 2021)

As a result, McKie continued:

> Pressure is mounting on the Joint Committee on Vaccination and Immunisation to approve the deployment of booster jabs for vulnerable people and the extension of vaccinations to most 12 to 15 year olds.

And, quoting Mike Tildesley, a member of the Scientific Pandemic Influenza Group on Modelling, he added:

Schools are no more risky than any other environment where people mix in close proximity to one another. But it's what happens around schools – when schools go back, parents tend to return to work and people mix in other environments. If we have high levels of vaccination across younger age groups, it should provide both direct and indirect protection.

This is a point that has been made at various points in this text and in *Lessons from Lockdown*. Schools are, of course, primarily, educational institutions, or at least that is their founding and stated public purpose. However, in reality, they perform a range of additional functions, often without acknowledgement, usually without credit: providing childcare to enable adult employment and to provide respite from full-time parenting (more recently augmented by the need to home-school), enabling children to both socialise and be socialised, acting as networking hubs for parents and community facilities for neighbourhoods. Thus, the full or partial closing of schools and their reopening serves as a barometer of normality, and adults in all sorts of settings adjust their behaviour accordingly. Certainly, in the first UK lockdown back in March 2020, it was the closure of schools to the majority of children and young people that sent out the signal that 'this is serious!'

Subsequently, across the 18 months since March 2020, the debate had swung back and forth between assessments of the educational importance of schooling to children (the 'missing out' or 'lost learning' thesis explored in Chapter 7 and throughout the text) and the health risks of full reopening. More recently, also explored across this text and in Chapter 7, concerns around the educational impact of lockdown had been increasingly augmented by more nuanced and harder-to-measure but arguably more profound issues around the impact on the socialisation of children and young people, their personal development and their well-being.

During the first lockdown, the subsequent cautious, clunky and, ultimately, partial exit from it, and also during early Autumn 2020, critics of school closures had wondered why the closing of schools was necessary or whether the need for it was sufficiently evidenced, given that this was an illness that predominantly appeared to be vested on the elderly, had an apparently limited impact on educational professionals, as well as the apparent impact of school absence on children and young people. One group of academics, writing in the *British Medical Journal*, contended that:

> The overall risk to children and young people from Covid-19 is very small and hyper-inflammatory syndrome is extremely rare. Studies

are under way to gauge the effect of post-Covid syndrome among children.

Although school closures reduce the number of contacts children have, and may decrease transmission, a study of 12 million adults in the UK found no difference in the risk of death from Covid-19 in households with or without children. Only 3% of people aged over 65 live with children.

In-person learning increases teachers' exposure and might be expected to increase their risk of becoming infected, but accumulating evidence shows that teachers and school staff are not at higher risk of hospital admission or death from Covid-19 compared with other workers. Teacher absence because of confirmed Covid-19 in England was similar in primary and secondary schools in the autumn term.

> (Sarah J. Lewis, Professor of Molecular Epidemiology, Alasdair P.S. Munro, Senior Clinical Research Fellow, Paediatric Infectious Diseases, George Davey Smith, Professor of Clinical Epidemiology, Allyson M. Pollock, Professor of Public Health: Lewis et al., 2021)

Indeed, a similar point was often made about the broader lockdown strategy, as one long-standing friend of the author put it, in less academic language, in the late Spring of 2020:

> This is all b*****ks. Why would you stop a fit 25-year-old truck driver from working, when the number of people under 40 contracting the disease is absolutely miniscule, and most of them are fine? The damage to the economy and the impact in terms of isolation and people getting into debt with unpaid mortgages and the like is likely to be far greater in the long term than the immediate impact of the illness itself; at least for this group. It's nonsense, and we'll be paying for it for years.
>
> (Alan McMahon, Senior constructional professional, In conversation with the author, May 2020)

By late Summer 2021, the picture had changed drastically. First the so-called 'Kent' variant of the virus had produced a surge in the virus at the turn of the year, and its reach in terms of the age profile of those impacted, as recorded in Chapter 4, had proved significantly wider, and this was swiftly followed by a number of other variants, notably the 'Delta' variant, which by mid-Spring appeared to be the dominant strain, again seeming to reach far beyond the elderly and those thought to be conventionally medically 'vulnerable'.

And by the time schools returned in Scotland in August 2021, and across the UK the following month, the disease was not just impacting on young people; it was most prevalent in school-age children, and the fear was that schools might become incubators of the illness, with children, and the broader sense of normality that the reopening of schools had helped to usher in, serving as conduits for the onward spread of the illness to those more likely to succumb to it, rather than brushing it off in the manner that healthy children and fit young people still appeared able to.

As reported in Robert McKie's *Observer* front-page article of 29 August, cited earlier, the pressure on the Joint Committee on Vaccination and Immunisation to approve the deployment of booster jabs for vulnerable people and the extension of vaccinations to those in the age 12–15 group had been considerable but, meeting later that week, the committee came to the conclusion that:

> The assessment by the Joint Committee on Vaccination and Immunisation (JCVI) is that the health benefits from vaccination are marginally greater than the potential known harms. However, the margin of benefit is considered too small to support universal vaccination of healthy 12 to 15 year olds at this time.
>
> (Public Health England, 2021)

However, this did not bring what had been a multi-cornered debate to a close, with resistance coming from disparate quarters. Some rejected the notion of an extension of the vaccine to what amounted to the majority of secondary school pupils on the basis that it had been unsuccessfully trialled on the young and the long-term impacts were, therefore, unknown. Some viewed this as either an intrusion on the rights of parents, or, alternatively, on the rights of young people, while others opposed the extension simply because they formed part of a numerically declining but vociferous 'anti-vax' campaign. Some, following the Joint Committee, simply opposed the extension because the specifically health-related impacts on the children themselves were likely, as the committee had argued, to be marginal. Still others saw the vaccination of those in disadvantaged countries overseas as a better use of what they felt were surplus supplies, either from an ethical point of view, and/or because the virus was a global phenomenon. From this standpoint, the disproportionate use of vaccine supplies by so-called 'developed' countries amounted to an act of selfish and pointless stupidity. One of the longest-standing champions of vaccine-sharing had articulated this perspective in a newspaper article in April 2021, citing the 'political leadership' that the UK might exercise thorough its Presidency of the G7:

Vaccinating the whole world isn't just the morally right thing to do – it's in every nation's scientific, public health and economic self-interest. The shores Covid now rages upon may seem distant to some, but the reality is that so long as the virus continues to spread in other countries, it continues to be a threat to everyone. If we allow Covid to keep spreading (in other settings internationally), it will go on evolving, increasing the risk of new variants that could cross borders and evade vaccines and treatments. With global infections at an all-time high, this is a very real risk. We are playing with fire. The first vaccines cannot be the preserve of the rich …

If countries who can afford to share [vaccines] choose not to, this pandemic will drag on, resulting in more deaths, suffering and economic hardship. We're in danger of creating a fragmented, unequal world of haves and have-nots, where it will be far harder to come together and address the shared challenges of this century.

(Dr Jeremy Farrar, Director, Wellcome Trust: Farrar, 2021)

In spite of these multiple concerns and recurrent calls to share vaccine 'overstocks', support for a domestic extension remained evident. Government ministers, if we are to believe a torrent of press leaks, were both intent on a 'return to normality' and remained cautious and concerned by the type of statistics cited by McKie in his *Observer* piece. In short, they wanted to see vaccinations extended to cover this mid-secondary school cohort. Conveniently, the Joint Committee had left the door open for them to pursue the possibility of this kind of risk mitigation, and to do so with the scientists on board. The second paragraph of the Public Health England Press Release, which revealed the Joint Council's judgement, stated that:

It is not within the JCVI's remit to consider the wider societal impacts of vaccination, including educational benefits. The government may wish to seek further views on the wider societal and educational impacts from the Chief Medical Officers of the UK's 4 nations.

(Public Health England, 2021)

Despite the disparate arguments launched against childhood vaccination outlined above and the marginal health benefits likely to accrue to the young people themselves as outlined by the Joint Committee, ministers needed little further encouragement, and they found it, in any case, with developments north of the border: the reopening of schools in Scotland in August had been accompanied by a surge in cases and, assuming at least some measure of 'cause and effect', this, ministers and their advisers feared, might, in the absence of preventative action, be replicated UK-wide in due course.

Anything, they figured, that could subdue the growth of the virus during the Autumn might deliver a less pressurised Winter for a trepidatious, and one might assume still exhausted, National Health Service.

Perhaps for this reason, with the Autumn Term in England, Wales and Northern Ireland entering what, for some, was its first full week, the Chief Medical Officers for England, Wales, Scotland and Northern Ireland, writing in a joint communique to ministers in the four UK jurisdictions, advised the governments of each jurisdiction that the vaccine should be made *available* (but not compulsory) for those children and young people aged between 12 and 15. They arrived at their decision by starting with an acknowledgment of rationale taken by their colleagues on the Joint Committee:

> The COVID-19 Delta variant is highly infectious and very common, so the great majority of the unvaccinated will get COVID-19. In those aged 12 to 15, COVID-19 rarely, but occasionally, leads to serious illness, hospitalisation and even less commonly death. The risks of vaccination (mainly myocarditis) are also very rare. The absolute advantage to being vaccinated in this age group is therefore small ('marginal') in the view of the JCVI. On its own the view of the JCVI is that this advantage, whilst present, is insufficient to justify a universal offer in this age group. Accepting this advice, UK CMOs looked at wider public health benefits and risks of universal vaccination in this age group to determine if this shifts the risk-benefit either way. Of these, the most important in this age group was impact on education … The UK CMOs, in common with the clinical and wider public health community, consider education one of the most important drivers of improved public health and mental health.

And continued:

> Evidence from clinical and public health colleagues, general practice, child health and mental health consistently makes clear the massive impact that absent, or disrupted, face-to-face education has had on the welfare and mental health of many children and young people. This is despite remarkable efforts by parents and teachers to maintain education in the face of disruption.
>
> The negative impact has been especially great in areas of relative deprivation which have been particularly badly affected by COVID-19. The effects of missed or disrupted education are even more apparent

and enduring in these areas. The effects of disrupted education, or uncertainty, on mental health are well recognised. There can be life-long effects on health if extended disruption to education leads to reduced life chances.

Before concluding:

> UK CMOs judge that it is likely vaccination will help reduce trans-mission of COVID-19 in schools which are attended by children and young people aged 12 to 15 years. COVID-19 is a disease which can be very effectively transmitted by mass spreading events, especially with Delta variant. Having a significant proportion of pupils vaccinated is likely to reduce the probability of such events which are likely to cause local outbreaks in, or associated with, schools. They will also reduce the chance an individual child gets COVID-19. This means vaccination is likely to reduce (but not eliminate) education disruption … [We] therefore recommend on public health grounds that ministers extend the offer of universal vaccination with a first dose of Pfizer-BioNTech COVID-19 vaccine to all children and young people aged 12 to 15 not already covered by existing JCVI advice.
>
> (Chief Medical Officer (CMO) for England, Professor Christopher Whitty, CMO Northern Ireland, Sir Michael McBride, CMO Scotland, Dr Gregor Smith, CMO Wales, Dr Frank Atherton: Whitty et al., 2021)

Especially with the removal of the majority of the 'bubbling' arrangements described in Chapter 3, the contention was that suppressing the rise of the virus in schools was vital because it reduced the likelihood of future disruptions to schooling – disruptions that it was now accepted would have an impact both on the education of young people and their well-being – and reduced the effectiveness of children as conduits for COVID. Perhaps it was unsurprising, therefore, that those representing both school leaders and classroom teachers welcomed the move:

> We welcome the recommendation to offer coronavirus vaccinations to 12 to 15-year-olds as a vital step forward in reducing educational disruption and keeping these young people in the classroom. This is particularly important in light of recently published evidence from the SAGE modelling group which warned that it is highly likely that exponential increases in infections will be seen in school-attending age groups in the autumn term. It is crucial that everything possible is

done to prevent this from happening and to prevent attendance from once again unravelling.

We are conscious of the debate that has been raging over vaccinations, but it is vital to see this issue in the context of educational disruption. While the evidence is that children are less likely than older age groups to suffer severe symptoms as a result of catching Covid, the damage caused by disrupted schooling is very real and very apparent, both in terms of learning loss and in the impact on mental health and wellbeing. Children from disadvantaged backgrounds have been particularly badly affected by the pandemic. We must put a stop to this disruption.

(Geoff Barton, General Secretary, Association of School and
College Leaders, press release, 13 September 2021)

The decision by the Chief Medical Officers to encourage the take up of vaccinations by 12–15 year olds will be another tool to help pupils sustain their access to education throughout the autumn and winter ... While vaccination is not needed generally to protect children and young people from severe illness, it will suppress transmission, but it is not the only story. There is still an important role for other mitigations, particularly ventilation and face coverings. So far [the] Government [has] been slow to roll out the promised CO_2 monitors which will at least help schools and colleges to identify where ventilation is poor.

(Dr Mary Bousted, Joint General Secretary, National Education
Union: Bousted, 2021c)

In addition to the National Education Union's call for the extension of vaccinations to sit within a broader battery of measures, this welcome came with a further vital caveat, one which articulated the concerns of school leaders and the wider profession about having to oversee a medical rather than educational process, and a highly politicised one at that:

It is essential that the government immediately confirms that the process surrounding vaccinations will be run and overseen entirely by the appropriate medical teams. Where parents have questions, including about important matters such as consent, these must be handled by those same medical teams. There must be no delay in confirming this, otherwise school leaders will be put in an impossible position of facing questions to which they simply do not have the answers.

> We are hearing reports of threatening letters being sent to school leaders urging them not to allow their school buildings to be used for vaccination, but these letters are misguided – it is not school leaders' decision to make, it is the government's and the NHS. School leaders are being put in an invidious position, stuck between government policy and public opinion, all while simply working to carry out their national duty.
>
> Schools must be allowed to focus on their core task of providing education to pupils. We would expect detailed guidance to be published by [the] government clarifying all this without delay.
>
> (Paul Whiteman, General Secretary, National Association of
> Head Teachers, press release, 13 September 2021)

> It is an NHS responsibility to carry out vaccinations on school sites, though schools are used to being sites for the vaccination programme … it is incumbent on the Department for Education to make clear and usable procedures for the necessary parental consent.
>
> (Bousted, 2021c)

The following day, it was confirmed that the vaccine programme would also be extended to other cohorts, with the announcement that the over-50s would receive booster jabs. Some months earlier as the Delta variant gained momentum, England's then Health and Social Care Secretary, Matt Hancock, spoke of 'a race between the virus and the vaccine'. August and September 2021 had offered key glimpses of post-lockdown normality: the reopening of schools had been accompanied by the reopening of sports stadia, theatres and nightclubs, and the implication was that the virus was winning the race. According to a January 2022 'Fact Check' in the *British Medical Journal*, those vaccinated were less likely to get the disease, less likely to pass it on, and less likely, if they were infected, to become seriously ill and hospitalised:

> The UK Health Security Agency (UKHSA) has recently started to report hospital admissions—not just those to intensive care—alongside vaccination status. The latest figures show that in the week to 29 December 2021 a total of 815 people with confirmed Omicron infection were admitted from an emergency department to hospitals in England. Of these, 74% had not had three doses of vaccine—including 25% (206) who were unvaccinated, 6% (49) who had received one dose, and 43% (352) who had received two doses. Twenty three percent (189) had received a booster dose, and the remainder were

unknown or had had their first dose less than three weeks ago. Further analysis by the agency has concluded that unvaccinated adults are as much as eight times more likely to be admitted to hospital than those who have been vaccinated and that booster doses are 88% effective at preventing hospital admission.

('Fact Check', *British Medical Journal*, 4 January 2022)

But messages remained mixed. On the day that the Chief Medical Officers published their recommendation on extending the vaccine to those aged between 11 and 15, and the day before the government confirmed that it had also accepted advice on the provision of booster jabs for all over-50s, England's new Secretary of State for Health and Social Care, Sajid Javid, stood down an earlier decision to roll out 'Vaccination Passports' for nightclubbers and attendees at other large social gatherings, a strategy that his colleagues had appeared committed to until hours before his announcement, and which his peers in other parts of the UK would subsequently go ahead with. Just over a year previously, one of Professor Whitty's colleagues on the government's Scientific Advisory Group for Emergencies (SAGE), Professor Graham Medley, cited in *Lessons from Lockdown*, had spoken of a choice between pubs and schools that the virus had forced upon us:

> I think we're in a situation whereby most people think that opening schools is a priority for the health and well-being of children and that when we do that we are going to reconnect lots of households. And so actually, closing some of the other networks, some of the other activities [that connect households] may well be required to enable us to open schools. It might come down to a question of which do you trade off against each other and then that's a matter of prioritising: do we think pubs are more important than schools?
>
> (Breslin, 2021a: 120–121)

Thirteen months on, the choice may not have been between pubs and schools, but a similar range of choices seemed to remain in play, albeit in the background and retained as part of what Prime Minister Boris Johnson described as a Plan B or C, should the virus take off and hospitalisations rise.

And as if to emphasise this scenario, newspapers and bulletins the following day, 15 September, led with dire warnings about the likelihood of a new surge in hospitalisations within a month or so, the possible need to bring back the aforementioned 'passports' later in the Autumn, that mask-wearing might yet return in several settings, that home-working was still very much on the agenda, and that 'bubbles' might, indeed, make a return to schools. Two of the experts that, in the UK, had become the face of the illness, were unambiguous in their messaging:

> People still need to take this disease very seriously.
> (Professor Chris Whitty, Chief Medical Officer,
> England, cited in Sparrow, 2021)

> When you make a move [against the virus], you have to go earlier than you want to and harder than you want to. It is important that measures are early enough and significant enough.
> (Sir Patrick Vallance, Chief Scientist, cited in
> Groves and Stevens, 2021)

Less than three weeks later, the Head at Watford Grammar School for Boys, who has been cited earlier in these pages and in *Lessons from Lockdown*, penned a letter to parents that underlined the point that Professor Whitty had made:

> Dear Parents and Guardians
>
> A return to normality has been very much appreciated by the school community and until recently, the number of positive Covid cases at Watford Boys has been relatively low. We have been fortunate. However, it was always likely that we would follow the pattern of many other schools in having to adapt as case numbers rise.
>
> Schools have been asked to develop plans in the event that the number of cases suggests that transmission may be taking place in the school setting. The threshold for implementing such plans is defined as:
>
> - 5 children, pupils, students or staff, who are likely to have mixed closely, test positive for COVID-19 within a 10-day period; or
> - 10% of children, pupils, students or staff who are likely to have mixed closely test positive for COVID-19 within a 10-day period.
>
> The first of the two threshold criteria has been met in Year 8 and in Year 11.
>
> This means that we will now require all students and staff to wear face coverings in communal indoor spaces and students in Years 8 and Year 11 should wear face coverings in school at all times when they

are indoors, including lessons. This arrangement will start from 12th October and will apply until the end of the half term.

We will continue to work with the Hertfordshire Public Health Team to adapt these plans as required. In the meantime, please reinforce the need for good personal hygiene and encourage your son to take the regular lateral flow tests – these have been invaluable as tools for identifying cases at an earlier stage.

Ian Cooksey
Headmaster

(Watford Grammar School for Boys, Letter to
parents and guardians, 11 October 2021)

The following day, a similar note landed in the inbox of parents and governors at a junior school a couple of miles away, with the almost invariably upbeat Head, Mary Ann Cooper, another school leader who we have cited elsewhere in these pages and in *Lessons from Lockdown*, lamenting that:

Over the last two weeks, there has been an increase in the number of cases in Year Six and with another confirmed case yesterday evening it took the numbers over the threshold within our risk assessment [at which point we] advise Public Health England and the Local Authority.

(Mary Ann Cooper, Federation Headteacher, Bushey Primary
Education Federation, email to Governors, 12 October 2021)

She continues:

[As a consequence] we have … cancelled the Year 6 trip to [a local secondary school] this afternoon for the local schools' Cross Country Run Competition and we have an event at Watford Colosseum [with] our Choir tomorrow afternoon, which we will also have to possibly cancel. Once again, it is hard for staff when we have to let down and disappoint our children at such short notice.

The emotional impact on staff of teaching and leading during such a period of uncertainty – especially against a backdrop of 'lockdown fatigue' and a yearning to re-introduce some of the curriculum enrichments that do so much to enhance day-to-day schooling – should not be underestimated. And with a much-needed half-term break less than a fortnight away, the threat to both family holidays (the prospect of which had begun to emerge again, at least for those who could afford them) and to staff-recuperation posed by the possibility of having to self-isolate during the upcoming break posed an additional worry. These concerns were underlined in the empathetic conclusion of a note to staff from Deputy Head, Shelley Bleau, pasted into Cooper's message to governors:

> This isn't about panic. It is an insight into how things will now work, and this way of working may be with us for some time. Let's support, reassure and help each other through calm and sensible mitigation, and ensure we all have a half term holiday where we are not confined to barracks. Thanks everyone.
>
> (Shelley Bleau, Federation Deputy Headteacher. Bushey Primary Education Federation, email to staff, 12 October 2021)

It was, indeed, proving to be a long road from lockdown, but one key player had departed the stage weeks earlier. On the afternoon of 15 September, the smartphones of policy watchers across the country pinged with the news that the Prime Minister was in the process of delivering a long-expected Cabinet reshuffle, one which pundits had envisaged would take place towards the end of the month. A second ping confirmed that Gavin Williamson, the gaff-prone Secretary of State for Education in England had been relieved of his duties, with his successor, the former and well-respected Vaccines Minister Nadhim Zahawi, duly announced later that evening.

The long-standing Schools Minister, Nick Gibb, who had first held the role under Michael Gove a decade previously, was also standing down, to be replaced by Robin Walker, a former aide to another ex-Secretary of State for Education, Nicky Morgan. For some education policy watchers, the end of Gibb's long association with the Department for Education was more significant than Williamson's departure in that many saw the former as both the guardian of the Gove legacy, and a relentlessly tough enforcer of the so-called 'standards' agenda.

But Williamson's departure grabbed the headlines – and a writer looking for a suitable chapter ending couldn't have hoped for a neater conclusion. Whatever the ultimate judgement on Williamson's tumultuous tenure – for which he was knighted in Spring 2022 – across an equally tumultuous and uniquely challenging period, journalists and researchers alike knew that, with this particular departing Cabinet Minister, they had lost a gift that just kept giving. Right to the very end.

Summary

In more settled times, the departure of Gavin Williamson may have heralded the opportunity for a post-lockdown reassessment of current educational practice in England. In truth, the political turmoil that was to bring a premature end to Boris Johnson's Premiership in the summer of 2022, has helped to scupper this, at least in the short term, with the revolving door at the Department of Education spinning at ever greater speeds. Nadhim Zahawi, Williamson's successor, who might have led such an appraisal, lasted ten or so months and was followed, in rapid succession, by Michelle Donelan and James Cleverley. We shall see whether Kit Malthouse, newly appointed as Education Secretary by the incoming Prime Minister Liz Truss, who takes up office in the week that the page proofs for this text are signed off, embraces such a challenge. Whatever, though, the political machinations, on the ground, the impact of COVID-19 will be long-standing and is likely itself to drive change, whatever the strategic leadership or direction offered by policymakers. As Senior Leader Shelley Bleau puts it above, whatever the system's leadership, in England, the UK or anywhere else, 'this way of working may be with us for some time.' The schooling 'system-shock' wrought by COVID will continue to be used as an opportunity to reflect on the effectiveness of pre-lockdown practice and the nature of future educational need.

For sure, individual schools will embrace different packages of 'COVID-Keeps' and some of these will, at least over time, be shared and become embedded system-wide. But the embracing of specific reforms on a piecemeal and school-by-school basis is not the same as strategic, planned, system-wide reform, to which the greatest barrier is not conservatism or complacency, but exhaustion and an over-zealous desire on the part of system leaders to establish the pre-lockdown markers of what has become educational normality in English schools: Ofsted, standardised testing towards the close of the primary phase, externally assessed examinations towards the close of the secondary phase, performance tables reflecting student outcomes at both levels, and the fulfilment of a range of re-established regulatory requirements, which system leaders were right to suspend during lockdown but would be wrong to rush the reintroduction of. Rather, schools need time to recuperate, repair and recover, and to get those other markers of educational normality back into place: assemblies, productions, trips, visiting speakers, after-school clubs, staff rooms and school gates that again flourish as *social* spaces. Well-being is organisational as well as individual, and one domain needs the other.

In short, if system leaders, governing boards and school leaders want to see a more deliberate approach to post-lockdown education reform, the priority must be to address the needs of actors at every level in the system – Heads, teachers, teaching assistants, support staff, children and their families – and the needs of the organisation itself, an exercise that is complex and one which needs time.

Recommendations

10.1 In the academic years after lockdown, system and school leaders will need to prioritise the well-being of children and staff at every level of practice.

10.2 If senior and middle leaders are to feel supported in prioritising well-being at school level, system leaders are likely to need to delay the reintroduction of a range of pre-lockdown performance measures and compliance requirements.

10.3 As well as addressing individual recovery, system leaders and school leaders need to focus on organisational recovery and well-being, if system-wide resilience is to be nurtured and developed.

10.4 System leaders, policymakers and school leaders need to resist the tendency to see the reintroduction of pre-lockdown performance measures and regulatory requirements as a marker of the return of normality itself.

10.5 Throughout this period, system leaders and those involved in functions such as inspection would be wise to focus on intelligence gathering, working in partnership with practitioners rather than rushing to judgements about their effectiveness at what remains a time best devoted to reflection and recovery.

Next steps

Leading schools out of lockdown

Just as this book started with a focus on the experience of school leaders in the establishment of 'bubble schools', it closes with their reflections on the 2020–21 academic year and the first term of 2021–22, the experience of beginning to lead schools out of lockdown, their hopes for the remainder of the academic year that lay ahead and their aspirations for the future of schooling – and learning – in the wake of the pandemic, a theme that we give initial consideration to here and which forms the core concern in the third text in this trilogy of lockdown studies, *Re-schooling Society after Lockdown*, which is set to be published in late 2023 or early 2024.

For the most part, media narratives over the 2020–21 academic year emphasised two things: the (undoubted) educational costs of lockdown, and the (false) universality of these. In short, the tale told has been one of monolithic educational armageddon. To repeat a phrase introduced early in this text and repeated at various points: no two children, no two families, no two schools and no two year groups have experienced the same lockdown. There is no singular lockdown experience. And the same can be said of school leaders and school governing boards. There is, though, one at least near-universal truth about educational practice during the lockdowns of 2020 and 2021, as articulated by this Northern Ireland-based Curriculum Leader, who while recognising the diversity of the focus group he found himself in, and which he had been instrumental in convening, picked out this common theme:

> The one thing that unites everyone here and what I've seen over the past year is that people have stepped up, not because someone has asked them to, but because it's the right thing to do. And as we've stepped

up, we've supported and helped each other. I've just come home from an earlier [Area] Learning Community meeting [a meeting of locally based school leaders and teachers] and it's just shown how much of a hunger there still is out there for us to learn from each other.

(Alistair Hammill, Curriculum Leader – Geography, Lurgan College, focus group – Northern Ireland-based educators, 8 June 2021)

Alongside an otherwise false universalism, these media narratives have also conveyed and amplified a nostalgia for practice prior to lockdown. As has been noted, I closed each of our focus groups and interview sessions by asking participants to reflect on practice immediately prior to the onslaught of the pandemic in February 2020 and to identify those things 'you can't wait to get back to' and those things 'you can't wait to leave behind'. I want to suggest that in education and in many other spheres, there has been an insufficient focus on the latter; instead, the past is a golden age of bustling shopping malls, busy, sociable workplaces, face-to-face GP appointments and crowded, happy city-centre coffee shops and bars.

There is, of course, an equally misleading representation of this pre-lockdown age, one of identical chain store-dominated malls, cramped, noisy workplaces reached only after tiresome commutes, GP waiting rooms where you are as likely to catch a cold as a cure, and soulless, corporate-owned coffee shops and bars devoid of individuality and, for that matter, distinctive beverages.

Unsurprisingly, ministers and headline writers alike, at various points across the period dominated by the pandemic, preferred the 'golden age' option and were keen to get back to this state of affairs. Thus, as 'Freedom Day', the day on which most COVID restrictions were initially lifted, in Summer 2021, the *Daily Mail* implored its readers to:

'Get back to the office, Rishi Sunak tells Britain amid fears over the economic impact of staying at home-- and young people missing out on career opportunities'

(Martin, 2021)

Later in the year, the then Prime Minister Boris Johnson was to use his Conservative Party conference speech to re-issue Sunak's summertime diktat, with the *Daily Mail* again happy to share the news:

PM will tell Britain to get back to work: Boris Johnson to use his Tory party conference speech to urge Britons to return to the office – amid growing confidence Covid will NOT spark another lockdown this winter.

(Groves, 2021)

In education, this translated into a desire for a return to face-to-face learning and the presentation of online approaches as the necessary poorer relation during a time of crisis. The response of then Education Secretary Gavin Williamson to the switch to online learning adopted by most Higher Education institutions across much of the 2020–21 academic year is a case in point:

> We do expect universities, unless there is an unprecedented situation, to be moving back to delivering lectures face-to-face … They are autonomous institutions. I don't have control over them, but I would expect universities to deliver a high quality teaching experience. If they are not delivering what students expect, they shouldn't be charging full fees.
>
> (Turner, 2021)

A month later, Williamson was to repeat the point in a speech to university vice-chancellors, at the *Universities UK* Annual Conference, in what would turn out to be one of his last interventions as Education Secretary:

> Above all students want the university experience to be the one they worked so hard for before COVID came along. We've all missed over the last few years, and students, I think they've missed the life on campus, the creative buzz they get, the thrill of discovering new friends, new ideas, new ways of seeing the world.

Warming to his theme, Williamson continued:

> Imagine trying to make sense of the subtleties of interpreting Chekov for the stage or carrying out complex molecular biology techniques over Zoom. I for one would need the full benefit of that in-person, world-class teaching that you and your members can rightly be so proud of.
>
> (Williamson, 2021c)

Press reports suggest his message was met with some disdain from this decidedly non-militant group of career academics – possibly because he delivered his criticism of online learning over the online meeting platform

Zoom. One online sub-editor couldn't resist the ironic tension between the means and the message, leading with the headline and byline:

> 'Gavin Williamson video calls uni bosses to tell them they must return to in-person teaching'
>> 'Do as I say, not as I do'
>
> (Shaw, 2021)

This nostalgia, and the resultant desire to get back to 'where we were', to 'get *back* to normal', carries a key risk: an insufficient focus on what the Hertfordshire-based governing body clerk Tracey Middleton, cited in the Preface to this book, terms 'COVID-Keeps', and, therefore, a lack of openness to the adoption for the long term of the many creative innovations developed during (and initially because of) the pandemic – a failure, in short, to learn and subsequently apply the *Lessons from Lockdown*.

This is not to champion online provision *over* face-to-face teaching or lecturing, short online parents' evening appointments over in-depth face-to-face discussions with teachers, or online conversations between subject leaders and link governors over traditional governor visits. It is to say that what started out as a package of pandemic-driven technologically-enabled adjustments may become complements to face-to-face practice, embedded into a 'new normal' *alongside* conventional, long-standing and highly valued face-to-face, onsite practice.

Thus, as we ponder next steps and seek to capture the creativity of the lockdown period, and the creativity of those involved in school and system leadership in particular, it is vital that the pull of pre-pandemic practice is not an uncritical and universal affair; the creativity of this period has both spawned and enabled new approaches to teaching and learning, new kinds of relationship between the home and the school, and a new empathy and respect for those who work in education, and a new status and prominence for digital practice. We owe it to our professionalism as educators, and to the children, young people and families that we support, to ensure that innovations in these and other areas of practice are not lost in a determination to return to 'normality', to go *back* to the future.

Let's start by exploring the potential of some of these innovations to become embedded in future practice, to become, as Middleton so adroitly puts it, 'COVID-Keeps'. Here, I offer not an exhaustive list (and it is for education professionals working in collaboration to construct context-sensitive lists of their own, not for a distant author to set them out in the manner of a prescribed and over-detailed curriculum), but a set of themes that appear to be prominent in the minds of those who have contributed to research that underpins this text and *Lessons from Lockdown*.

1. New approaches to teaching and learning
    The challenges of the pandemic have demanded new (or at least sub-stantively new for most schools) approaches to teaching and learning. On the one hand, these have been innovative and progressive, harnessing technology as never before. On the other hand, the need for social spa-cing has seen a move away from group and other forms of collabora-tive working in favour of teaching in rows, often at separate desks, the classroom morphing into a miniature version of the examination hall. Indeed, the irony that written examinations – the one area of school life that is intrinsically and necessarily always socially spaced – were can-celled, was not lost on some observers.

    Moreover, the distancing has not just been between one pupil and another, but between pupils and teachers, and between those children with identified needs and the teaching assistants and peripatetic tutors who work with them to address these needs. For those who favour didactic, instructional approaches the pandemic has provided a setting in which their favoured pedagogies can be trialled and assessed. However, it has also meant a concurrent shift away from those strategies that depend on closer contact between the educational professional and the pupil.

    In Chapter 7, we drew on the identified progress of some of those so-called 'vulnerable' children during the second substantive lockdown to make the case for greater curricular personalisation and the use of pedagogies often originally developed and role-modelled by SEND specialists. This distancing, if retained, would present a significant bar-rier to the delivery of such an aspiration.

2. A newly empathetic relationship between the home and the school
    To some degree, the period starting with the first lockdown in March 2020 and concluding with the first half-term break of the 2021–22 aca-demic year (as I drew the substantive primary research for this text to a close), is a tale not of 'lockdown' but of several different lockdowns, national and local, total and partial. Throughout this period, we have seen qualitative and substantive changes in the relationship between education professionals and those they serve – children and young people, and their families.

    The data from our focus groups and interviews seems to suggest that in the main, schools and families have not only built stronger relationships across the totality of this period, but the journey has not been unequivocally in a single direction. Much of the research for both this text and *Lessons from Lockdown* has pointed to a greater closeness between what the educationalist J.W.B. Douglas, one of the founding fathers of the Sociology of Education, termed simply as 'the home and the school' (Douglas, 1964). On this, the observation offered by Zak Jalil, Head of Sixth Form at the secondary school in North West London that I had attended as a pupil, remains illuminating and is worth repeating in full here:

> The most insightful part of this situation was phoning home of every student in my year group. In my previous role I knew the backgrounds of those in my form and believed I knew a lot about their home life. I was confident that I would be able to utilise this skill in my new role [across the] year group. I was naive. I called every single [sixth former's] home … numerous times during lockdown. I heard about the numbers of people living in a small space, I got to know their sleeping habits, I learnt about their families' work lives. I had conversations with students and their parent's or carers where they [felt] able to be vulnerable. I was told [about] family histories, their fears, their aspirations. I heard about the hobbies that they picked up, their views on the news. I was asked questions, I was told jokes, I was cried at. I thought that I knew my students well before this process, I now know that I had no idea … We have seen the human side of each other, and [I feel they will feel] more willing to come to me in future.
>
> (Zak Jalil, Head of Sixth Form, Newman Catholic
> College, Brent, written submission, 29 August 2020)

As always, though, the reality is complex and nuanced. This Headteacher reflects on having deeper relationships with many families but worries about the lower daily visibility that local and national lockdowns and bubble schooling have delivered:

> I think we know the families much better than before, I think we know the children better, [but] I think with some of the children and their families we haven't made the connections in the usual way through school, through information sessions, through parents' evening. For me, I find it very difficult that there are children in Year 2 whose names I don't know and I don't know their families. In the normal pathway of school life you'd know the child's name and you could picture their

family and you [could] understand the context of that child, and I find it difficult that I don't.

(Headteacher, reproduced on condition of confidentiality,
research interview, October 2021)

However, especially in those later focus groups and interviews, held towards the close of the 2021 Summer Term and early in the following Autumn Term, when a more general 'lockdown fatigue' was at its height amongst parents and pupils *and* amongst educational professionals, there was some evidence of a change of mood, and this played out in the relationships between the two, as Jalil's Headteacher, Daniel Coyle, a long-standing supporter of the research detailed here and in *Lessons from Lockdown*, illustrates:

> In this job you have to be eternally optimistic [but] there is a general weariness with the ongoing nature of the pandemic … It's just been a massive drain of energy and there's the frustrations of staff. I detect bitterness, anger and frustration in the profession. I've had more passive aggression from parents in the last few months than in thirty years in the profession – so, general discontent.
>
> (Daniel Coyle, Headteacher, Newman Catholic College, Brent,
focus group – secondary educators, 6 July 2021)

Re-establishing and subsequently sustaining the sense of mutual empathy that blossomed, albeit sometimes briefly, between the home and the school prior to the onslaught of this fatigue ought to be a priority for all engaged in education, wherever they sit in the schooling landscape; it ought to be a 'COVID-Keep' that we can all agree on.

3. A reconsideration of what it means to be a 'school'
   Notwithstanding the challenges that will always be involved when professionals are involved in the education of *other* people's children – a reality of formal education systems the world over – and that, as outlined above, pupils, parents and education professionals, one outcome of the new relationship between the home and the school outlined above is the emergence of what could become the seedcorn for a redefinition and reconceptualisation of schooling itself.

   In some cases, the foundations for this new empathy were rooted in schools going far behind their stated core business of educating the children and young people in their care. Throughout this text and in *Lessons from Lockdown*, the case has been made for acknowledging the range of functions that schools – especially but not exclusively schools in disadvantaged areas – undertake, that stretch beyond the formally and narrowly educative. A couple of weeks after schools in England, Wales and Northern Ireland returned in September 2021, the Chief Inspector opined that this may have caused something akin to 'mission drift' and a loss of focus:

> In a lot of schools it felt as though their attention went very rapidly to the most disadvantaged children, into making food parcels, going out visiting. They put a great deal of attention into the children with greatest difficulties which is admirable, but in some cases that probably got prioritised – certainly last summer, the summer of 2020 – which may have meant that they did not have the capacity left to make sure there was some kind of education offer for all children.
>
> (Amanda Spielman, Chief Inspector for Schools, cited in Weale, 2021b)

The reaction of many in the profession was swift and highly critical, not least amongst those who spoke on behalf of school leaders:

> From the very start of the crisis, staff looked after the most vulnerable pupils as the country went into lockdown; they effectively reimagined the very concept of 'school' as they worked to implement a remote learning offer. There is no doubt that this vital work helped to shield large numbers of children from the worst effects of the pandemic. Schools learned much more quickly than policymakers about what worked and what pupils needed.
>
> (Paul Whiteman, General Secretary, National Association of Head Teachers, cited in Weale, 2021b)

> Schools have worked very hard throughout the pandemic to juggle many demands which have often been unfamiliar and required entirely new approaches and processes to be put in place. Our experience is that they have done extremely well in balancing these demands and doing the best they can for all their students at all times.
>
> (Geoff Barton, General Secretary, Association of School and College Leaders, cited in Weale, 2021b)

But, against the backdrop of a preceding period of some three decades in which schools had been judged entirely on the basis of academic outcomes, something that the new inspection framework ushered in by Spielman in September 2019 and developed during the early years of her tenure, had sought to correct, this disapproval was not universal;

> Look, I admire those schools that have done the food parcels and all of that – and I lead a school in a 'disadvantaged' setting, so I know how vital it has been, but I also firmly believe that learning is our core business, and I think there might, therefore, be something in what the Chief Inspector says.
>
> (Headteacher, speaking on condition of confidentiality, 15 September 2021)

This, of course, takes us back to a point made throughout this text, and it echoes Whiteman's comments about the way in which some education professionals had 'reimagined the very concept of 'school' during the course of the pandemic – that lockdown has exposed the *multiple* functions of schools: as centres for learning (of course), but also as sites for children's socialisation, as community hubs, as facilitators of parental employment and as providers of what amounts to respite from full-time parenting. This multiplicity of functions has been highlighted during lockdown, but like so many other issues, it pre-existed the pandemic. And, in turn, this reminds us of a comment made by Daniel Coyle, reflecting on the early weeks of the pandemic in Spring 2020, cited in *Lessons from Lockdown*:

> Tony, this makes clear to me the sheer range of our work that goes way beyond the educational; we're the ones that end up doing it, so maybe the system needs to acknowledge that. We do this stuff and, if we didn't, who else would?
>
> (Danny Coyle, Headteacher, Newman Catholic College, Brent, cited in Breslin, 2021a: 32)

Perhaps the Chief Inspector and her colleagues would do well to ponder this point. The logic of it is that those inspecting and otherwise appraising schools might want to consider the development of the kind of broader 'score-card' recommended in *Lessons from Lockdown* at that time:

> The score-card on which schools are judged needs to be much broader, taking into account contextual factors, and issues such as wellbeing, learner experience and inclusion.
>
> (Breslin, 2021a: 44)

And none of this denies or minimises the traditional and core educational function of schools or the primacy of this, but it *begins* to acknowledge that broader issues of both context and purpose exist *alongside* this educational role, and impact profoundly on it; the Chief Inspector may have a point about what I have reframed here as 'mission-drift', but one thing is clear: hungry children don't learn. The toil of delivering food parcels may indeed have exhausted and distracted school leaders and their colleagues, and it may have impacted on their effectiveness as teachers, whether this be in the classroom or online, but it may also have done more than anything else to enable any learning that did take place. Undoubtedly in many settings, it helped to develop the newly empathetic relationship between the home and the school, or at least between some homes and some schools described earlier. Perhaps ironically, the new inspection framework introduced in English schools in the run-up to the pandemic (Ofsted, 2019; 2021), developed, championed and ushered into place under Amanda Spielman's leadership, gives a new prominence to issues of pupil and staff wellbeing, and to building inclusion. In speeches ahead of its launch, Spielman had emphasised the importance of the need to move away from a culture driven solely by examination outcomes, arguing that:

> There is more to a good education than league tables. Vitally important though a school's examination results are, we must not allow curricula to be driven just by SATs, GCSEs and A levels. It is the substance of education that ultimately creates and changes life chances, not grade stickers from exams.
>
> (Spielman, 2017)

Further, in a comment widely cited in those helping schools to prepare for the new framework, Spielman reminds us that:

> … teaching to the test and [the] narrowing of the curriculum have the greatest negative effect on the most disadvantaged and the least able children.

These statements, and the new framework itself, would seem to offer at least some prospect of an acknowledgement of the efforts of those who departed the classroom to deliver food parcels, or undertake comparable activities, during the course of this pandemic. And maybe it is this more holistic approach to teaching and learning, and a recognition of the 'substance of education', and its facilitation, that we ought to want to retain long after this dreaded pandemic has passed.

4.   A new status for digital practice
     Necessity is the mother of invention goes the phrase, and, certainly, this has been true of the period covered in this book and in *Lessons from Lockdown*. The upsurge in the confidence and competence of education professionals is likely to provide a lasting and positive legacy of the pandemic but, if it is to do so, it is surely vital that system leaders move away from a deficit language that takes, as its starting point, the limitations rather than possibilities offered by digital practice. These comments, from England's then Secretary of State for Education Gavin Williamson, referring to practice in universities after the first educational lockdown, and its Chief Inspector for Schools are illustrative. As such, they appear to position online learning as a necessary second-choice solution in extreme circumstances, rather than something that might have merit in itself:

> While the switch to online teaching was a necessary and vital way of keeping young people learning in as safe a way as possible, we have now moved on and students quite rightly expect that they can study in person alongside other students.
> (Gavin Williamson, Secretary of State for Education, cited by Singh and Hymas, 2020)

> It's increasingly clear that for most children, remote education can never replace the classroom, however hard teachers try. It was a necessary stop gap, but one that reinforced just how important it is for children to be in school – for academic, social and health reasons.
> (Amanda Spielman, Chief Inspector for Schools: Spielman, 2021c)

Almost six months later, addressing a community of educational researchers, Spielman was to underline the point:

> It was abundantly clear that remote learning is a sticking plaster at best for most children. We saw that even the most well-thought-out offer couldn't replace classroom learning, despite everyone's best efforts. Equality of access was a problem.
> (Spielman, 2021d)

To locate digital and online practice, as Spielman appears to do, as primarily a necessary 'stop gap', is to deny the transformative potential of such technology on how we both teach and learn, while to compare it (negatively) to input provided by an expensively and extensively trained and experienced educational professional is to assume that the two are alternatives rather than complements. The point is that while they have often, and necessarily, been alternatives in a landscape of lockdowns and bursting bubbles; in a landscape *without* these features, they can, and ought, to be complements. Teachers can do things when utilising such technology that they cannot do without it, and COVID has enabled the discovery of this. Moreover, if access is the problem, as for the most disadvantaged children and young people it often is, the challenge is to address the access issue (as we suggest in Recommendations 9.4 and 9.5), not to reject the technology.

In this context, would it not be more helpful for system leaders to acknowledge the potential of the technologically enabled and assisted pedagogies in post-lockdown settings, rather than to equate them with sticking plasters, to be restored to the First Aid kit now that their need has passed? And ought not education departments and inspection frameworks and the broader apparatus of the performity culture seek to encourage digital innovation and creativity of this type? After all, it was the Department for Education that, as the 2021–22 academic year approached, had re-issued a Legal Direction that would require schools to:

> … offer immediate access to 'high-quality remote education' when pupils need to self-isolate.
>
> (Carr, 2021)

One thing is for sure:, a number of the teachers who have contributed to the research detailed in these pages, and to that set out in *Lessons from Lockdown*, have no intention of confining the innovations of this period to history, and their ambitions are supported by a vibrant, and re-energised EdTech community, itself encouraged by the launch of a review into the use of technology in education led by the one-time New Labour education adviser, Sir Michael Barber. The usually digitally sceptical Gavin Williamson welcomed the review, acknowledging that:

> All our learners, whether at school, college or university, have been able to continue with their studies even when they were not able to have in person teaching. I want to take the opportunity to thank you all for this incredible response. I know adapting to it has been really challenging.
>
> But something positive has come out of it. Technology has come into its own and is one of the few causes of celebration in an otherwise

grim pandemic. Over the past year we've seen nothing short of a revolution in the way people learn.

(Williamson, 2021b)

This potential and these ambitions must be harnessed for a post-lockdown landscape, and that this harnessing be led by practitioners in schools, rather than those formally defined as 'system leaders', may be as it should be. Nonetheless, it would give a nudge to others if those charged with measuring and quality assuring educational experiences and outcomes were to catch up, and to catch on.

5. A new concern for wellbeing
    The inspection framework for English schools launched in September 2019 and updated, partly in light of the pandemic, in both July 2021 and July 2022 cited earlier (Ofsted, 2019; 2021, 2022), signalled a significant change in the lens through which school performance would be appraised. Contrary to many early misreadings of the framework, the inspectorate had not dropped their abiding concern for educational standards. Rather, it augmented this with a new concern – one for the wellbeing of both students and staff, and, alongside this, reintroduced curriculum to the heart of the framework.

    Prior to the pandemic, concerns about the impact of student and teacher wellbeing on educational outcomes were rising, with the so-called 'standards' agenda – and its range of associated accountability levers – often held responsible for this. Whether or not this charge was fair is contestable, but the revised inspection framework cited earlier acknowledged these concerns. Thus, in terms of student wellbeing, those schools judged to be 'Good' would need to demonstrate, for instance, that they provide 'high-quality pastoral support', and that:

    > Pupils know how to eat healthily, maintain an active lifestyle and keep physically and mentally healthy [and that] they have an age-appropriate understanding of healthy relationships [and that] … the curriculum and the school's effective wider work support pupils to be confident, resilient and independent, and to develop strength of character.
    >
    > (*Education Inspection Framework*: Ofsted, 2021)

In terms of staff wellbeing, the expectation is also explicit, with those schools judged to be 'Good' having to demonstrate that their leaders 'protect staff from bullying and harassment', and:

> … engage with their staff and are aware and take account of the main pressures on them. [Leaders] are realistic and constructive in the way they manage staff, including their workload. This includes managing staff workloads proactively in response to COVID-19 … .
>
> (Education Inspection Framework: Ofsted, 2021)

This focus by the inspectorate on wellbeing is surely correct, but the analysis it offers is insufficient and incomplete. We must move away from a system characterised by a false binary between, on the one side, attainment and standards, and on the other, inclusion and wellbeing. As I have demonstrated in *Lessons from Lockdown*, the relentless pursuit of the standards agenda is a necessity in an underperforming education system with the capacity to do better. However, in a system performing at capacity, in which success is the norm, but a minority are persistently underachieving, the relentless pursuit of standards enhances further the performance of the already successful while confirming the exclusion of the minority group or groups. Nevertheless, to simply seek to 'do' inclusion and attainment alongside each other is not enough (and this is the gap in the Ofsted analysis). The challenge for practitioners is to understand the relationship between the two, as most educational professionals intuitively do, such that enabling the achievement of these excluded and inevitably socially demarcated cohorts is rooted in ensuring their inclusion. Thus, for these cohorts, attainment (counter-intuitively) does not flow from the pursuit of attainment-first strategies, it flows from the pursuit of inclusion-first strategies (Breslin, 2001).

The work of schools with children defined as 'vulnerable' in the second schools lockdown in early 2021 is illustrative. The data assembled to facilitate the writing of this book and *Lessons from Lockdown*, suggests that some of these children and young people made greater progress and gained greater enjoyment from their learning in a setting characterised by smaller groups and closer teacher-student relationships, but became anxious on learning that school would be returning to normal. 'Normal' schooling had been the schooling with which many of these learners had struggled pre-lockdown. Pre-lockdown, the focus had been on attainment (which in turn shone a spotlight on their persistent lack of attainment). During the second lockdown, assisted by a softer, more open, less public definition of 'vulnerability', the focus was explicitly on inclusion. And for the perennial 'underachiever' (so often a child that also carries the badge of 'vulnerability' and a particular intersection of disadvantages), inclusion is a prerequisite for attainment, not its poor relation.

Retaining the SEND-informed inclusion-first practice that flows from this analysis ought to be a COVID-Keep system-wide. Given the new vulnerabilities revealed by the virus, and the acknowledgement of these by schools 'on the ground' and according to local context in the second schools lockdown in early 2021, it is an analysis that is likely to reach – and likely to be needed by – a significantly larger number of children and young people.

6. A new focus on educational purpose
    'Big' systems such as those delivering energy, healthcare, or national security (both militarily and in terms of policing) reproduce themselves over time. Education systems and, in particular, *schooling* systems fall into this category. As noted elsewhere in these pages, and in *Lessons from Lockdown*, they change as a result of system shocks, such as that provided by the pandemic. These shocks can, therefore, open up the potential for transformation but, as we have acknowledged, in exhausting the professionals involved, they can cause the dissipation of the capacity and patience required to see the change through. There is, though, a light on this horizon. System-shocks may both open up the space for change and deny us the energy to deliver the change, but they do leave a vital residue in that they make us think about long-established approaches like never before, as Headteacher Jill Allen outlines in one of our focus-group discussions:

> One of the great things about this is we have been asking questions about what is great learning and what is the point of school ... school's not just about doing Maths and English.
> (Jill Allen, Headteacher, St Wilfrid's Catholic Primary School, Ripon, focus group – primary educators, 14 July 2021)

Having the confidence to address this 'what is the point of school?' question is vital if we are to genuinely learn from this period in educational history because it takes us to the much-ignored issue of educational purpose. The history of education policy is a succession of tactical tweaks to a pre-organised system: an adaption of the examination system here, a change to the mode of reporting to parents there, a new curriculum every generation or so, a change to the governance of schools or the way in which they collaborate or compete, an initiative to deal with this or that area of underperformance, or to address the needs of this or that disadvantaged group.

In all of this, the *purpose* of education is rarely, if ever, explored; it is taken as a 'given', but that given is rarely stated and, in any case, means different things to different players in the landscape. For the most part, modern education systems have their foundations in the nineteenth and early twentieth centuries, surely making such an exploration long overdue. Maybe, just maybe, COVID, for all its awfulness – and the visceral human suffering that it has wrought, especially but not exclusively on those who were already suffering multiple disadvantages before the virus emerged on the horizon – might prompt a reappraisal of educational purpose.

Yes, as educational professionals, we may be too weary to implement the changes that might flow from this in the immediate future – and we should not rush to change in any case – but it might be that the innovations and accommodations of this period will ultimately point the way to a new educational future, with schools evolving to address this purpose. Our shared experiences of the pandemic, and its associated lockdowns, have clarified how much we need our schools, not that we don't. But the question as to what exactly we need them *for*, and what form we will need schooling to take, as we approach the middle of the twenty-first century, remains an open one.

Education for a greener and post-industrial future?

The six themes outlined above are among those that might help us to reshape and reorientate modern schooling systems for a world facing (usually richly connected) local and global challenges that were not on the horizon (although their seeds were being sown) when most modern schooling systems were initially devised. Here, five challenges are especially pertinent. They are notable, not in so much as they flow heavily through the data discussed in these pages – perhaps surprisingly they are either absent or do not feature as strongly as might be expected – but because they are increasingly prominent in the meta-discourses beyond the education sphere. The five challenges might be summarised as being about how we provide education for:

A. Personal development and wellbeing
B. Citizenship, civic engagement and political participation
C. Climate change and the resultant climate emergency
D. Creativity and entrepreneurship
E. More than employability.

These themes feature strongly in the third book in this trilogy, *Reschooling Society After Lockdown*. In bringing *this* book to a close, it is worth discussing each briefly at this stage.

A. Education for personal development and wellbeing

I have already noted that the re-emergence of wellbeing as a concern for both practitioners and policymakers pre-dates the pandemic, as exemplified, for instance, through the new prominence given to student and staff wellbeing in the most recent revisions to England's Ofsted inspection framework (Ofsted, 2019; 2021; 2022). However, the case advanced by those campaigning for a stronger focus on the 'whole child', on wellbeing (especially the mental health of children), on neuro-diversity and on personal development have been bolstered by the challenges that have emerged, or been given a new visibility, during the national and local lockdowns and the bursting bubbles spurred by COVID-19.

Thus, in English schools, and across the UK, as well as in the revised inspection framework, we have seen the emergence of revised curricula in areas such as Relationship and Sex Education (RSE) (DFE, 2021D), Personal, Social and Health Education (PSHE) (DFE, 2021e), and Careers Information, Education, Advice and Guidance (CIEAG) (DFE, 2015) and enhanced guidance in areas relating to the safeguarding of children, drawn together in the document, *Keeping Children Safe in Education* (DFE, 2021f) and in areas such as healthy eating (DFE, 2021g) and the mental health of children (DFE, 2021h). Alongside these, we have also seen the rise of Character Education and the growing interest in related areas such as personal resilience and self-esteem (DFE, 2019) and a body of work around trauma and attachment (see, for instance, Adoption UK, 2019; 2021) and a range of initiatives arising from enduring concerns around identity and inclusion. These have been thrown into sharp focus in recent years – and in the build-up to and during the pandemic – by the emergence and growing profile of movements and campaigns such as Black Lives Matters, Pride and Me Too, many of which have spawned interest from and been driven by young people, a significant number of school age, especially but not exclusively in the upper secondary (or high) school years:

Each of these areas, and several others, might be represented on a Venn Diagram shared with those elements of the wider social curriculum that we discuss next, and partly bridged by the 'umbrella' provided by Personal, Social and Health Education and, in England, the broader duty on schools in England to enable children and young people to access a 'Broad and Balanced' curriculum and to attend to the Spiritual, Moral, Social and Cultural (SMSC) development of those in their care.

The challenge, clearly, is to find a way to give coherence to this welter of areas while resisting the temptation to simply bundle them together in some low-status corner of a curriculum dominated by 'traditional' subjects. While frameworks have been proposed for doing so, not least by this author

(Breslin, 2014; Breslin and Dufour, 2005), the new prominence that, post-lockdown, these areas are at last receiving, demands a much more defined and identifiable place, both in the school curriculum (and *on* the timetable) and in the wider life of schools.

B. Education for citizenship, civic engagement and political participation

Some readers will be aware that I have retained a career-long commitment to the social sciences, to Personal Social and Health Education (PSHE) and to Citizenship Education, both in the classroom and through holding a range of roles beyond the classroom, as a Principal and Chief Examiner and a Chair of Examiners in Sociology, Social Policy and Social Sciences, as the Chair of the Association for the Teaching of the Social Sciences, as a Founding Trustee of the Association for Citizenship Teaching, as the first Director of the Orwell Youth Prize, and as CEO at the education and participation charity, the Citizenship Foundation (now Young Citizens). For me, both the personal development curriculum and the wider social curriculum have been too long overlooked and marginalised, and what Cecil Wright Mills famously termed the 'sociological imagination', too often ignored.

The acclaimed British actress Maureen Lipman captured this marginalisation in one of a popular series of television advertisements for the UK telecommunications provider BT that aired around the time that I was cutting my educational teeth as a young sociology teacher in the late 1980s (British Telecommunications, 1987). 'At least it's an "ology"', she opined when her grandson broke the news to her (in a phone call, how else?) that he had passed just one examination – Sociology, of course. At the time, Advanced Level Sociology students in England, Wales and Northern Ireland recorded the highest number of E (bottom) grades and the lowest number of A (top) grades – hardly the expected outcomes for an 'easy' subject, but the messaging cut through in spite of the evidence.

And so it was to prove with Citizenship Education, introduced as a statutory subject to the secondary National Curriculum that the majority of English schools were required to implement in 2002 (QCA, 2002), following the report of an all-party advisory committee led by the late Professor Sir Bernard Crick (QCA, 1998). Two decades later, Citizenship appears on a small minority of secondary school timetables as an identified subject, and this in a highly inspected schooling system. Would the inspectors note the absence of Mathematics or English, or accept the claim when the absence is noted, that 'Oh, we do that *across* the curriculum', with a similar complacency? Strong cross-curricular delivery of the Citizenship, PSHE and the wider social curriculum is a marvel to behold, but one notable for its scarcity. As I once noted to a Select Committee Enquiry into Citizenship Education, 'Too often, everywhere is nowhere.'

Post-lockdown, and given persistent concerns about a diverse range of issues often *only* dealt with within the social curriculum – spanning, for instance, childhood wellbeing and mental health, low levels of financial literacy and the apparent growth of an antipathy to the political and public sphere in an increasingly atomised society – the social curriculum, and all of its constituent elements, however constructed or reconfigured, must surely be given a more prominent seat at the curricular table. The re-emergence, in England, of a concern for curriculum-related matters in the inspection framework could be one lever for this, but a better one might rest in the conclusions reached by Sinead Harmey and her colleagues (Harmey and Moss, 2021) at the UCL Institute of Education and cited elsewhere in these pages: that, through using a thematic approach, the curriculum might enable children and young people to make sense of this interruption to their learning, and to recover from it, especially in terms of wellbeing, in a manner that many of the 'catch-up' strategies proffered by others cannot hope to achieve.

C. Education for sustainability against the backdrop of climate emergency

In an otherwise positive review of *Lessons from Lockdown*, Steve Thurnbull, writing in *Schools Week* in February 2021, a month or so after that book's publication, bemoans the absence of any discussion of the sustainability or 'green' agenda in its pages, and argues that:

> … [the book's] 'reset' argument actually doesn't go far enough. There is plenty of talk about resilience within its pages, but not a single mention of environmental sustainability. Yet, to my mind, the most important lockdown lesson of all is that we simply have to join the dots between zoonotic pandemics, the catastrophic loss of biodiversity caused by rampant industrialism, and climate change. And we must allow children to see the big picture that emerges about the 'normal' that created Covid.
>
> (Turnbull, 2021)

It is a fair point, and one which, as author, I entirely agree, about an issue thrown into even sharper focus by the build-up to, and staging of, a climate emergency-focused COP26 in Glasgow in November 2021, the United Nations-convened gathering of national leaders, policymakers and aspirant policy shapers, and the UK's prolonged drought of Summer 2022.

The non-coverage of environmental matters in *Lessons form Lockdown* was a consequence not of a lack of author-interest, or an unwillingness to consider these matters to be important, but because of the failure of such issues to emerge in focus groups and interviews that were deliberately not guided by a fixed schedule of questions. Again, and even with the backdrop in the UK of COP26, and a series of widely reported extreme weather episodes – in the UK and globally – an analysis of the transcripts of the interviews and focus groups that inform the analysis offered here does not reveal a single direct reference to the Climate Emergency, and only a handful of passing references to the wider sustainability agenda.

But this should not be taken as a lack of interest in sustainability, or a lack of concern for the climate amongst those in education. The discussions in these pages are necessarily time limited, and most of those that engage educational professionals are with senior and middle leaders seeking to navigate their way through completely unforeseen circumstances, while leading their colleagues and the school communities within which they sit through this landscape.

Moreover, educators and educational researchers have been active in this area throughout lockdown, and some of those who have participated in this activity have also been involved in the research documented here and in *Lessons from Lockdown* are likely to be individuals who have been involved in this process. One output from this activity is a newly published 'Manifesto for Education for Environmental Sustainability', co-produced by 'over two hundred young people, teachers and teacher educators' and published by a Research Commission funded by the British Educational Research Association in Movember 2021 (BERA, 2021), which calls for a range of responses (or 'solutions') at the levels of the classroom, the school and the community. At the level of the classroom, the manifesto identifies the need to:

- Resource teachers of all subjects to engage in sustainability-focused professional development to develop confidence.
- Use more sustainable resources and practices across both the curriculum and extra and co-curricular contexts
- Provide students with the space and time to learn about climate change and environmental sustainability that is not linked to assessment.
- Encourage students to research and take action on sustainability.

As we create a schooling system fit for the middle decades of this century, we cannot ignore the climate emergency; the BERA Research Commission's Manifesto, and a range of other initiatives, underline this. The challenge will be to educate young people such that they are empowered to address this crisis, while not adding to the trepidation of a generation who have, thanks to the COVID years, already had a lifetime's worth of anxiety.

D. Education for creativity and entrepreneurship

There is something oxymoronic about attempting to promote creativity and entrepreneurship in a (necessarily) highly structured setting such as that provided by the modern secondary school. Nonetheless, the research detailed in these pages makes clear that, whatever their educational effectiveness in the narrowest of terms, the school plays a vital role as a community hub, in the border socialisation of children, in enabling parental participation in the workforce, and in providing respite from full-time parenting. And schools, whatever the level and constraints of their internal structures, have to be spaces in which the creativity of children and young people and all who work with them must be enabled to thrive.

Again, amongst the backdrop of the chaos and tragedy of COVID, there may be a positive legacy. This text, and *Lessons from Lockdown*, have already celebrated the innovation and creativity of school leaders, teachers and the school workforce in responding to the pandemic. The challenge now is two-fold: first, to resist the 'pull-back' to pre-COVID realities, such that no space is left to build on the innovations of this period; second, to use these, as a foundation for a system that better enables and embraces creativity and entrepreneurship. With regard to the second part of the challenge, the Cultural Learning Alliance, which 'champions a right to arts and culture for every child', is clear on the potential, and need, for change:

> There is a wealth of evidence to show that studying the arts fosters creativity, innovation, empathy, and resilience; that the arts are crucial for our economic prosperity; and that the arts enrich lives, making us happier and healthier.
>
> But children's access to arts and culture is declining. In England's secondary schools the numbers of arts teachers and the hours the arts are taught is declining. Arts GCSEs and A-level entries continue to decline, and access to arts provision for the most disadvantaged children is narrowing.

> This is a social justice issue: research shows that children with an arts deficit are disadvantaged educationally and economically while their more fortunate peers who do participate in the arts are more resilient, healthier, do better in school, are more likely to vote, to go to university, to get a job and to keep it. Participation in the arts fuels social mobility.
>
> (Cultural Learning Alliance, 2021)

One thing is clear, if our schools are overly constrained by a need to *conform* and *comply*, especially to externally set regulations and expectations rather than those agreed with professional peers, the compliance culture will feed through to a classroom conservatism that will struggle to model creativity and innovation amongst children and young people, a creativity that they will need to navigate a much less predictable post-school world. The seeds that are most likely to produce the creative, innovative and entrepreneurial adults who will thrive in the middle decades of the twenty-first century are unlikely to be sown in schooling systems themselves driven by a culture of compliance.

E. Education for more than employability

In our discussion of the examination system so disrupted by the virus, three things became clear: first, that while vital, a clutch of strong examination grades does not, in itself, constitute either a full education or readiness for the world of work. Second, the dependence, in most modern education systems, on a single or dominant mode of examination at any one level narrows the curriculum and disables young people from displaying the breadth of their potential to prospective employers or to those who make decisions on school or college admissions, and – as such – limits their future options. Third, such an approach relegates those matters not captured in an examination, or not seen as contributing *overtly* to future employment prospects, as less important and, often, somehow frivolous. I have argued as much elsewhere:

> Skills for jobs? Yes. But, with employment likely to be less stable, work playing a lesser role in the lives of many (if not all) and careers increasingly fluid and multiple, education – compulsory and post-compulsory – needs to be for much, much more than just the workplace.
>
> (Breslin, 2021b)

There is an irony in all of this: in creating a system that quantifies young people's educational achievement so that employers and admissions tutors may make sense of it and, therefore, make decisions about their employment or course access, we have created a system that, arguably, does not always equip young people well for the challenges of the employment or the college place itself. Why? Because the so-called 'soft skills' (an unfortunate title as they are, invariably, the hardest to grasp) and personal qualities that modern employers, business opportunities and courses in further and higher education require are rarely captured sufficiently in examination grades, especially given the narrow range of examination methods that, in non-COVID times, we typically use, and to which our schools returned in Summer 2022.

Moreover, there is an even bigger challenge: the increasingly precarious relationship between educational success (quantified and defined through *examination* success) and success, howsoever defined, in the labour market. The first reason for this is set out above – an examination and grading-driven system doesn't necessarily produce employment-readiness in any given setting, a reality that modern employers increasingly recognise. The second reason is more profound: structurally, the economy is moving away from a 'career for life' model and all the securities (and limitations) that this offers, and probably towards a model in which employment (in whatever form it takes) may be just as important in our lives but will be less all-dominating in terms of time. In any case, the very predictability and causality that underpins the education-employment relationship is fast declining – the schooling required for such a fast-moving world is, arguably, very different to that which might prepare the young person for a conventional career, less still a 'job for life', and the pace of change should not be understated. In my capacity as Chair of the Governing Board at Bushey Primary Education Federation, I give an annual address to parents thinking of selecting our schools for their children. At the core of my message, which draws on an earlier report (Breslin, 2016) is one passage that barely changes from year to year:

> Children entering Reception Class this autumn will need to be prepared for a world that is ever-changing; they will need a new agility and adaptability, they will find their careers in industries that don't yet exist, and they will need to engage in learning as a lifelong, life-wide project.

Even in a world where economic wellbeing and financial security may be underpinned by models such as that provided by Universal Basic Income

(Painter, Thorold and Cooke, 2018; Painter, 2020), irrespective of employment status, employment will retain a range of social functions, just as schools will do, even when there are many other sources of education.

Thus, employment will remain important and a good, largely school-based education will remain vital at least to initial entry into the workforce. However, the *causal* link between educational qualifications gained in youth and employment and career destinations will weaken. In short, to over-stress the link between education and employment, when such a 'contract' is hard to fulfil – because of structural changes in employment and in the way that we work – may not be a smart move.

Endnote: Towards a scorecard for educational change

The weariness of an exhausted profession, and the yearning for stability and normality in the wake of COVID-19, has already been noted. The observation that highly organised and structured settings – as schools, especially secondary or high schools, necessarily are – tend towards reproducing procedure and practice over time in spite of efforts at (usually top-down) policy reform has also been a constant refrain. Both of these themes – exhaustion and a tendency towards the repetition of established practice across generations – sit in contrast with a third theme, that of the opportunity for change presented by the system shock delivered by COVID-19.

Reconciling the first two themes with the third is a difficult circle to square but the answer may lie in seeking to frame the key objectives for the re-equipping of our educational and schooling systems post-lockdown – we are back to the primacy of long-term and considered educational purpose over short-term tactical reform. If a set of high-level objectives – not necessarily those suggested here and developed in *Reschooling Society After Lockdown* – can be agreed, might it not be possible to embed these in a kind of score-card against which national, local and school-based progress might be evaluated? A task perhaps for repurposed inspectorates, ones that do not shy from objective judgements, but which accompany these with a range of developmental assistance, and which are themselves supported by a range of agencies focused a *little* less on current performance and a *lot* more on future development, an Office for School *Development* (or even school *enhancement*), rather than one concerned with inspection alone, as my long-standing friend, co-worker and professional mentor, Mike Moores, suggested in one of the many conversations that we have had during the drafting of these pages and which is embedded here as one of our recommendations.

This is not an argument against the gathering of data, and other forms of evidence, on the success of our schools, colleges and other educational institutions; nor is it an argument against measured, objective and external inspection – public transparency demands this. It *is* about re-balancing such activity, such that, to put it in the language of assessment, the exercise is for-mative rather than summative, one that supports the future development and enhancement of our schools (and, for that matter, the full range of agencies, centres and institutions that support our learning, lifelong and life-wide, and across every phase and context), encouraging and rewarding cre-ativity and entrepreneurship amongst school, college and university leaders and those they lead, granting them agency rather than demanding their compliance.

Such an outcome would represent an enduring product of a torrid time, a positive legacy from an awful episode. For all who have been impacted by COVID-19, for all of *us* – and for our children and young people – we are surely duty bound to give it a go.

Appendix A
Research methodology

As with the book that precedes it, *Lessons from Lockdown: The Educational Legacy of COVID-19*, this text is a blend of ethnography (albeit in a constantly changing landscape), part quasi-journalistic account of the experience of lockdown and the telling and retelling of COVID-19 stories, and part research study. As I remarked in the earlier text, for purists of one parish or another, this book may, therefore, fail on all three counts, but the attempt has been to produce a second text that does two things that otherwise excellent and rigorous 'academic' texts sometimes fail at: first, to give voice to those at the heart of these stories: pupils, parents, teachers, support staff, teacher educators, school leaders, school governors and system leaders; second, to cross-over to those beyond what we sometimes think of as a 'target audience'; of course, publishers require prospective authors to identify such target audiences, and they are right to, for a book written for everybody risks appealing to nobody. But, as with *Lessons from Lockdown*, my ambition here is that we might meet the aspirations of our target market – education professionals, those preparing to enter the education professions or to progress further within these professions, and those enabling them to do so, school and system leaders and those who aspire to these roles, school governors and trustees, and policy shapers and policymakers – and go a little further and reach parents, community leaders and those in other professions with no more than an interest in education. After all, as I remarked at this point in the predecessor text, and as I doubtless will in the final book in the trilogy, *Reschooling Society After Lockdown*, an education is for nothing if it is not for sharing, and sharing beyond our own particular ghetto.

And so our methodology has sought to be inclusive and investigative, systematic rather than strictly 'scientific' (whatever that now means), and inquisitive and questioning but without anything as constraining as a questionnaire, hoping that in the process we might 'find the answers to questions, we might not have thought to ask' (Foote-Whyte, 1943). Against this background, we have hosted more focus groups than for *Lessons from Lockdown* (17 instead of ten), each of approximately ninety minutes in length, involving between five and twelve participants, but fewer one-to-one and small group discussions, six in total as against 16 for the earlier text, each lasting about an hour. In each of these conversations, we have sought to capture the essence of schooling during lockdown.

Again, each of these recorded and subsequently transcribed Zoom discussions were structured around three deliberately broad questions:

1. How did you, and your colleagues, respond as the 2020 Autumn Term progressed and schooling, again, became increasingly disrupted?
2. How did you respond to the subsequent national lockdowns of the 2021 Spring Term and to the challenges posed during the latter part of this term and the Summer Term that followed it, and how was this experience different to the national lockdowns, and the attempts to recover from these, of almost a year earlier?
3. What lessons do you draw from the experience of schooling during the pandemic, as we seek to re-establish schooling in the wake of it?

Again, with respect to the third question, we wanted to know what our research participants couldn't wait to get back to, what they couldn't wait to leave behind, and, thus, how lockdown might reshape schooling for the future. And, in surveying responses to these questions, we were able to compare the insights offered with those already 'banked' through the research for *Lessons from Lockdown*, research that we revisited frequently and necessarily.

In addition, and as we had been in researching the earlier text, we were invited into a series of additional online discussions and meetings concerned, at least in part, with similar themes hosted by a number of organisations, notably the international professional development portal Leadership Lemonade and the Fabian Society Education Group. Finally, in terms of primary research, we have, again, taken a small number of written submissions, notably from those who have wanted but not been able to take part in the focus group or interview sessions.

Throughout, the relationship between research and writing has again been iterative rather than sequential. *Lessons from Lockdown* had been commissioned on 1 June 2020 with the first full draft submitted to the publisher exactly three months later, on 1 September. This time we had slightly longer, with the book commissioned at the start of March 2021 and the draft text submitted just before Christmas that year. Originally, the intention had been to complete the text at the end of August 2021, as had been the case the year before, but it felt right to extend the research so that it covered the first term of the 2021–22 academic year. We could not complete the story without taking some account of the return to school, and the success with which all adjusted to what was at least intended to be the resumption of normal schooling.

The originally planned additional time – that is, the earlier start – enabled the staging of several additional focus groups and, notably, a second focus group involving colleagues from primary, secondary and SEND and alternative provision settings at the close of the 2021 Summer Term. However, the luxury of extra time did not reduce the intensity of the process, with the final research discussions taking place in the week before the submission of the first draft. Of course, as with *Lessons from Lockdown*, the story kept changing right up to that point and, indeed, up to the point when the book entered the production process, a period that brought with it several changes in Education Secretary, a new Prime Minister and a new Monarch.

In addition to the primary research, we have attempted to capture media coverage across a range of newspapers, magazines and broadcast networks, and been asked to contribute to this coverage on various occasions, in particular to pieces carried by LBC, BBC Radio 4, BBC Radio 5 Live, Sky News, GB News, Times Radio, the *I* and the *Daily Telegraph*. We have also sought to capture debates in the educational press and on social media, notably Twitter and a range of blogging spaces. Again, the British Educational Research Association (BERA) blog has proved invaluable.

As with *Lessons from Lockdown*, I have, throughout the process, drawn on a range of distinct educational literatures. As well as the emergent educational literature on lockdown, of which this book forms a part, we have drawn on those literatures concerned with attachment and trauma, assessment and qualifications, curriculum studies, governance, inspection, school leadership, and educational technology.

Finally, as a parent of two boys at state secondary schools, one who undertook his GCSE examinations in Summer 2022, as a Chair of Governors in a Local Authority-maintained federation and as a Trustee at a Multi-Academy Trust, and as somebody married to a Headteacher, and with a rich array of educationalists of one form or other strewn across our friendship groups, I continue to exploit the networks and knowledge that these roles have presented, and to draw on my own experience as a (sometimes reluctant) participant observer in these landscapes, conscious that my own experience might not be representative or typical, but that it does offer several perspectives from which lockdown might be assessed.

Appendix B
Research participants

We are grateful to each of the 112 participants who have taken part in the range of research acivities – including focus groups and one-to-one interviews – that have informed the analysis offered in this book, and list each of the participants, alphabetically, below.

Whether we have directly cited the contribution they have made in the text or not, those listed below have played a vital role in informing our thinking and the analysis that we offer:

Alan McMahon, Parent and Senior Construction Professional, Taiwan

Alex Bell, Founder and Convenor, Leadership Lemonade, UK

Alice Faulkiner, Class Teacher, Crabtree Junior School, Harpenden, Hertfordshire

Alistair Hamill, Senior Leader, Lurgan College, Lurgan, Northern Ireland

Allyson Dobson, Headteacher, Dalkeith High School, Dalkeith, Scotland

Andrew Dunne, Deputy Headteacher, Designated Safeguarding Lead, Newman Catholic College, Brent

Andy Bell, Deputy Head, Newman Catholic College, Harlesden, North West London

Andy Funnell, Head of Geography, Omagh High School, Omagh, Northern Ireland

Ann Berisford, Deputy Head, Whitehill Primary School, Hitchin, Hertfordshire

Ann Bowen-Breslin, Headteacher, Hillingdon Primary School, Hillingdon, Middlesex

Annette Szymaniak, Consultant Headteacher, Monks Risborough Church of England Primary School, Buckinghamshire

Betty Merchant, Professor of Education, University of Texas at San Antonio, USA

Boaz Waruku, Programme Manager, African Network, EFA Campaign, Nairobi, Kenya

Campbell Hornell, Headteacher, Lasswade High School, Edinburgh, Scotland

Caroline Graham, Parent, Northamptonshire

Christopher Harris, Teacher of English, Highams Park School, Waltham Forest

Ciara Hunter, Head of English and Integration Coordinator, Fort Hill Integrated College, Lisburn, Northern Ireland

Colin Platt, Chair of Governors, Monks Risborough Church of England Primary School, Buckinghamshire

Cosette Reczek, Director, Permuto Consulting

Dan Hall, Director, Information Technology Services, Girls' Day School Trust, UK

Daniel Kerbel, Head, Grange Primary School, Harrow

Danielle McKirnan, Digital Learning and Communication Lead, St Patrick's Academy, Dungannon, Northern Ireland

Danielle McKirnan, Digital Learning and Communication Lead, St. Patrick's Academy, Dungannon, Northern Ireland

Daniel Coyle, Headteacher, Cardinal Wiseman Catholic School, Greenford, Middlesex (formerly, Headteacher, Newman Catholic College, Brent)

David Miller, Headteacher, Pebble Brook School, Buckinghamshire

Deborah Outhwaite, Director, Derby Teaching Schools Alliance

Denny Tennyson, Senior Teacher, St. Joseph's Grammar School, Donaghmore, Northern Ireland

Donna Hubbard-Young, Head of School, Chesterton Community College, Cambridge

Emma Knights, Chief Executive, National Governance Association, UK

Eugene Dapper, Strategic Coordinator, Foundation for Education Development, UK

Faizan-Wali Ahmed, Year 10 Student Council Leader, Newman Catholic College, Brent (Name reproduced with parental and school permission)

Fiona Ellis, Parent, Surrey

Gemma Absalom, Assistant Head, Parmiters School, Watford, Hertfordshire

Georgia Holloran, Independent SEND Consultant, Buckinghamshire

Girish Patel, Parent and General Practitioner, Manchester

Glen Amoah, Teacher of English, Ministry of Education, Dubai, UAE

Hayley Hardy, Head of Year 7, Newman Catholic College, Brent

Helen Naughton-Green, Independent International Educationalist, UK

Helen Shirley, Pastoral Lead and Staff Governor, Bushey Primary Education Federation, Hertfordshire

Jacqueline Gray, Head of Chemistry and School Governor, Strathearn School, Belfast, Northern Ireland

James McClintock, Director of Evaluation and Development, Dunclug College, Ballymena, Northern Ireland

Jane Lovis, Deputy Head Pebble Brook School, Buckinghamshire

Jill Allen, Headteacher, St. Wilfrid's Catholic Primary School, Ripon

Joe Hallgarten, Chief Executive Office, Centre for Education and Youth, UK

Juan Nino, Associate Professor of Education, University of Texas at San Antonio, USA

Judith Bennett, Teacher, School Governor and Examiner

Kathleen McGillycuddy, Principal, Broadoak Academy, Weston-Super-Mare

Kathryn Wilkinson, School Governor, Hardy Mill Primary School, Bolton

Kerry-Jane Packman, Chief Executive, Parent Kind, UK

Kyle McCallan, Vice Principal, Lurghan College, Lurgan, Northern Ireland

Lee Jerome, Associate Professor of Education, Middlesex University, UK

Lizana Oberholzer, Programme Leader, Leadership in Education, University of East London

Lucy Barnes, Principal and Co-founder, Beach Lodge School, Buckinghamshire

Malcolm Leigh, Trainer and Consultant on School Exclusions, Herts for Learning Governance Services

Marcus Bhargava, Head, School of Education, Kingston University, UK

Marina Costa, Education Psychologist, Hertfordshire

Mark Williams, Parent and SEND Specialist, Fabian Society Education Group

Mary Ann Cooper, Federation Headteacher, Bushey Primary Education Federation, Hertfordshire

Max Fishel, SEND Teacher and Adviser, Fabian Society Education Group

Michael Callanan, Delivery Director, Orwell Youth Prize, and Teacher of English, Parmiters School, Hertfordshire

Michael McGarvey, Managing Director, The Key for School Leaders, UK

Neil Strain, Head, Stony Dean School, Buckinghamshire

Nichole Walters Head of Year 8, Newman Catholic College, Brent

Nick Johnson, Chief Executive, British Educational Research Association

Nikki Lye, Counsellor, Bushey Primary Education Federation, Hertfordshire

Noreen O'Neil, Head of Year 11, Newman Catholic College, Brent

Paddy O' Leary, Site Manager, Bushey Primary Education Federation, Hertfordshire

Phil Bowen, Parent, Edinburgh, Scotland

Rachel Lofthouse, Professor of Teacher Education, Leeds Beckett University

Rafael Hernandez, Parent and CEO, Human Data Research, Barcelona, Spain

Richard Lord, Headteacher, The Deepings School, Peterborough

Ronan Sharkey, Head of Year, St. Ronan's College, Lurgan, Northern Ireland

Rosemary Hoyle, Chair of Governors, Wrawby St. Mary's Primary School, Lincolnshire

Ruth Dwight, Parent, Brighton

Sally Knighton, Assistant Head, Pebble Brook School, Buckinghamshire

Sam Shellcross, Teacher of Computing, Bromley High Junior School, Kent

Sarah Morgan, Governor, Bushey Primary Education Federation, Hertfordshire

Sarah Walsh, Head of Year 10, Newman Catholic College, Brent

Sheila McKenzie, Chief Operating Office, Anthem Schools Trust, UK

Shelley Bray, Parent and Headteacher's PA, Buckinghamshire

Shula Tolland, Parent and Teacher, Kent

Sian Davidson, Head of English and Literacy Lead, Grosvenor Grammar School, Belfast, Northern Ireland

Stephen Cowden, Head of Mathematics and Senior Teacher for Learning and Teaching, Nendrum College, Belfast, Northern Ireland

Steve Edmonds, Director of Advice and Guidance, National Governance Association, UK

Steve Mills, Head, Whitehill Primary School, Hitchin, Hertfordshire

Steven Kolber, Teacher of English, Brunswick Secondary School, New South Wales, Australia

Sue Gallop, Chair, GATHER School Governors' Network, East Riding and Hull

Susan Grace, Assistant Headteacher, Newman Catholic College, Brent, and Chair, Brent Borough of Sanctuary

Tony Thorpe, Co-founder, Citizenship Foundation and Governor, Hall Cross Academy, Doncaster

Tracey Middleton, Governance Clerk, HFL Governance Services, Hertfordshire

Tracey Price, Chair of Governors, Moulsham High School, Chelmsford

Vanetta Richards-Lindo, Head of Year 9, Newman Catholic College, Brent

Vangie Aguilera, Coordinator, Centre for Educational Leadership, Trinity University, San Antonio, Texas, USA

Victoria Pendry, Chief Executive Officer, The Curriculum Foundation, UK

Will Durham, Regional Director, Governors for Schools, UK

Zak Jalil, Head of Sixth Form, Newman Catholic College, Brent

Zoe White, Trainee Teacher, Lurgan College, Lurgan, Northern Ireland

In line with safeguarding guidelines, I am not publishing the names of the young people who have supported my research, or that of their schools, unless I have express parental consent to do so, but their input has been invaluable. Special thanks are due to the child or children of every parent and the pupils of every teacher that has spoken with me in the course of the research for this book; they are the inspiration behind these contributions.

In particular, I am especially grateful to Daisy, Louisa and Lucy for their openness in sharing the reality of undergraduate life during lockdown and to members of the Student Council at Newman Catholic College in Harlesden, North West London and the teacher who coordinates student voice at the school, Susan Grace, Assistant Headteacher.

Appendix C
Recommendations

Chapter 1: The optimism of September

1.1 If we are to sufficiently personalise learning post-lockdown, research into the educational impact of COVID needs to be focused on capturing the very different and nuanced experiences of different children, families and school communities and, therefore, there should be a focus on in-depth, qualitative research tasked with revealing the intensely personal stories that sit behind lockdown statistics.

1.2 'Catch-up' strategies need to embrace the various curriculum enrichment activities and experiences that children have missed out on during lockdown – activities and experiences that may not feature in the lists of content to be covered in traditional curriculum statements.

1.3 Policymakers and system leaders ought to grasp the new, and undeniable, visibility given by the pandemic to the impact of poverty on educational attainment as an opportunity to reflect on the effectiveness of pre-lockdown policy and practice in 'closing the gap' or 'diminishing the difference' in a post-lockdown world.

1.4 Policymakers and system leaders ought also to grasp the new, and undeniable, visibility given to the impact of other long-standing non-educational factors on educational attainment as a result of the pandemic, as an opportunity to address these socially patterned outcomes.

1.5 Policymakers and system leaders ought to reflect on the 'new vulnerabilities' revealed by COVID and the impact of these on educational outcomes so that strategies may be developed and piloted to address these new vulnerabilities.

Chapter 2: After the grading crisis

2.1 UK-based students who progressed to Further and Higher Education in September 2020 were drawn largely from the cohort that had experienced the grading crisis of the previous summer; educational researchers should be supported and funded to track the fortunes of this group through to at least their late twenties, as the longer-term impact of their lockdown experiences, at school, college and university, are unlikely to be known until then.

2.2 There may be a case for financially compensating those who have had to pay for Further or Higher Education during the academic years blighted by the pandemic, not because they have not received an education, or the wider university experience, but because they have received something very different to what they had thought they were signing up to – national governments and the university and college sectors ought to give urgent attention to this issue and explore the means through which learners might be remunerated if it is found that there is a case for doing so, without threatening the viability or sustainability of the institutions concerned.

2.3 Policymakers, especially those concerned with widening participation, need to consider the risks associated with the emergence of a bipartite university system made up of elite (or 'selecting') universities on the one hand and new (or 'recruiting') universities on the other, each attended by students from different social cohorts.

2.4 System leaders, school leaders and those involved in overseeing university application processes need to promote the value of Higher Education across a border matrix of benefits rather than simply those associated with future employment or earnings.

2.5 System leaders should give serious consideration to the establishment of a national or international Commission on the Future of Further and Higher Education, exploring its purpose, those who engage in it, how participation might be funded and the multiple forms, or optimal form, that it might take.

Chapter 3: It all ends in tiers

3.1 The models of school organisation developed in response to the local lockdowns and bursting bubbles of the Summer and Autumn Terms of 2020, and sustained across the duration of the pandemic, need to be documented and shared system-wide so that the practices undertaken during this period, and the emergent lessons from these, are captured for utilisation in the future.

3.2 At the level of practice, school and curriculum leaders, school improvement advisers and inspectors, and those involved in school governance ought to be encouraged to identify those specific competencies and strategies, developed during the pandemic, that have the potential to become 'COVID-Keeps' as schools emerge from lockdown.

3.3 Retaining elements of the 'calmness' witnessed by many school leaders and young people during lockdown in the post-lockdown landscape ought to be an objective for all schools, as this clearly supports the learning of some children.

3.4 Recapturing the 'trial and error' creativity of Autumn Term 2020 ought to be an objective for all school-based education professionals, but if they are to be successful in this regard, school-based educators will need to feel that they have a licence to innovate from advisers, inspectors and policy leaders.

3.5 As schools emerge from lockdown, and as educational professionals seek to make sense of this period, they need to place a special emphasis on student and parental voice, so that the post-lockdown recasting of schooling is informed by multiple perspectives and a diversity of experiences.

Chapter 4: Crisis at Christmas

4.1 Policymakers and system leaders would be wise to draw up a code of conduct for working with the professionals who deliver educational and other public services on the ground, and this ought to preclude threatening those professionals with legal action in all but the most extreme of circumstances.

4.2 Policymakers and system leaders need to give school leaders and those involved in school governance at a local level far more autonomy on decisions about the opening and closing of school sites in line with local circumstances, while continuing to hold Heads and school-based boards to account for the continuing provision of education for all students.

4.3 There should be a greater focus on the development of study skills in school, college and university curricula, especially in the upper primary, secondary, Further and Higher Education phases.

4.4 Development work undertaken, and skills developed, by teachers during this period so that they are better placed to support home learning, need to be built on with Continuing Professional Development (CPD) programmes that enhance these often new-found capabilities.

4.5 The enhancement in the digital literacy of teachers and learners during this period needs to be utilised as one of the foundation stones for a system that makes optimal use of digital technologies in the post-lockdown era.

Chapter 5: Better connected?

5.1 While practitioners and policymakers are right to be concerned about what children will have missed out on during lockdowns and other disruptions to schooling, both in curricular and developmental terms, it is important that schools capture, and are encouraged to capture, the learning that children and young people have undertaken during this period, seeing this as a resource on which to build.

5.2 Building on the positive experiences of those who thrived in the bubbles and smaller classes of lockdown ought to be a priority for schools as activities return to scale.

5.3 Where schools have formed richer relationships with parents, especially those hitherto defined as 'hard to reach', it is vital that senior leaders understand the precise and local factors that have generated this new closeness, such that this learning is applied to school-home relationship building post-lockdown.

5.4 School leaders, and all working at school level, ought to continue to address the needs of those newly revealed as vulnerable during lockdown, while bringing the needs of these cohorts to policymakers' attention.

5.5 Policymakers ought to pay particular attention to those hitherto unseen or lesser-seen cohorts who have been either rendered vulnerable by the virus, or who had pre-existing vulnerabilities exposed by it, so as to ensure that future policy reforms capture their needs.

Chapter 6: 'Examining' the class of 2021

6.1 Policymakers, policy influencers and senior education professionals ought to take responsibility for consciously leading a shift in mindset, such that increased educational success, however defined, is seen as something to be celebrated, without reservation, rather than rationed or claimed as evidence of falling standards; such a shift requires a re-commitment to an assessment and examination framework that is criterion rather than norm referenced.

6.2 The work undertaken by teachers in the development and application of assessment systems based on Centre Assessed Grades (CAGs) and Teacher Assessed Grades (TAGs) has made a significant contribution to their professional development; school and system leaders need to give serious consideration as to how to best utilise this as schools navigate the long road from lockdown.

6.3 The pandemic has opened a window on a much greater diversity of assessment practice; system leaders need to retain and build on this diversity and multiplicity of assessment methods, and to take the opportunity that it presents to begin to explore the potential of a much broader range of qualifications, especially in the professional and vocational domain.

6.4 As with other areas of educational reform, the approach taken in any reconsideration of educational assessment should be gradual, focused on clear objectives and driven by a profession, supported by expert agencies, including one focused on the curriculum and its assessment, themselves staffed by expert practitioners.

6.5 Systems and qualifications designed to measure student achievement have become mechanisms, through the aggregation of individual performance, for the assessment of teacher and school performance, and are likely to remain so post-pandemic, but they should never again be allowed to become seen, at least by some, as the sole measure of such performance.

Chapter 7: Beyond lockdown

7.1 At school level, education professionals should be encouraged and enabled to move away from the deficit language of 'catch-up' and 'recovery' and towards approaches that are diagnostic, personalised and proportionate.

7.2 Both at the level of classroom practice and in the national narrative, the social and emotional wellbeing of children and young people should be given at least as much prominence as matters of curriculum content.

7.3 Policymakers, system leaders and educational researchers should be encouraged to draw on the literature of 'learning disruption' rather than just that focused on 'learning loss' in framing responses to the challenges now facing school leaders, curriculum managers and classroom practitioners.

7.4 School-based professionals should be encouraged to utilise the principles and practice of family learning as they navigate the long road from lockdown, building on the positive relationships developed during this period with families that had sometimes previously been defined as 'hard to reach'.

7.5 Practical policy responses need to be developed to meet the needs of young people who have transitioned from schooling into either Further and Higher Education or into training programmes or employment during this period, such that their experience is as positive as it can be, and education and training providers and employers ought to be prepared to demonstrate how they have done this.

Chapter 8: Leadership and governance in a hybrid world

8.1 Policymakers and system leaders ought to pivot the range of educational agencies that they oversee or lead away from compliance and towards development, such that the creativity sparked by the pandemic is captured and developed in post-lockdown landscapes.

8.2 With specific regard to the inspectorate in England, policy makers ought to explore the kind of developmental focus discussed in *Lessons from Lockdown*, possibly reframing and rebranding Ofsted as an 'Office for School Development'.

8.3 The Department for Education in England, and equivalent departments and agencies elsewhere, ought to commission research with 'lockdown starters' – those in the school workforce, governors, parents and pupils who have started in education, or in a new educational phase during lockdown – so as to reveal the specifics of their experience and insights.

8.4 At every level, the potential impact on the retention of education professionals in general, and school leaders in particular, ought to be guiding consideration in the framing of schooling policy.

8.5 System leaders, school leaders, those involved in school governance and educational researchers need to collaborate so as to provide a much richer understanding of leadership and governance in mult-school settings, identifying how and where this works well, and where it does not.

Chapter 9: Personalising learning for all

9.1 At every level, policymakers and shapers, system, school, curriculum and pastoral leaders, and those involved in initial and continuing teacher education need to give far more attention to SEND pedagogies, if the aspiration of a more personalised schooling experience is to be delivered for all.

9.2 Policymakers, system and school leaders, and classroom practitioners and all who support them should seek to make sense of the educational impact of COVID-19 less in terms of 'lost learning' and more in terms of 'learning disruption', a lens that enables practitioners to escape a deficit narrative that risks generating negative self-fulfilling prophecies, system-wide, but which will weigh heaviest on the shoulders of those already suffering the greatest disadvantage.

9.3 Urgent attention ought to be given by policymakers as to how excellence in digital pedagogy is identified and shared system-wide, where possible on a peer-to-peer basis, and supported by national efforts to develop and accredit the growing digital literacy of educational professionals.

9.4 Partnerships formed during lockdown with technology suppliers and those in related industries need to be developed as part of a national Every Child Connected initiative, possibly part-funded through a levy on the profits of the so-called 'tech-giants'.

9.5 Policymakers, at national, regional and local level, need to elevate Internet connectivity and device access to the same level as that pertaining to access to electricity, fuel, gas and water.

Chapter 10: Autumn's return

10.1 In the academic years after lockdown, system and school leaders will need to prioritise the wellbeing of children and staff at every level of practice.

10.2 If senior and middle leaders are to feel supported in prioritising wellbeing at school level, system leaders are likely to need to delay the introduction of a range of pre-lockdown performance measures and compliance requirements.

10.3 As well as addressing individual recovery, system leaders and school leaders need to focus on organisational recovery and wellbeing, if system-wide resilience is to be nurtured and developed.

10.4 System leaders, policymakers and school leaders need to resist the tendency to see the reintroduction of pre-lockdown performance measures and regulatory requirements as a marker of the return of normality itself.

10.5 Throughout this period, system leaders and those involved in functions such as inspection would be wise to focus on intelligence gathering, working in partnership with practitioners rather than rushing to judgements about their effectiveness at what remains a time best devoted to reflection and recovery.

Appendix D
Recommendations from
Lessons from Lockdown

We reproduce below, for ease of reference, the fifty recommendations offered in *Lessons from Lockdown: The Educational Legacy of COVID-19* (Routledge, 2021), which is the prequel to this text and curates the experience of the first lockdown in the Spring and Summer terms of 2020.

Chapter 1: Schools during lockdown

1.1 There needs to be greater cooperation between policymakers, system leaders and schools to collectively respond to the multiple impacts of COVID-19.

1.2 The Department for Education should urgently provide legal advice on the respective responsibilities of Heads, Governing Boards, Trustee Boards and Local Authorities in the event of a future suspension of schooling.

1.3 Plans should be put in place for the possibility of future local lockdowns or school closures at the earliest opportunity.

1.4 There must be much greater recognition of, and sensitivity to, how policy announcements impact on capacity and confidence across the education sector.

1.5 Policymakers must find far more effective ways to directly engage with, and respond to, the experiences of practitioners.

Chapter 2: Parental engagement and the experience of learning at home

2.1 Schools ought to be encouraged to periodically reassess the multiple ways in which they can build parental engagement.
2.2 Engagement with parents on pupil progress and attainment should go beyond parents' evenings and attainment updates.
2.3 Schools should endeavour to place the principles of family learning at the heart of their work with parents.
2.4 Online engagement ought to be a part of the parental engagement mix.
2.5 Schools should endeavour to facilitate and improve vehicles for parental voice.

Chapter 3: Economics, education and inequalities

3.1 Closing the gap must remain a driving principle of educational provision.
3.2 Funding streams and mechanisms should reflect this priority.
3.3 The practicality of remodelling school campuses as multi-service community hubs should be explored, with the community-hub model informing new build projects wherever practical.
3.4 The score-card on which schools are judged needs to be much broader, taking into account contextual factors, and issues such as wellbeing, learner experience and inclusion.
3.5 The Department for Education ought to establish a Standing Commission on Education to map out what a post-lockdown education system could and should look like.

Chapter 4: Breadth, balance, the curriculum and its assessment

4.1 The return of curriculum to inspection frameworks is welcome and long overdue, but the inspectorate needs to conceptualise the curriculum as more than a list of subjects.
4.2 Future reforms to the curriculum need to critically examine how breadth and balance are achieved, not just across the range of subjects offered but in the variety of types of learning that learners are exposed to.

4.3 Schools should be encouraged to develop practice beyond the specifically academic, such that there is a stronger focus on the development of character, resilience and the whole child.

4.4 Policymakers should urgently address the neglect of the social curriculum, and notably areas like Citizenship Education, Economic and Financial Literacy, and Personal, Social and Health Education.

4.5 The Department for Education ought to give serious consideration to re-introducing an expert advisory body with qualifications and the curriculum as its central concern.

Chapter 5: Making the grade: The class of 2020

5.1 Future reforms to the qualifications structure across the UK ought to seek to re-introduce elements of teacher assessment and coursework alongside external assessment and marking.

5.2 The Department for Education and its agencies, awarding organisations and the profession need to work together to produce an agreed model to be implemented in the event of the cancellation of timetabled exams.

5.3 Decisions about whether and when to stage written examinations in 2021 should be made and announced without delay.

5.4 The government ought to commission a major longitudinal study tracking those who would have sat Standard Attainment Tests and written GCSE and A level papers in 2020, tracking wellbeing, academic success and early career progress.

5.5 It is vital that there is a full and transparent enquiry into the 2020 examination grading crisis in each of the UK jurisdictions.

Chapter 6: Catching up on 'lost' learning

6.1 Schools ought to be encouraged to take a diagnostic approach to ensure that both the learning losses and the learning gains of lockdown are captured.

6.2 Catch-up programmes need to be tailored to the needs of specific cohorts and individual students.

6.3 Funding streams need to be affirmatively structured so that provision is targeted at those with the greatest need.

6.4 External interventions, such as mentoring programmes, should complement the work of schools in addressing identified gaps in learning.

6.5   School-level practitioners need to be enabled to work with those providing tutoring services, to deliver bespoke solutions in a cohesive manner.

Chapter 7: Pupil wellbeing and emotional recovery

7.1   It is vital that the emotional, psychological and attachment needs of children and young people are not ignored in the pursuit of academic catch-up.

7.2   Schools, system leaders and policymakers should pivot their efforts towards inclusion-first and well-being-focused strategies, both in the immediate aftermath of the pandemic and in the longer term.

7.3   Schools must be enabled to better develop an understanding of trauma and attachment and how vulnerabilities in these areas might be addressed, an understanding that is likely to be vital in supporting the needs of children returning to school.

7.4   Education professionals must recognise that some students have thrived during lockdown and therefore develop strategies that sustain their flourishing in a school setting.

7.5   System-wide, there needs to be a much stronger focus on matters of staff wellbeing, including that of Heads and senior leaders, if schools are to retain the capacity to enable the children and young people in their care to thrive.

Chapter 8: Leadership and governance

8.1   The positive profile of the teaching profession as it emerges from lockdown ought to be used as the foundation for future recruitment and retention campaigns.

8.2   Initial and continuing teacher education providers need to be enabled to capture the Lessons from Lockdown for teachers' initial training and professional development, and enabled to innovate in doing so.

8.3   Access routes to the teaching profession should reflect the needs of potential teachers, teachers and schools in a digitally enabled, post-lockdown age.

8.4   System-wide, the wellbeing of school leaders ought to be an absolute priority, guiding the approaches of school governors, system leaders and policymakers alike.

8.5 System leaders ought to commission a study of the role and effectiveness of different school governance frameworks and strategies in independent, maintained and non-maintained schools during lockdown.

Chapter 9: Inspection, research and system performance

9.1 Any reinstatement of inspection and accountability measures should take account of the context and consequences of lockdown and retain this approach in the event of any future periods of suspension.

9.2 Building on the principles underpinning the visits programme to English schools in Autumn 2020, consideration ought to be given to the pivoting of school inspection away from a judgemental and towards a developmental ethos.

9.3 Consideration should be given to the prospect of re-constituting and re-branding school inspectorates across the UK, in light of this proposed change in ethos.

9.4 The Department for Education should work in partnership with the British Educational Research Association, University Schools of Education and similar bodies and a range of philanthropic foundations to fund and deliver a range of studies designed to capture the many and varied Lessons from Lockdown, including the major longitudinal study proposed in Recommendation 5.4.

9.5 This body of investigative work should enable the engagement of school leaders, teachers and other frontline educational professionals in the research process.

Chapter 10: Recasting the learning blend: Technology and pedagogy

10.1 Unilaterally raising the capacity and quality of digital and online provision to that of the best schools needs to be a national policy priority, and a priority within every Local Authority and every Multi-Academy Trust, and amongst comparable bodies in the independent sector.

10.2 In due course, and within an agreed time frame, schools should be required to develop and periodically update a blended learning strategy that clearly outlines how digital and online technologies support learning in and beyond the classroom, assessment and liaison with parents.

10.3 It should be recognised as a priority by policymakers that closing the digital divide is key to closing the attainment gap between advantaged and disadvantaged children.

10.4 Forthcoming inspections should capture the use of digital technologies in schools and their impact on learner outcomes.

10.5 Consideration should be given to the development and funding of dedicated adult and family learning programmes for parents and professional development programmes for school staff, so as to build digital literacy, capacity and confidence system-wide.

Appendix E
Critical reaction to
Lessons from Lockdown

Pre-publication endorsements

Tony Breslin's highly readable and engaging book works on three levels.

First, it offers a comprehensive chronicle of the impact of lockdown on our education system. Through clarity of narrative and the voices of a wide range of participants, we are reminded of the multi-layered and capricious events of Spring and Summer 2020. I have a strong sense that those interested in education will return to these pages for many years to come.

But *Lessons from Lockdown* provides much more than a captivating narrative of schooling during the pandemic. Breslin is a knowledgeable and experienced educator and articulates several decades of change within education, thus contextualizing the various responses to the closure of schools across the UK.

Finally, and most powerfully, the book makes a series of clear-eyed, well-balanced recommendations. These stimulating suggestions will, unquestionably, be discussed in staff rooms across the nation and, if we are to have the future we desire for our children, by those in power.

Daniel Coyle, Headteacher, Newman Catholic College,
Brent, North West London

This book captures a vital moment in time and offers a highly readable and engaging account of what happened when education was thrust into lockdown early in 2020.

But it goes further than that, placing the decisions taken in a broader context of educational policy and practice. Therefore, it should not be a surprise that it tells a tale of how many individual schools and teachers were left largely alone to make the best of the situation. In many ways *Lessons from Lockdown* demonstrates how the pandemic has shone a light on the injustices, inequities and poor political leadership that are endemic in our education system.

Tony Breslin's extensive research, drawing on the immediate experiences of a range of key players in the education sector, does us all a service in making sure that those decisions, actions and consequences are not all left to be reimagined with the benefit of hindsight, but chronicled here and now.

As we see the longer-term impact of lockdown on our children, our schools and on the wider educational community, researchers of the future will be intensely grateful for this book's ability to present a broad and deep narrative of what the lockdown of the first part of 2020 felt like to those involved.

The arguments that Breslin marshals from these experiences to challenge us all to reimagine what our education system should seek to achieve and how it should be structured are provocative and engaging.

Nick Johnson, Chief Executive, British Educational
Research Association (BERA)

A lesson or class is a structured period of time where learning is intended to occur. *Lessons from Lockdown: The Educational Legacy of COVID-19* opens wide many doors to learning at the same time: principals' and policymakers' office doors, staffroom and classroom doors and, in particular, the doors to pupils' homes.

Drawing on extensive discussion and research, Dr. Tony Breslin argues that one impact of COVID-19 lies in the way that the resultant lockdowns have challenged the success of traditional educational practice. As such, there are opportunities for change in every classroom, every school and every schooling system, and in local and regional agencies.

Lessons from Lockdown provides an immediate provocation of the work to be done while at the same time acknowledging the critical driver of such change: the collective capacity of all of those involved in supporting young people to thrive.

Breslin calls for direct engagement between policymakers and experienced educators, and identifies opportunities for change that span parental engagement, family learning, the development of schools as community hubs, the need for a stronger social curriculum, the wellbeing of both students and staff, and the growth of digital literacy, and offers detailed recommendations on each.

This book will help us to achieve the educational outcomes that we all hope for. If acted on, its recommendations have the power to create a new culture of schooling, a culture where 'flourishing' is a regular descriptor of not only the experience of students, but of staff, schools and their communities.

Ross Dean, Teacher Educator, School Leadership, School
Improvement and Adolescent Wellbeing Consultant,
and Researcher, Learning Focused Communities, and
Founder, Victorian Educational Leadership Consortium,
Australian Education Union, Melbourne, Australia

This book arrives just in time, as a new school year begins – albeit haltingly – under the continuing threat of the COVID-19 virus which, only a few months ago, abruptly interrupted educational systems around the world and created unprecedented chaos in the teaching and learning process.

In exploring the implications of this health crisis, Tony Breslin focuses on the interrelatedness of factors that exert a collective and profound effect on all aspects of the educational system. As such, the book includes both a retrospective analysis of specific policies that shaped the pre-COVID-19 educational system and a rich description of the ways in which a broad cross-section of stakeholders experienced the recent school closures and ensuing confusion associated with the virus. This is followed by a thoughtful examination of the inequities inherent in the current educational system that have been laid bare by the pandemic. Readers are asked to consider the significant and potentially permanent nature of societal changes associated with this and future global health crises, and to resist the compulsion to return to the familiar. They are urged, instead, to view the crisis as an auspicious opportunity for re-thinking taken-for-granted educational policies and practices and collaborating with all relevant stakeholders, for the purpose of creating a more equitable education for all.

Although this ground-breaking book focuses on a specific national context, the themes that emerge from this work are remarkably similar to those that are surfacing in schools across the globe, making *Lessons from Lockdown* a particularly informative and valuable book for all those concerned with schooling, regardless of the country in which they live.

Betty Merchant PhD, Henrietta Frances Zezula Lowak
Endowed Distinguished Professor, Department of Educational
Leadership and Policy Studies, College of Education
and Human Development, University of Texas
at San Antonio

Schooling in England needed a reset before anyone had heard of Covid-19, but that ongoing crisis has also shone an unforgiving light on the limitations of the system. In this incisive and timely piece of research and analysis Tony Breslin makes a powerful case for us to use the experience of crisis to pursue reform in areas ranging from school governance, to parental engagement, to social inclusion.

Matthew Taylor, Chief Executive, Royal Society of Arts,
Manufactures and Commerce (RSA)

In the rush to reopen schools after lockdown, the temptation to 'get back to normal' and simply catch up on the months of lost learning appears to be overwhelming.

Tony Breslin argues this must be resisted. Instead, now is the time to rethink the entire system, from the starting age of formal education to the currently limited opportunities to learn in later life, to what is taught, how and why. For too long, changes to the education system have been driven by political considerations, short -term difficulties and even, at times, nostalgia. *Lessons from Lockdown* sets out why this piecemeal approach to reform needs to stop and provides an invaluable contribution to the debate that now must take place.

Rosemary Bennett, Former Education Editor, *The Times*

It has become somewhat fashionable to talk about building a better and a different education system following the pandemic. The fact that Tony Breslin has already written an informative and challenging book on the subject is evidence that he has been thinking of these things long before the recent difficulties caused others to also do so.

This is, therefore, a well thought out account of some of the questions we need to address and a good guide as to how to begin to put them into action. Tony Breslin's experience and commitment to children and young people, as ever, underpins everything that he writes.

Estelle Morris, Baroness Morris of Yardley, Former
Secretary of State for Education

Post-publication reviews and reactions

A highly thought-provoking and significant contribution to the emerging educational literature on lockdown.

Steve Turnbull, *Schools Week*

Breslin weaves in media releases, policy shifts, his own knowledge, and testimonies to provide an important historical account of what happened to the UK education systems, with a particular focus on England, during the spring and summer of 2020 … The book will be of value to school leaders, policy makers, and researchers alike.

Sinéad Harmey, *Educational Review*

On hearing about [*Lessons from Lockdown*], I could not wait to get a copy. How Tony Breslin and Ryan McMahon (his researcher) managed to compile and analyse so much valuable qualitative data on the experiences of so many in such a short time is beyond me. However, thank goodness they did as the book speaks volumes about what we need to learn and take away from the experience of education during an unprecedented event in history.

Hans Svennevig, *Teaching Citizenship*

A good book full of insights and ideas, which takes a thorough look at the impact of the pandemic, from the practicalities of returning to teaching face-to-face to the long-term effects on our learners' future education.

Anne Davis, *InTuition Magazine*

As a parent rather than a teacher or academic, I've found this book really informative and inspiring. It's beautifully written and easy to read, and full of insights that are very recognisable, alongside recommendations that it would be wonderful to see put into action. Highly recommended.

Caroline Graham, Parent, Amazon Customer Reviews

I can't think of a better text for our new Secretary of State for Education, Nadhim Zahawi, and his team at the Department for Education to reflect upon right now.

Isobel Bryce, Education consultant and former secondary
school Head (via Twitter on the news of the appointment
of Nadhim Zahawi as Secretary of State for Education
in September 2021)

References

Adoption UK (2018) *Bridging the Gap: Giving Adopted Children an Equal Chance in School*, Oxfordshire: Adoption UK.

Adoption UK (2019) *The Adoption Barometer 2019*, Oxfordshire: Adoption UK.

Adoption UK (2021) *The Adoption Barometer: A stocktake of adoption in the UK – June 2021*, Oxfordshire: Adoption UK.

Ashord, K. (2021) A Return to Real Exams is Essential for Restoring Fairness in Our Education System, in *The Daily Telegraph*, 29 July. www.telegraph.co.uk/news/2021/07/29/return-real-exams-essential-restoring-fairness-education-system/ Retrieved 21 August 2022.

Baker, K. (2020) Children Will Suffer if Exams Aren't Axed, in The Sunday Times, 9 August.

BBC (2021) Simon Thomas in conversation with Nihal Arthanayake on the latter's daily afternoon show on BBC Radio 5 Live, 26 January.

Bousted, M. (2021a) Comments on Government's Education Recovery Plan, National Education Union, 2 June, https://neu.org.uk/press-releases/governments-education-recovery-plan Retrieved 24 April 2022.

Bousted, M. (2021b) Comments on Resignation of Sir Kevan Collins, National Education Union, 3 June, https://neu.org.uk/press-releases/resignation-sir-kevan-collins Retrieved 24 April 2022.

Bousted, M. (2021c) Chief Medical Officers Recommend Vaccinations for 12–15 Year Olds, National Education Union, 13 September, https://neu.org.uk/press-releases/chief-medical-officers-recommend-vaccinations-12-15-year-olds Retrieved 24 April 2022.

Breslin, T. (2014) From Great Aspirations to Effective Practice: Towards a Strategy for Supporting Student Development and Wellbeing in Schools, in Peterson, A.,

Lexmond, J., Hallgarten, J. and Kerr, D. (eds.), *Schools with Soul: A New Approach to Spiritual, Moral, Social and Cultural Education*, London: RSA.

Breslin, T. (2016) *A Place for Learning: Putting Learning at the Heart of Citizenship, Civic Identity and Community Life*, London: RSA.

Breslin, T. (2017) Who Governs Our Schools? Trends, Tensions and Opportunities, London: RSA

Breslin, T. (2021a) *Lessons from Lockdown: The Educational Legacy of COVID-19*, Oxford: Routledge.

Breslin, T. (2021b) Why Building the Capacity for Lifelong Learning Can't Wait Until School's Over!, Workers Educational Association, www.breslinpublicpol icy.com/uncategorized/why-building-the-capacity-for-lifelong-learning-cant-wait-until-schools-over/ Retrieved 13 December 2021.

Breslin, T. and Dufour, B. (2005) *Developing Citizens: A Comprehensive Introduction to Effective Citizenship Education in the Secondary School*, London: Hodder Education.

Breslin, T., Harris, K. and Moores, M. (2013) A Series of Doors: Young People Talking about the Experience of Poverty, Office of the Children's Commissioner, Hertfordshire: Breslin Public Policy Limited.

British Educational Research Association (BERA) (2021) *Manifesto for Education for Environmental Sustainability*, British Educational Research Association. November 2021.

British Telecommunications (1987) At least it's an 'ology, the inaugural advertisement in the It's Good to Talk campaign featuring Maureen Lipman as 'Beattie', London: British Telecommunications.

Busse, M. (2021) Call for Stability in School Education – Letters to the Editor, in *The Times*, 25 August.

Camden, B. (2022) Apprenticeship Starts Recovering to Pre-pandemic Levels, DfE Data Shows, in *FE Week*, 27 January.

Camper, Z., Tavssberger, J. and Weisburgh, M. (2021) *An Opportunity to Reimagine Learning*, RSA Augmented Society Network www.thersa.org/globalassets/rsa-global/rsa-us/resources/asn-learning-reimagined-v1.pdf Retrieved 11 September 2022.

Carr, J. (2021) DfE Reintroduces Remote Learning Legal Duty for 2021–22 Academic Year, in Schools Week, 26 August.

Chambers, S. (2020) *Evidence Submission to the House of Commons Education Committee, Getting the grades they've earned – COVID-19: the cancellation of exams and 'calculated' grades: First Report of Session 2019–21*, 14 June, House of Commons.

Collins, K. (2021) *Evidence to the Education Select Committee Enquiry into Educational Recovery (HC452), 29th June 2021*, House of Commons.

Coughlan, S. (2021) School Catch-up Tzar Resigns Over Lack of Funding, BBC News, 2 June, www.bbc.co.uk/news/education-57335558, Retrieved 24 April 2022.

Cultural Learning Alliance (2021) *About Us* https://culturallearningalliance.org.uk/about-us/ Retrieved 13 December 2021.

Department of Education – Northern Ireland (2021) *Frequently Asked Questions – Education Restart*, www.education-ni.gov.uk/frequently-asked-questions-education-restart Retrieved 17 October 2021.

DFE (2015) *Careers Guidance and Access for Education and Training Providers: Statutory Guidance for Schools and Colleges on Providing Careers Guidance*, London: Department for Education.

DFE (2019) *Character Education: Framework guidance*, London: Department for Education.

DFE (2020a) *Governance Handbook: Academy Trusts and Maintained Schools*, London: Department for Education.

DFE (2020b) *Governing in Challenging Circumstances: Business Continuity and Holding Virtual Meetings*, London: Department for Education.

DFE (2020c) *Pupil Absence in Schools in England: 2018 to 2019*, London: Department for Education.

DFE (2021a) New Commissioner Appointed to Oversee Education Catch-up, www.gov.uk/government/news/new-commissioner-appointed-to-oversee-education-catch-up Retrieved 23 August 2021.

DFE (2021b) *Schools COVID-19 Operational Guidance*, 27 September, https://assets.publishing.service.gov.uk/government/uploads/system/uploads/attachment_data/file/1057106/220224_Schools_guidance.pdf Retrieved 24 April 2022.

DFE (2021c) Education Secretary Sets Out School Contingency Plans for England, Statement to the House of Commons, 30 December, www.gov.uk/government/speeches/education-secretary-sets-out-school-contingency-plans-for-england Retrieved 23 August 2022.

DFE (2021d) *Relationships Education, Relationships and Sex Education (RSE) and Health Education: Statutory Guidance for Governing Bodies, Proprietors, Head Teachers, Principals, Senior Leadership Teams, Teachers*, London: Department for Education.

DFE (2021e) *Personal, Social, Health and Economic Education*, London: Department for Education.

DFE (2021f) *Keeping Children Safe In Education*, London: Department for Education.

DFE (2021g) *Standards for School Food in England: Guidance on the Standards for Planning and Providing Food in Cchools*, London: Department for Education.

DFE (2021h) *Promoting and Supporting Mental Health and Wellbeing in Schools and Colleges*, London: Department for Education.

Dickens, J. (2021) Sir Kevan Collins Appointed 'Education Recovery' Tzar, in *Schools Week*, 3 February.

Douglas, J.W.B. (1964) *The Home and the School*, London: MacGibbon and Kee.

EdCentral (2021) The Impact of E.D. Hirsch on the UK Education Curriculum, https://edcentral.uk/edblog/this-week-in-edresearch/the-impact-of-ed-hirsch-on-the-uk-education-curriculum Retrieved 9 August 2021.

Elliot Major, L., Eyles, A. and Machin, S. (2021) Learning Loss Since Lockdown, in *Centre Piece*, Autumn 2021.

Farrar, J. (2021) Political Leaders Must Ensure Covid Vaccines Aren't the Preserve of the Rich, in *The Guardian*, 28 April.

Fazackerley, A. (2020) UK University Student Halls Too Full to be Safe, Experts Warn, in The Guardian, 2 October.

FE News (2021) Attendance in Education and Early-Years Settings during the Coronavirus Outbreak, www.fenews.co.uk/press-releases/72058-attendance-in-education-and-early-years-settings-during-the-coronavirus-covid-19-outbreak-23-march-2020-to-1-july-2021 Retrieved 17 October 2021.

Garner, R. (2002) The Teachers' Leader Who Spoke In Soundbites, in The Independent, 28 March.

Gaughan, C.H., Razieh, C., Khunti, K., Banerjee, A., Chudasama, Y.V., Davies, M.J., Dolby, T., Gillies, C.L., Lawson, C., Mirkes, E.M., Morgan, J., Tingay, K., Zaccardi, F., Yates, T. and Nafilyan, V. (2022) COVID-19 Vaccination Uptake Amongst Ethnic Minority Communities in England: A Linked Study Exploring the Drivers of Differential Vaccination Rates, in *Journal of Public Health*, 6 January https://doi.org/10.1093/pubmed/fdab400 Retrieved 23 August 2022.

Gregory, A., Stewart H. and Sample, I. (2021) NHS Chiefs Urge 'Plan B-Plus' Amid COVID Surge, in *The Guardian*, 20 October.

Gregory, A., Stewart H. and Walker, P. (2021) Javid Warns of 100,000 Daily Cases and Urges MPs to Lead by Example, in The Guardian, 21 October.

Griffiths, S. and Das, S. (2021) Ghost Children of Covid: 135,000 Pupils 'Disappear' From School, in The Sunday Times, 3 October, www.thetimes.co.uk/article/ghost-children-of-covid-135-000-pupils-disappear-from-school-vj5q7d96j Retrieved 22 August 2022.

Groves, J. (2021) PM Will Tell Britain to Get Back to Work: Boris Johnson to use his Tory Party Conference Speech to Urge Britons to Return to the Office – Amid Growing Confidence Covid will NOT Spark Another Lockdown This Winter, in *Mail Online*, 4 October, www.dailymail.co.uk/news/article-10058841/Get-work-Boris-Johnson-use-Tory-conference-speech-urge-Britons-return-office.html Retrieved 13 December 2021.

Groves, J. and Stevens J. (2021) Chief Scientist, Surprise! It's Back to Panic Stations, in Daily Mail, 15 September.

Harmey, S. and Moss, G. (2021) Learning Disruption or Learning Loss: Using Evidence From Unplanned Closures to Inform Returning to School After

COVID-19, T&F Online, 17 September www.tandfonline.com/doi/full/10.1080/00131911.2021.1966389, Retrieved 25 August 2022.

Hastings, C. (2021) Why Sunday Night Viewers Are All Set To Go Wild About Aggi, in The Mail on Sunday, 3 October.

Hayward, L. (2021) The Independent Assessment Commission www.neweraassessment.org.uk Retrieved 2 October 2021.

Hazell, W. (2021) Gavin Williamson Says GCSEs are Here to Stay-- and Reveals He Gets 'Lobbied' on Schools During 'Pillow Talk', *The I*, 12 March.

Henry, J. (2021) Britain's Covid-era University Students May Suffer 'Impostor Syndrome', in *The Observer*, 26th September 2021.

Herts for Learning (2021) *Knowing Your School and Ofsted: Towards Outstanding,* Hertfordshire: HFL Governance Services.

HMRC (2020) Coronavirus Job Retention Scheme Statistics: August 2020, 21 August www.gov.uk/government/statistics/coronavirus-job-retention-scheme-statistics-august-2020/coronavirus-job-retention-scheme-statistics-august-2020 Retrieved 23 August 2022.

House of Commons, Health and Social Care, and Science and Technology Committees (2021) *Coronavirus: Lessons Learned to Date, Sixth Report of the Health and Social Care Committee and Third Report of the Science and Technology*, 12 October. FpSoV2T1.pdf Retrieved 23 August 2022.

ImpactEd (2021) *Lockdown Lessons: Pupil Learning and Wellbeing During the COVID-19 Pandemic: Final Report from Impact Ed's Longitudinal Study of Over 60,000 Pupils in England*, ImpactEd, February.

Jones, H. (2021) This Year's GCSE and A Level Exams Cancelled, Gavin Williamson Confirms, in The Metro, 5 January.

Kirkwood, J. (2020) Returning to School After Lockdown, Children's Parliament, www.childrensparliament.org.uk/returning-to-school-after-lockdown/ Retrieved 27 October 2020.

Knights, E. (2020) Planning for a Year of Liberation, Birmingham: National Governance Association, 17 July.

Leahy, F., Newton, P. and Khan, A. (2021) Learning During the Pandemic: Quantifying Lost Time, Ofqual, 12 July www.gov.uk/government/publications/learning-during-the-pandemic/learning-during-the-pandemic-quantifying-lost-time--2 Retrieved 24 August 2022.

Lewis, S.J., Munro, A.P.R., Davey Smith, G. and Pollock, A.M. (2021) Closing Schools is Not Evidence-based and Harms Children, in British Medical Journal, 23 February, https://doi.org/10.1136/bmj.n521 Retrieved 5 September 2022.

Long, D. and Danechi, S. (2022) Home Education in England, London: House of Commons Library, 28 March.

Lough, C. (2021) COVID: DFE Legal Threat to Schools an 'Insult' to Heads, in *Times Educational Supplement*, 5 November.

Madeley, P. (2020) Gavin Williamson to Sign Off on 2021 Exam Delays, in *Express and Star*, 3 October.

Major, L. E., Eyles, A. and Machin, S. (2021) Learning Loss Since Lockdown, in Centre Piece, Autumn.

Martin, H. (2021) Get Back to the Office, Rishi Sunak Tells Britain Amid Fears Over the Economic Impact of Staying at Home – and Young People Missing Out on Career Opportunities, in *Mail Online*, www.dailymail.co.uk/news/article-9771 105/Get-office-Rishi-Sunak-tells-Britain-amid-fears-economic-impact-staying Retrieved 13 December 2021.

McKie, R, (2021) COVID Cases are 26 Times Higher than a Year Ago, in *The Observer*, 29 August.

Medley, G. (2021) Speaking on the Today Programme, BBC Radio 4, 1 August.

Mulholand, M. (2021) Mind the 'Gap' Trap, in *Times Educational Supplement*, 15 October.

NAHT (2021) Fixing the Leadership Crisis: Time For Change – Making School Leadership a Sustainable Career Choice, December.

NEU (2021), Education Unions Call for a Pause to Routine Ofsted Inspections, 9 December https://neu.org.uk/press-releases/education-unions-call-pause-rout ine-ofsted-inspections Retrieved 23 August 2022.

NIACE (2013) *Family Learning Works: The Inquiry into Family Learning, October 2013*, Chaired by Baroness Howarth of Breckland OBE https://learningandw ork.org.uk/wpcontent/uploads/2020/05/Family-Learning-Works-The-Inqu iry-into-Family-Learning-in-England-and-Wales-Summary.pdf Retrieved: 23 October 2021.

Ofqual (2020a) Ofqual Welcomes DfE Announcement on 2021 Exams. 12 October, www.fenews.co.uk/resources/ofqual-welcomes-dfe-announcement-on-2021-exams-2/ Retrieved 24 April 2022.

Ofqual (2020b), *Results Tables for GCSE, AS and A level Results in England, 2020*, Coventry: Ofqual.

Ofqual (2021), *Summer 2021 results analysis and quality assurance – A level and GCSE*, Coventry: Ofqual.

Ofsted (2019) *Education Inspection Framework*, London: Office for Standards in Education.

Ofsted (2021) *Education Inspection Framework (Update, July 2021)*, London: Office for Standards in Education.

Painter, A. (2020) The Case for Universal Basic Income after COVID-19, *RSA Bridges to the Future* blog www.thersa.org/blog/2020/05/ubi-basic-income-covid#comments Retrieved 15 November 2021.

Painter, A., Thorold, J. and Cooke, J. (2018) Pathways to Universal Basic Income: The case for a Universal Basic Opportunity Fund, 16 February, London: RSA.

Pollard, A. (2007) Editorial: The UK's Teaching and Learning Research Programme: Findings and Significance, *British Educational Research Journal 33* (5): 639–646.

Pollard, A. and James, M. (eds.) (2004) Personalised Learning: A Commentary by the Teaching and Learning Research Programme, Swindon: Economic and Social Research Council.

Public Health England (2021), JCVI Issues Updated Advice on COVID-19 Vaccination of Children Aged 12 to 15, London: Public Health England.

QCA (1998) *Education and the Teaching of Democracy in Schools*, London: Qualifications and Curriculum Authority.

QCA (2000a) *National Curriculum Programme of Study: Citizenship Key Stage 3*, London: Qualifications and Curriculum Authority.

QCA (2000b) *National Curriculum Programme of Study: Citizenship Key Stage 4*, London: Qualifications and Curriculum Authority.

Richardson, H. (2021) Exams: Covid Grade Inflation to be Wound Back After Two Years, *BBC News*, 30 September www.bbc.co.uk/news/education-58734418 Retrieved 30 September 2021.

Richardson, J. (2021) Supporting Children Returning to School After the Lockdown, *Nip in the Bud*, https://nipinthebud.org/returning-to-school-after-the-lockdown/ Retrieved 9 December 2021.

Roberts, J. (2020) COVID: DFE Legal Threat to Schools an 'Insult' to Heads, in Times Educational Supplement, 12 December.

Roberts, J. (2021), Call to Halt Ofsted Inspections for Heads' Wellbeing, in Times Educational Supplement, 25 October.

Russell, W. (1980) *Educating Rita*, London: Royal Shakespeare Company.

Russell, W. (2003) *Educating Rita*, London: Methuen.

Russell, W. and Gilbert, L. (1983) *Educating Rita*, London: Acorn Pictures.

Ryan, M. (ed.) (2022) *Pandemic Pedagogies: Teaching and Learning During the COVID-19 Pandemic*, New York: Routledge.

Sandhu, S. (2021) Sir Kevan Collins: What the Education Tsar Wanted for the School Catch-Up Plan Versus What Children Will Get, in The I, 3 June.

Schools Week (2021) The 2021 Summer Exams Plan: Everything You Need to Know, in Schools Week, 15 January.

Severs, J. (2015) I've Been Misunderstood from Day 1 in *Times Educational Supplement (TES)*, 6 November.

Severs, J. (2021) Teachers are Running on Empty – We Must Help Them to Refuel, in Times Educational Supplement, 15 October.

Shaw, D. (2021) Williamson Video-calls Uni Bosses to Tell Them They Must Return to In-person Teaching, *The Tab*, 9 September https://thetab.com/uk/2021/09/09/gavin-williamson-video-calls-uni-bosses-to-tell-them-they-must-return-to-in-person-teaching-222445 Retrieved 22 September 2021.

Sibieta, L. (2021) The Crisis in Lost Learning Calls for a Massive National Policy Response, London: Institute for Fiscal Studies.

Singh, A. and Hymas C. (2020) Schools Must Reopen for Sake of Children, Says Gavin Williamson, in The Daily Telegraph, 16 May.

Slater, J. and Dean, C. (2001) Proper Jobs Need Proper Staff, in Times Educational Supplement, 16 November.

Sleigh, S. (2020) Government is Committed to GCSE and A Level Exams Taking Place Next Year, Says No.10, in *Evening Standard*, 30 September.

Sleigh, S. (2021) Gavin Williamson Accused of 'Cobbling Together' Exam Alternatives, in Evening Standard, 22 January.

Sleigh, S. and Davis, B. (2020) Gavin Williamson Says Exams Will 'Absolutely' Go Ahead in 2021, in *Evening Standard*, 3 December.

Smyth, C. (2021) Javid Warns Daily COVID Cases Could Hit 100,000: Public Urged to Get Booster Jab and Wear Masks, in The Times, 21 October.

Sparrow, A. (2021) Act Urgently or Face Up to 7,000 a Day in Hospital, Scientists Tell PM, in The Guardian,15 September.

Spielman, A. (2017) Speech to the Association for School and College Leaders' Annual Conference, 10 March.

Spielman, A. (2021a) Speech to the Festival of Education Conference, 24 June.

Spielman, A. (2021b) Address to the Institute of Government, 14 September.

Spielman, A. (2021c) Speech to the Association for School and College Leaders' Conference, 17 March.

Spielman, A. (2021d) Speech at *researchEd* National Conference 2021, 6 September.

Stewart, W., and Clews, M. (2021) Exclusive: Sir Kevan Collins Resigns Over Catch-up Plans, *Times Educational Supplement*, 2 June www.tes.com/magazine/news/general/exclusive-sir-kevan-collins-resigns-over-catch-plan Retrieved 21 August 2022.

Thorpe, D. (2020) Response to the Government Regarding Schools, www.royalgreenwich.gov.uk/news/article/1755/response_to_the_government_regarding_schools Retrieved 19 October 2021.

Timmins, N. (2021) Schools and Coronavirus: The Government's Handling of Education During the Pandemic, Institute for Government, August.

Turnbull, S. (2021) Review: Lessons from Lockdown by Tony Breslin, in Schools Week, 14 February.

Turner, C. (2021) Gavin Williamson: Students 'Deserve' Top A-level Grades, in The Daily Telegraph, 9 August.

Weale, S. (2020), Heads Angry After Two Councils Forced to Back Down Over Covid School Closures, in The Guardian, 15 December.

Weale, S. (2021a) Transition Year for GCSE and A-level Pupils in 2022, in *The Guardian*, 14 September.

Weale, S. (2021b) Ofsted Head: Schools' Focus on Food Parcels May Have Hit Learning, in *The Guardian*, 14 September.

Weale, S. and Quinn, B. (2020) Government Launches Legal Action Against Greenwhich School Closures, in *The Guardian*, 19 October.

Webster, R. (2021) A Shift in Support, in Times Educational Supplement, 24 September.

Whitaker, D. (2021) Does the Zero-tolerance Approach to Behaviour Management Work?, in *Education Executive* https://edexec.co.uk/does-the-zero-tolerance-approach-to-behaviour-management-work/ Retrieved 12 December 2021.

Whiteman, P. (2021a) NAHT Comments on Government's Education Recovery Plan, National Association of Headteachers, 2 June www.naht.org.uk/News/Latest-comments/Press-room/ArtMID/558/ArticleID/1055/NAHT-comments-on-governments-education-recovery-plan Retrieved 24 April 2022.

Whiteman, P. (2021b) NAHT Comments on Announcement of Vaccinations for Younger Teens, National Association of Headteachers, 26 August www.naht.org.uk/News/Latest-comments/Press-room/ArtMID/558/ArticleID/1187/NAHT-comments-on-possibility-of-Covid-vaccinations-for-younger-teens Retrieved 24 April 2022.

Whittaker, F. (2022), 270 Million In-person School Days Missed Due to Covid Last Year: Absences Rose More Than Five-Fold in First Year of the Pandemic, in Schools Week, 24 May.

Whitty, C., McBride, M., Smith, G. and Atherton, F. (2021) Universal Vaccination of Children and Young People Aged 12 to 15 Years Against Covid-19, 13 September www.gov.uk/government/publications/universal-vaccination-of-children-and-young-people-aged-12-to-15-years-against-covid-19 Retrieved 24 April 2022.

Williams, K., Papadopoulou, V. and Booth, N. (2012) Prisons' Childhood and Family Backgrounds: Results from the Surveying Prisoner Crime Reduction (SPCR) Longitudinal Cohort of Prisoners, London: Ministry of Justice Analytical Services.

Williamson, G. (2021a) Letter to Simon Lebus, Chief Regulator, Ofqual, 23 February www.gov.uk/government/publications/simon-lebus-responds-to-the-secretary-of-states-direction-of-23-february-2021 Retrieved 24 April 2022.

Williamson, G. (2021b) Education Secretary Speaks at Launch of Digital Learning Review, 25 February, Department for Education www.gov.uk/government/speeches/education-secretary-speaks-at-launch-of-digital-learning-review Retrieved 24 April 2022.

Williamson, G. (2021c) Speech at Universities UK Annual Conference, 9 September, Department for Education www.gov.uk/government/speeches/education-secretary-speech-at-universities-uk-annual-conference, Retrieved: 22nd September 2021.

Williamson, G. (2021d) Speech to the Foundation for Education Development National Education Summit, 1 March www.gov.uk/government/speeches/education-secretary-speech-to-fed-national-education-summit Retrieved 22 September 2021.

Index

Note: Page numbers in *italic* denote figures.

Milton Keynes UK
Ingram Content Group UK Ltd.
UKHW022227121023
430501UK00008B/63